Odds on Favorite

Book Two of the

Winning Odds Series

MaryAnn Myers

Sunrise Horse Farm
11872 Chillicothe Road
Chesterland, Ohio 44026
440-729-0930
www.sunrisehorsefarm.com

First Edition
10 9 8 7 6 5 4 3 2 1

This is a work of fiction. Names, characters, places, and incidents
either are the products of the author's imagination or are used
fictitiously, and any resemblance to actual persons, living or dead,
events, or locales is entirely coincidental.

1. Fiction 2.Horses 3. Love Story 4. Thoroughbreds 5.Sports

Formatted to save paper

Odds on Favorite is the much-anticipated continuance of

Favored to Win

Welcome back to Nottingham Downs!

Sunrise Horse Farm is an organic, sustainable enterprise. It is an equine retirement sanctuary; it houses a bevy of dogs, and lives in harmony with the environment.

www.sunrisehorsefarm.com

Chapter One

Who would have believed it? Dawn and Randy now have two children. Ben Miller is the picture of health, even at his age. Beau Born was named the leading sire of winning two-year olds in Ohio last year. And Tom got religion. "Praise the Lord!" It was practically a perfect world until today.

"Ladies and gentlemen," Bud Gipson, the track announcer said, his voice trembling. "It is with a heavy heart that I inform you of the upcoming closing of Nottingham Downs." He paused to clear his throat. "Our last day of racing will be this coming Saturday. We want to thank you for your patronage and support these past sixty-two years, and wish you well."

"What the hell?" Tom said. It was already Thursday and this was the first anyone on the track had even heard mention of this, anyone aside from the powers-that-be in the upper office that is. "I'll tell you why they didn't say anything sooner." Tom nodded knowingly. "They wouldn't have filled a damned race for Saturday. It'd be a stampede to get outta here."

A blanket of silence spread across the entire backside. This announcement would not only affect the owners and the trainers, the grooms and the horses, but all the other racetrack employees, and the vendors, the public, the surrounding businesses, the veterinarians.

Randy pulled up next to the barn in his truck and sat behind the wheel looking at Ben and Tom. "Can you believe this?"

"Bastards," Tom said. "The sons of bitches."

Ben sighed. "At this church you go to, do they allow you to swear like that? Aren't you disobeying a commandment or something?"

Tom shrugged. "Joke all you want, old man. This is serious shit."

"Where's Dawn?" Randy asked.

"I don't know. She was here just a minute ago."

"Tell her I'll be back in about an hour. We're supposed to go to lunch."

Ben nodded.

"Are you okay?" Randy asked, hesitating.

Another nod. Ben always knew one day he'd have to retire. In the midst of his having that stroke some years back, he'd worried it would be then. "I'll be fine," he said. "I'm too old to pull up roots now." He had no desire to relocate to another racetrack.

Dawn came around the corner, looking as if she'd seen a ghost. A child perched precariously on each of those skinny hips of hers. "Here, go to Daddy," she said, handing first one to Randy and then the other. "Linda's in labor. I have to go."

"What about lunch?"

"What about labor coaching?"

Randy smiled. "Where's Harland?"

"Down-under."

Tom made googley faces at the children, both hugging their daddy. Randy Jr., nicknamed "D.R." by Ben, just turned three last week. Little Maeve was eighteen-months old. They both had lots of auburn hair like their mother.

"Where's Carol?" Carol was their nanny.

"In Flagstaff. Gees, Randy, don't you remember anything?"

Randy chuckled, giving kisses to both his children. "Bad daddy."

"Did you hear the news?" Tom asked.

"What news?" Dawn gathered up sweaters, toys, Maeve's diaper bag.

"Just now, over the p.a."

Dawn shook her head. A minute ago she was changing Maeve's diaper and singing along, "I love you, you love me...." It's hard to hear anything but D.R. when he's singing that song. He sings it at the top of his lungs.

"They're closing the track."

"What? Why? Was there an accident?"

"No, I mean for good," Tom said. "As of this Saturday."

"You're kidding?"

Tom shook his head.

Dawn turned to Ben and then Randy. Both shook their heads. "Can they do that?" she asked. "How can they do that? Where will everyone go?"

"It's a cinch not Mountaineer. They're fucking full."

"Tom...." Dawn sighed. "The children."

"Sorry, kids," he said.

The children weren't paying any attention at the moment. But, just last week D.R. piped up with a doozy of a swear word at his birthday party and everyone in attendance pointed a finger at Tom.

"I gotta go." Dawn kissed Randi good-bye and left.

With the initial shock of the announcer's news escalating into a near panic, it wasn't long before the secretary's office was overflowing with bodies, elbow to elbow. It looked like something right out of the Depression era - the racing secretary Joe Feigler resembling George Bailey outside the bank trying to calm an angry mob in the movie, "It's a Wonderful Life."

"Settle down. We will be posting a complete explanation in the HBPA office within the hour."

"What about our money?"

Winning purses took three days to clear.

"Are you going to be here Sunday morning or will the offices be locked up and empty?"

"We'll be here."

"How can we be sure? You've been lying all along."

9

"Now wait a minute. That's not fair and you know it! You all aren't the only ones having the rugs pulled out from under you. We're in the same boat as you."

"Oh yeah? Well I'm floating a little dinghy and you're sitting on a big-ass yacht. Who do you think's going to sink faster?" one of the old-time trainers said. "What the hell's going on here?"

"I'm not at liberty to say, but let me reassure you...."

"Bullshit!"

"Why weren't we told of this sooner?"

"Where are we supposed to go?"

"What are we supposed to do?"

"Damn you!"

The racing secretary took a step back. "Again, as I said. There will be an explanation posted in the HBPA office in about an hour. I'm sorry."

"You're sorry?"

"Yes. And remember, I am only the messenger here. This was not my decision. I had nothing to do with it."

"Yeah, well let me tell you something," another trainer said.

"No, Dave. Just listen. It wasn't but ten years ago, I was training here as well. You all remember that. So I know how you feel."

"No, you used to know how we feel."

"Fine. Whatever." Joe sighed in frustration. "But if it'll make you all feel any better, I just found out this morning myself."

A momentary hush fell over the room, one that seemed to summarize the belief that he was telling the truth. "What are we going to do, Joe?" asked Jeannie Simpson, the leading woman trainer for the past six years. "Where do we go from here?"

The racing secretary shook his head. "I don't know."

Ben had been quiet up until this point. "Joe, why don't you just tell us what's going to be posted in an hour?" Everyone nodded in support of that.

10

"I would if I could, Ben. But I'll be reading it for the first time right along with you."

"Well then," Ben said. "I guess we'll see you over there."

When the infamous hour came, Dawn was across town, doing her very best to try to make Linda as comfortable as possible. She placed pillows where they helped, cool washcloths for her neck and forehead, soothing words of encouragement. Her cousin was eight centimeters dilated and understandably rather anxious to get this delivery over with. Dawn relied on stories of their childhood to help take her mind off her contractions.

"Do you remember the time we ran away to the basement?"

Linda laughed and then grimaced - another contraction on the horizon.

"Breathe. Breathe. Breathe."

"I can't stand this," Linda said, on the downside of that one. "Tell me it doesn't get any worse."

"Okay, it doesn't get any worse."

"Are you lying?"

"Yes and no."

"Oh, God!"

Dawn mopped her brow. "Come on, you're doing great! You're almost there. Right?" She turned to the nurse and midwife. Both nodded. Thank heaven. "Okay, so we ran away to the basement and...."

"We called and ordered takeout Chinese. And when it came, Dad brought it down to us."

Dawn laughed. Linda laughed.

"Do you remember why we ran away?"

Linda shook her head.

"Me neither."

"Oh no." The start of another contraction.

"Breathe.... That's it, breathe.... Breathe...."

"All right," the midwife said, with that contraction over and upon exam. Ten centimeters. "It's showtime!"

11

"I'm scared," Linda said. "Can we hold off a minute?"

Dawn smiled supportively. "I remember feeling the exact same way."

The midwife adjusted the lights, softening them, and softened the surround-sound music. How apropos that Linda's favorite classical song was playing. "The Blue Danube."

"I can't do this."

"Yes, you can. You're doing it now."

"All right, when I say push, I want you to...."

"Ohhh....."

"Okay, go ahead and push. That's good. That's good. You're doing good, very good. Okay, okay, let's take a break."

Dawn leaned close to Linda's ear. "Think of the names. Alice Marie, if it's a girl, Harland Matthew, if it's a boy. "

Linda nodded, panting, waiting for the okay to push again. "How much longer?"

Dawn glanced anxiously at the midwife. The woman smiled. "We've crowned."

"It will all be over in a few minutes."

"A few minutes?!"

"Minutes are seconds."

"Writer! Words!"

Dawn smiled, wiping her cousin's forehead.

"All right, you're going to push again. Remember to push from the waist down. Remember to swallow, no tightening up. That's good. Let's push!"

"I'm going to scream! I'm going to scream - I'm going to scream - I'm going to scream!" Linda said, her voice getting louder and louder.

"Go ahead, scream. Scream 'I am about to become a mother.'"

"I'm about to become a mother!"

"Say it again and push!"

"I am about to become a mother!!"

"Push a little more! There you go! There you go!"

"Oh my God! This hurts so bad!"

"One more. Shout for the world to hear."

"I am about to become a mother!!!"

"Yes!" The midwife said, smiling. "Yes! I've got the head. Rest a second." She and the nurse cleared the baby's mouth and nose.

"Breathe," Dawn coached. "Breathe. You're doing awesome."

"All right, we're going to go for the shoulder. The first one you'll feel, the second one, will be a piece of cake."

Dawn glanced from the midwife to Linda and back, waiting, waiting....

"All right, Linda. We need you to push again. You're doing great. You are a mother. Let's make this little one proud of you! That's it. Push. Push...."

"Oh my God! Oh my God. Oh my God!" Linda kept saying. "Oh my God!" Her cries of motherhood mingled with the sounds of a tiny voice that had been within her for nine months.

"Waaaaaaa....."

"It's a girl! A beautiful little girl." The midwife laid the baby on Linda's stomach. "It's a girl!"

"Waaaaaaa....." It was the sweetest little sound - the sweetest little baby, testing her lungs and searching for her mother. Linda reached for her. "Oh, look at you," she said, she and Dawn crying. "Look at you." Alice Marie wiggled and squirmed. "Look at you."

Dawn picked up the phone immediately, as promised, and dialed Harland's cell phone. She held the phone to Linda's ear. "It's a girl, honey. It's a girl."

"Tell him you did wonderful," the midwife said.

"I did wonderful," Linda said, with even more tears flowing. "No, no, I'm fine. She is so precious. I love you."

Dawn smiled, with tears running down her face like water. "I'm going to go tell your mom and Uncle Matt."

Randy got a call a few minutes later. He left the children with Ben and Tom and stepped out of the meeting at the HBPA office to talk.

"It's a girl. Both mother and baby are fine. She did great!"

"I told you it was a girl."

Dawn laughed. He predicted the sex of their two children, and Ginney's three as well. "How are things going?"

"Not good. Swingline is filing bankruptcy Monday morning."

"Chapter thirteen?"

"No, chapter seven. According to the press release, he says he's done."

"Wow," Dawn muttered. "Is Ben okay?"

"Yeah, he's fine. He wants us to come to dinner tonight. He says he needs to talk to you."

"What about?"

"Buying the racetrack."

"You're kidding? Right?"

"Nope. He's dead serious."

Chapter Two

Dawn sat looking at Ben; one of the wisest men she had ever known. Yet what he was proposing was totally out of the question. Even if they could or would buy the racetrack, neither one of them knew the first thing about running one. Even more importantly, how would they run it successfully? The attendance was at an all-time low and the handle; the daily wagering, was way down. The barns were in disrepair. The grandstand was outdated. The caliber of horses was dwindling. All these thoughts ran through her mind. "And if you own a racetrack, are you still allowed to run there? Wouldn't that be a conflict of interest?"

"Good questions," Ben said. "We'll have to find out."

Years ago, veterinarians weren't allowed to own a horse and race at the same track where they practiced medicine. How would a racetrack owner be any different? They could be accused of fixing the races when their horses ran. Who needs that negative energy? Nor would she want any association with the racetrack and her family. She was very protective of her privacy to the point of paranoia, and even more now with

D.R. and little Maeve. "I don't know, Ben. There are just too many things to consider, plus look at the time frame. How could we even come up with a proposal between now and Monday? And that's if Swingline will even consider selling."

"He will. I asked. The man's bankrupt. I doubt he'll be quibbling over price. Time is on our side."

Dawn sat back, obsessing.

Ben smiled. "Here's what I think you should do. Write all your questions down and we'll go over them in the morning. I have a meeting set up with Swingline at ten."

Dawn paused. "You're really serious about this, aren't you?"

"Yes. Only since everything I own is essentially yours and Tom's and at my age God only knows how long I'll live…."

Dawn shook her head, smiling. "Don't even go there." He was a father to her, a friend, her best friend, her business partner. When he had a stroke and almost died a few years ago, she was devastated. She couldn't imagine life without him then and certainly couldn't now. He was a grandfather to her children. He was their neighbor. He was family. "What does Randy think about all of this?" she asked.

"He's all for it, but says it's up to you."

"Where's Tom?"

"At bible study with George and Glenda."

Dawn nodded and yawned. "Oh, that's right; it's Thursday." Randy and the children were due any minute. Ben had a spaghetti dinner ready. He'd turned into quite the chef lately. Dawn had stopped at his house straight from the hospital and found herself too tired to leave. The home she and Randy built at the back of Ben's property was less than a quarter of a mile away, and yet it seemed as far as another state at the moment. Oddly enough, she'd been thinking the last couple of weeks of slowing down, doing less. It had been years since she'd done any serious writing. She'd been kicking around the idea of writing another novel.

She didn't dare tell Ben that; he'd suggest she write another book about the racetrack, this time about "buying" a

15

racetrack. She yawned again. While Ben checked on dinner, she lay down on the couch and closed her eyes. She wasn't the least bit interested in owning a racetrack. She didn't want any part of it.

"Mommy!" D.R. ran through the living room and jumped on her. "Mommy! Mommy!"

Dawn wrapped him in her arms, laughing. "How's my boy?"

Randy piled Maeve on top of them and plopped down in the chair, equally as exhausted. Dawn looked at him. "I love you," she said.

He smiled. "No, I love you."

"I love Mommy!" D.R. said.

Dawn laughed. Little Maeve wanted in on the act as well. "I wuv Mommy even mo'!" This was an ongoing "I love you" game, ever since D.R. learned to talk.

"Where's Tom?" Randy asked.

"At bible study. He'll be home soon." Both Dawn and Randy were thrilled when Tom decided to move in with Ben two years ago. He was good company for Ben and could keep an eye on him as well.

It wasn't long before they were all seated at the dining room table and eating. D.R. sat in a booster seat next to Randy, and Maeve, in the highchair next to Dawn. Ben definitely had an agenda. "How's the sauce?" he asked, practically before anyone had even taken a bite.

"Delicious."

"Here, have some bread."

Randy laughed. Ben was so obvious. If they were drinkers, he would be plying them with booze. What a guy! He glanced at Dawn. "Have you talked to anyone since you left the hospital?"

"Yes. They're both fine. She did so well."

Randy smiled. He had to admit, when he first met Dawn and Linda he couldn't imagine either one of them going through childbirth. He actually could see them hiring someone to do it for them.

"What's the baby's name?" Tom asked, shoveling spaghetti into his mouth.

"Alice Marie."

"My baby," little Maeve said.

"D.R., eat," Randy said. He'd just stuck the tip of his nose in his plate and looked like Bozo the red-nosed clown.

"Ignore him," Dawn whispered.

Tom laughed. "These two here are why I never had kids."

"Excuse me," Randy said. "You never had kids because every woman alive knows they'd end up looking just like you."

Tom laughed again.

"Anyone ready for dessert?" Ben asked.

They hadn't even finished their meal yet. Randy couldn't stand it, and had to laugh again.

"Ice cream?"

D.R.'s eyes lit up.

"None for you until you finish your dinner," Dawn said. "Randy, wipe his nose."

"What? I think it's kind of cute."

Little Maeve noticed her brother's red nose for the first time. She giggled, then promptly went about dipping her finger in her plate and trying to make her nose look the same. "Wow, look at that," Randy said. "That's disturbing." She was trying to touch her nose, but kept hitting her cheek. "I'll bet she gets that from your side of the family."

Dawn smiled. "Very funny."

"All right," Ben said. "Listen. We all need to talk. We can talk while you're eating, because as you can all see, I'm done."

"Pass the spaghetti, please." Dawn said, ignoring the suggestion.

Ben sighed and handed the bowl to her. She could be pretty stubborn when she wanted to be, such as now. "I could see where you would have some apprehensions. It would be a huge undertaking."

"The track's not making any money, Ben," Dawn said.

"Right, and we'd have to turn that around."

"How?"

"Well, for one, we can add a double-or-nothing race each day. Tell them, Tom. It was your idea."

"It was just a thought," Tom said, looking hesitant all of a sudden for the very first time. "I wouldn't exactly call it an idea. It was just a thought."

Ben sat back and crossed his arms. "How is it I'm all alone here? Are you all ready to give up racing? Because that's what's going to happen if we don't step in and do something."

Randy shook his head. "I'm staying out of this."

"What? Are you telling me this isn't going to affect you?"

"No, I'm not saying that." Randy reached for another piece of bread. "Actually, it's going to all but kill me. Sixty percent of my business is done at the track."

Dawn looked at him. "That much?"

"I'm a racetrack vet, Dawn. It's what I do. It's what I love."

"What are you saying? Do you think this is a good idea?"

"I don't know." Randy shrugged.

Dawn moved the butter from in front of D.R. He'd set his sights on it. "Does anyone have any idea how much the racetrack would even sell for? Or how much it takes to operate one?"

"We'll find out tomorrow," Ben said.

The following morning, Dawn had a list a mile long. Rudolph Swingline, the current owner, appeared ill. His two lawyers did all the talking. The selling price was three million. That alone was enough to take the wind out of Ben's sail.

"Why so much?" Dawn asked.

"Well, if Rudolph files bankruptcy he won't gain anything. But he also won't be losing anything. He will essentially walk away free and clear."

"I see," Dawn said. She looked at Ben. "Well, so much for that."

Ben just sat there.

Dawn sighed. There were so many other things she'd rather be doing at the moment. It had been a particularly busy training morning. She was tired; she was hungry. She glanced at her watch, ten-fifteen. There was a knock on the door, right on time. "That'll be my Uncle Matt," she said.

Swingline had never laid eyes on her Uncle Matt before, but his lawyers certainly had. The color drained from their faces. "Matthew," first one and then the other said, standing to shake his hand.

Dawn's Uncle Matt introduced himself to Rudolph Swingline. "I'm Matthew Fioritto." He looked at Ben and nodded with a faint smile on his face. "Mind if I sit in?"

"No, not at all," Ben said. "We were just talking price."

"I see." Uncle Matt motioned to his assistant, a handsome young man; all testosterone and business. "Do you have that figure we worked up?"

The man nodded, reached into his lapel pocket and handed Uncle Matt a folded piece of paper. He passed it to Dawn; she opened it, glanced at it briefly and passed it to Ben.

"So," Uncle Matt said. "Before I get involved in this, if that figure's higher than what's been put on the table...."

Ben smiled. He wasn't used to dealing in millions, but certainly had done his share of horse-trading over the years. He folded the paper and sat back. "It appears bankruptcy is the way Rudolph wants to go."

Rudolph Swingline shook his head. "That's not true," he said, glancing sheepishly at both his attorneys, who did not look pleased in the least at his speaking out.

Uncle Matt motioned for Ben to hand him the paper and edged it toward Swingline. "As you can see, we have your debts listed. We have your profits. And down below...." He motioned. "That's the figure of your mortgage."

"I don't have a mortgage."

Uncle Matt paused, looking somewhat apologetic, but only for a second. There was no mistake. "You have a house in Reno if I'm correct, a condo in Tampa, and a houseboat in Seattle, plus a little-known cabin, family included - from what I understand, that's in the Ozarks."

Swingline looked closer at the numbers.

Uncle Matt glanced from one attorney to the other. "Time is of the essence here, gentlemen. This is going to be your call. We can go back and forth for hours and talk until we're blue in the face, but in the end, we're still going to come back to that same figure. It is a fair amount, the best for both sides. So what'll it be, an early lunch or a late dinner?"

Dawn was rather pleased when it turned out to be an early lunch, Ben too. "My treat," he said. When they sat down to eat at The Rib, they were the proud new owners of the essentially bankrupt Nottingham Downs. Purchase price: One million two hundred and thirty seven thousand dollars plus a debt of nine hundred thousand and counting.

"Salude!" Uncle Matt said.

Ben raised his glass. "Salude!"

"Dawnetta?"

Dawn looked at her Uncle Matt and then at Ben. Ben was ecstatic. She raised her glass. "Salude!"

Chapter Three

The news traveled fast. By race time Friday afternoon just about everyone on the backside had heard the racetrack had been sold and that it looked as if maybe it wasn't going to close after all. An hour or so later, they all knew who had bought the racetrack, Ben Miller himself. Some seemed surprised that he had that much money. Others figured with as many good horses as he'd had over the years and the stable he was racing now with Beau Born the leading sire in Ohio that it wasn't all that hard to imagine he could afford it. After all, they speculated, if the racetrack was bankrupt, how much could the asking price have been? The average guess was around a hundred thousand dollars. Some said that wasn't nearly enough, some said it was too much.

Fortunately, the Miller barn didn't have any horses running that afternoon. Ben and Tom were holed up in the secretary's office. Joe Feigler, the racing secretary, sat across from them at the table. Joe was sweating bullets, as the saying goes. Losing his job was one thing. Having to fight to get it back was quite another.

"It's a simple question," Ben said. "Considering the status of Nottingham as is it today, tell me why you think you're the best man for the job."

"Well...." Joe hesitated.

Tom leaned back in his chair, a toothpick dangling from his teeth.

"I've done the best job I can."

"Oh?" Ben said.

"I know what you're thinking."

"Possibly." Ben shrugged. "But I'm more interested in what you're thinking."

"Honestly?"

Ben nodded.

"I think I'm the best man for the job because...." Joe hesitated again. "Because I've seen it all go bad. I've seen the absolute worst it can get."

Ben motioned for him to continue.

Joe looked from one to the other. There probably weren't two more respected men on the racetrack than Ben and Tom, even with Tom and his preaching the bible of late. Yet they were both known for being a little hardheaded, set in their ways. "I think because I know what we've tried and what didn't work."

Are you to blame for any of this?" Ben asked.

Joe paused. He wasn't a bad man, in fact, quite the contrary. But he'd been a yes man for years now and Ben had no use for yes men.

"I think I can take a fair share of the blame," Joe said.

"All right." Ben liked that answer. "It comes back down to this. If you were me, sitting in my chair, what would you be saying right about now? Now remember, I'm you and you're me."

"Well." Joe leaned forward and cleared his throat. "I think I'd be saying, Joe, I've got no faith in you. I think you took the

21

easy way out these past couple of years and I think you know that. I think you had your heart in the right place once upon a time, but I think you forgot you're a horseman. I think you forgot how you got started in this business and why. I think once upon a time you loved horseracing. And that lately, it's been just a job. I think from where you're sitting now, pretty close to rock bottom, that you should get down on your knees and beg for another chance. Because I think this just might be your only chance to prove you still have it in you to do what's right. I think you owe it to yourself, and I think you owe it to the horsemen on this racetrack. I think you can do a good job."

Tom glanced at Ben and nodded slightly. It sounded sincere to him, worth a shot. And he wasn't necessarily a big Joe Feigler fan.

Ben looked at the man long and hard. "Well now, if I were you and speaking on your behalf at the moment, I'd be saying thank you for the opportunity to prove myself."

Joe stared at Ben for a second or two and then lowered his head, trying hard to swallow the lump forming in his throat. "Thank you."

Ben gave him a moment, and then presented him with a list of things he needed done today. Top of the list: Damage control. "I want you to head out to the barns and talk to everyone there, the trainers, owners, grooms, hot walkers, everyone. I want you to reassure them that we're going to do everything possible to turn this track around. And I want you to make sure they know they're going to be part of the success."

"How?"

"I don't know that yet." Ben scratched his head and chuckled. "But it's going to be your job to convince them we have a plan."

"Wait a minute. Isn't that a little like how it's been going?"

"No, well, maybe a little. But this is different. We're going to make it happen. We just don't know how we're going to go about doing it yet."

"Our plan," Tom said, with a laugh. "Is to come up with a plan. By the way, Joe, do you know the Lord?"

"Excuse me. The Lord?"

There was a knock on the door. "Sorry to interrupt," said Dave Horneck; the assistant racing secretary. "But we have a problem. The gate crew's threatening to walk off the job."

"Why?" Ben asked.

"Because a change of ownership negates their contract."

"No, it doesn't," Joe said. "That's bullshit."

Tom rose to his feet. "I'll take care of this. Am I done here?"

Ben smiled. "Yes."

"Don't worry about a thing,"

When Tom walked out, Ben motioned for Dave to close the door after them and waited until he and Joe were alone. "What's your feelings on Dave?"

Joe hesitated, reconsidering what would have been his initial yes-man response. He answered honestly. "I think he's shady. I don't like him."

"Me neither," Ben said. "He's outta here."

"Anyone else?"

"Not at the moment, but I'll let you know." Ben paused. "How do you feel about our General Manager?"

Joe shrugged. Ben's sentiments exactly. Randy was waiting for Ben at the barn for an update, and looked concerned when Ben sat down in the tack room and heaved a heavy sigh. "You okay?"

Ben nodded. "What have I done?"

Randy laughed. "I remember feeling pretty much the same way when I bought Doc Jake's Vet Hospital. It all got so complicated."

Ben smiled. Doc Jake had been his best friend. "He'd be proud of you."

"Thanks," Randy said. "I miss him."

"Me too."

"So what do you have to do now?"

"Well...." Ben told him about his morning thus far. "And now I've got a meeting with the accountant in about an hour. I don't want to shake things up too much, although there's certain people that have to go. What do you think about Spears?" Spears was the General Manager.

"I don't know. I haven't had any personal dealings with him. I've run into him a couple of times at the club, that's about it."

"There's something about him that doesn't sit right with me. It's like he doesn't belong here."

"What did Uncle Matt have to say about him?"

"Well, he doesn't seem real high on him. The problem is who do you replace him with? And then, do we really want to rock the boat at this point?" They heard voices down the shedrow and turned to see Joe, the racing secretary, talking to Gibbons; the trainer on the other end of the barn.

"What's he doing?" Randy asked.

"Making nice - nice," Ben said.

Joe stopped to talk to a groom hanging leg wraps out to dry, and worked his way down to the tack room.

"How's it going?" Ben asked.

"Good," Joe said, and smiled as he nodded to Randy. "Everybody's relatively upbeat."

"Did you get any good suggestions from anybody?" Ben asked, motioning to the notepad he carried. The man was always carrying a notepad.

"A few," Joe said, grinning as he glanced at it. "You'll get a kick out of them." He tipped his hat. "I'll see you later."

Randy watched him walk away. "I don't think I've ever seen that man smile so much before. He seems pretty happy with things."

"Yeah, but does he know the Lord?"

Randy laughed. Tom. "Tell me he didn't?"

Ben nodded. "He did. He's probably asking everyone on the gate crew right about now."

"Nah, I think he's asked them all before."

Ben shook his head. "You know, that's what I don't understand about people and religion. Why can't they just keep it to themselves?"

24

Randy shrugged and stood up to leave. "I gotta go. Do you need me for anything?"

Ben shook his head, but then called after him. "Do you think we're doing the right thing?"

"I don't know." Randy smiled. "Time'll tell."

"Thanks." Ben said, laughing. "What the hell good are you?"

Randy chuckled. "You're doing the right thing, Ben. It's the only way you know how."

Ben's expression grew serious. He needed to hear that. Randy was like a son to him. He needed to hear that from a son. "Thank you."

The accountant could have talked in riddles and it would have made more sense to Ben. "Wait a minute. There's either enough money to clear the purses today or there's not."

"Not necessarily."

Ben sighed.

"What I'm trying to explain is that it all depends on today's handle."

Ben stared. Today's handle? The fact that there was racing going on at the moment seemed like another lifetime, one quickly slipping away. "But these purses are from three days ago? What happened to the money from the handle three days ago?"

"Operating expenses."

"This *is* an operating expense," Ben said, getting red in the face. "This is the horsemen's money. It's their bread and butter."

"And that's all fine and dandy, Mr. Miller. But if we don't have electricity in the grandstand or toilet tissue in the ladies rooms, the horsemen will be putting on a show for themselves. We play the odds. The handle today, pays the horsemen from three days ago."

Ben shook his head in utter disbelief.

"On a good day, the interest alone would pay the purse monies."

"When's the last time we had a good day?"

The man hesitated. "It's been a while."

Ben sat, thinking, agonizing. "If Swingline had filed bankruptcy on Monday as planned, that would mean the horsemen running their horses Thursday, Friday, and Saturday would have essentially been running for nothing. Talk about odds. And if a horse broke down, it'd be double nothing, triple, because it was for nothing to begin with."

"I don't think you can think like a horseman in this situation, Mr. Miller. The sad reality is this isn't really about the horses or the horsemen anymore. You could simulcast and still get the same crowd."

Ben held up his hand. He'd heard enough. "How old are you?"

The man hesitated, wondering what his age had to do with anything. "Thirty-three."

"There was a time, and not all that long ago, when the horses *were* all that it was about."

"I'm sure it was. But like I said, those days are over."

"I don't think so. I just think we need to figure out how to get them back."

The man shrugged. "Good luck."

Ben sat back. "You don't think we have a prayer, do you?"

The man's answer was written all over his face.

Ben had heard and seen enough. "I'm getting the impression you're thinking you'd like to bail out of here."

"I do have another job offer."

"Then I suggest you take it. As much as I'd like to have you around when we get back on our feet so I can say I told you so, I need people on the job that do the same kind of math I do."

"I'm sorry, Mr. Miller."

"So am I."

Tom was waiting outside the office for Ben. The young man walked out ahead of him. Tom read between the lines. "What'd you do, old man, fire another one?"

Ben shook his head. "I had no idea."

Tom smiled and put his arm around Ben's shoulder. "I'll tell you what, Ben. If there's one thing I know, it's this. You've got to go with what's in your heart, because in the end your heart is all that matters."

Chapter Four

Dawn and Ben's stable consisted of five horses; a two-year old colt appropriately named "Beau Together" that was out of All Together and sired by Beau Born, a three-year old filly named "Born All Together" also of the All Together and Beau Born parentage. Two other three-year old fillies named "Wee Born" and "Winning Beau" from other broodmares on the farm, sired by Beau Born, and a three-year old Beau Born colt named "Native Born Beau" that they bought at a sale along with the dam. All were Ohio breds.

Between Dawn's pregnancies and Ben's slowing down a little with age and the aftermath of the stroke, they'd decided to keep the number of horses in training at a manageable five or under and concentrate on furthering Beau's tenure at stud. Dawn loved the racetrack, but loved being at home on the farm during the winters almost as much. This was a good compromise, the fewer horses the better and they only trained for themselves now. No more public stable. This way, for the most part, if they weren't running a horse that day, Dawn was only at the racetrack four hours or so each morning.

Wee Born was in the 7th race on Saturday; what would have been the last day of racing had Ben and Dawn not bought the racetrack. "I want everything in your name," Dawn insisted. "For all practical purposes, I don't want any ownership involvement." This was much like the day they'd bought All Together at the Vandervoort sale. Randy preferred it this way as well. The money and notoriety Dawn's family had afforded many things, but it also brought vulnerability.

In all of Ben's years at Nottingham Downs, he'd never once been to the upper offices. The racing secretary's office was as far as he ever needed to go. He drew a deep breath as he stepped off the elevator and for a second felt a little lightheaded. He glanced at his reflection in the glass panel outside the General Manager's office and without realizing it at first, had tucked in his stomach and puffed up his chest. He laughed to himself. "You old fool," he thought. "Boy, wouldn't Meg get a kick out of this."

His wife Meg had been dead for years. His first love, his only love. He recalled the times he'd tuck his stomach in wanting to show off and look muscular for her, and how she'd laugh. Ben was strong as an ox, but a muscle man? No. "Mr. Miller," she'd say. She always called him Mr. Miller. "Who do you think you're kidding?"

Oh how he loved that woman. He wondered if she'd be proud of him taking on the racetrack. Or would she think...?

Spears' secretary greeted him with an air of disdain. "Can I help you?"

"I have an appointment to see Spears."

The woman's rather sour expression turned instantly into a forced smile. "I'm sorry. Are you Mr. Miller?"

Ben nodded.

"It's so nice to meet you."

Ben simply nodded again. She wasn't fooling anybody. A second ago he was just a racetracker who'd possibly lost his way; not somebody she'd want to meet at all. As he followed her into Spears' office, he wondered if it would be considered power mongering if he up and just fired her on the spot.

"Ben," Richard Spears said, walking around from behind his desk to shake Ben's hand. "It's nice to see you."

Spears had been Nottingham Downs' General Manager for three years now and yet the two men had never laid eyes on one another until this very moment. Under the circumstances, Ben thought saying something like "Nice to *meet* you," would have been more appropriate. Meg, he thought, why am I picking apart everything everybody says? "Go with your heart," he could hear Tom saying. "Go with your heart."

28

"Well," Ben said, sitting down across from Spears when the man offered him a chair. "Where do we begin?"

"Can I get you something? Coffee? Water? A glass of wine?"

"No, thank you," Ben said, noticing the cocktail on the man's desk. "I'll be wanting to go over just a few things with you today. My main concern is the handle."

"Rightfully so," Spears said.

"I suppose if we had time we could hire a consultant to come in and do a study as to what went wrong, how we got to be where we are today or what could go wrong from here, or even what it is we might try and do. But we need to turn the situation around fast. The way I see it, this is a business that revolves around a racehorse and yet no one upstairs here seems to give a damn about racehorses."

"This isn't the county fair, Ben. The horse is just the means to the end."

Ben nodded. "I wonder if that attitude's trickled down through the floor to the public."

The man shrugged. "Listen, Ben, you have some fine horses and we have a dozen or so other horses here that are a draw. But for the most part, the average horse led over here to race...."

Ben shifted his weight. "Before we go any further and you piss me off, here's what I want you to do. I want you to find yourself a pair of jeans and get out on the backside."

"Excuse me...?" Spears chuckled, amused by such a juvenile suggestion. "Mr. Miller, I think I understand where you're coming from, but...."

"No." Ben said, stopping him right there. "Not another word. You've already pissed me off."

"I'm sorry."

Ben glanced at his watch. In just a few more minutes racing would be over for the day, too late for now. "Show up at my barn in the morning. We start at five. Come dressed like you belong there. I'll have the coffee on." Ben stood, no handshake, and walked out.

"Ma'am," he said, nodding to the man's secretary as he passed her desk.

Spears appeared at her side, shaking his head in disbelief. She looked up at him when Ben boarded the elevator and the doors closed.

"I need a pair of jeans," he said. "And some boots."

The woman hesitated. "Uh…what size?"

"I don't know. Call my wife."

It never occurred to Ben to check out the owner's office while he'd been upstairs. It was the furthest thing from his mind then and the furthest thing from his mind now as he walked through the grandstand. The horses in the last race were just about to break from the starting gate. He saw televised images of the action everywhere he looked. All eyes were on the monitors. He supposed that was a good thing, but it saddened him. It was a gorgeous sunshiny day and yet as he walked outside there weren't but a dozen or so spectators in addition to the trainers and the grooms watching the race live. To make matters worse, the race was a flat mile and starting right in front of the grandstand. There was a time not so very long ago when the excitement of the horses breaking from the starting gate that close would have drawn a crowd.

Ben stood and watched the race by himself. No one approached him, not even people he considered friends. He couldn't remember feeling so alone. The day Meg died? The day he buried her? The day he and Dawn argued years ago…?

The seven horse won the race. "Congratulations," he told its trainer, Bill Branagan.

"Thank you," the man said. No smile, no nothing.

Ben found Bill's lack of emotion both puzzling and irritating. What was happening to the Sport of Kings? He walked back to his barn with a heavy heart. What made him think he could do this? His moment of anguish was about to get worse. As he started down the shedrow he saw a note nailed to the tack-room door.

It read. "Ben Miller! You are a fool!"

Ben crumpled it and threw it into the trashcan. "Tell me something I don't know."

He heard a voice in his head, a familiar voice, a soft voice. "Mr. Miller, since when do you let other people get you down?"

Ben drew a breath and sighed. "Am I doing the right thing, Meg?"

"I don't know."

Ben chuckled. "I thought maybe you could tell me."

"No." He could almost feel the soft touch of her hand. "But I can tell you this. No one will try harder to make it work than you. I'm proud of you. Do your best."

Ben nodded. "I've got to admit I'm little scared."

"So am I," she said. "Don't let me down. As your wife, I have a reputation to uphold."

Ben laughed to himself. Was he really talking to Meg? He could never really know for sure, not as long as he was alive at least. But that comment right there sounded so much like something she *would* say. It had to be Meg. He was smiling as Tom came around the corner of the shedrow.

Ben looked up at him. "What are people saying about me?"

Tom shrugged. "You mean the ones I beat up or the ones I let walk away?"

Ben's smiled widened. "Never mind."

Tom nodded. "You okay?"

"I'm fine," Ben said, and half believed it.

Ben's farm always gave him that welcome-home feeling when he turned into the driveway. He appreciated that feeling even more today. He pulled past the main barn and parked by the house. A sense of warmth and well-being washed over him, but then just as quickly it vanished. He wondered if he shouldn't be doing something? But what? It's not as if he'd ever owned a racetrack before and knew what needed to be done. He sat in his truck, thinking. It seemed ludicrous to him to have driven home, as if it were any other ordinary day and he had nothing better or more important to do.

31

He looked around. This had been his home for close to thirty years now. He built the house; he built the barns, the pastures and the paddocks, the training track. He had everything he needed right here to train and run off the farm. What did he want with a whole damned racetrack? He'd never been one to make snap decisions. Why did he have to go and pick something this big to start now? He shook his head and sat scratching the back of his neck. The lawyer said they had three days to change their minds? It wasn't too late to back out. Though if he did, he had to admit he'd really look like a fool then. If people aren't talking to me now, they certainly wouldn't want to talk to me then.

Meg had asked a good question. Since when did he start caring so much about what other people thought? But that was just it. He wasn't doing this just for himself or strictly for Dawn or Tom or Randy either for that matter. He'd put everything he owned on the line for each and every person at Nottingham Downs. How could he not care? He was going to need the help of each and every person there if they were going to succeed.

A smile crossed his face as he watched Beau Born grazing lazily in the north pasture, one of the finest Thoroughbreds he'd ever laid eyes on. He started humming one of Meg's favorite tunes. "To Dream the Impossible Dream." Beau had been an impossible dream. All Together was too. He waved to George and Glenda, the couple that took care of the horses at the farm. They too were counting on him. And the horses. And the dogs; all six of them came running. He got out of the truck, singing in his deep baritone, "And I know if I'll only be true, to this glorious quest." The dogs barked and howled and vied for his attention. "That my heart will lie peaceful and calm, when I'm laid to rest."

Chapter Five

Dawn's phone rang and D.R. ran to answer it. Dawn got there first. "Hello."

"I just had a thought," Ben said, standing in his kitchen. "Do you still have personnel contacts at the newspaper?"

"A few. Why?"

"I'm thinking we need to make people care about what's going on at the racetrack."

"You don't mean about us buying it?"

"No, I'm talking about the people, the owners and the trainers, the horses. I'm thinking you can use your contacts at the paper and maybe get a daily article run."

"Daily? I don't think, uh…."

"All right, weekly. And I want you to write it."

Dawn smiled. "Did Randy put you up to this?"

"No. Why?"

Dawn hesitated. "Oh, I've just been thinking I would like to get back to writing."

"Well then," Ben said, as if it were a done deal. "This is perfect."

"I'll see what I can do. I'm not even sure who the sports editor is anymore."

"I don't think you should write it for the sports section. You need to get it where everyone will read it. And something else I've been thinking, I think we should start the racing at two instead of one and have two daily doubles. One for the people that come at two and one for the people who come after work, maybe the last two races of the day and move the trifecta up. And I think we should look into changing the time frame between races."

Dawn sat down on the couch, giving thought to all this, and admittedly, was starting to get just a little excited with the possibilities.

"Spears is going to be in the barn at five in the morning. I want him to spend some time seeing what it is we horsemen do."

"Okay, but I'm going to have the kids tomorrow. Carol won't be home until early afternoon."

"So, that's even better. I'll see you in the morning."

Five o'clock the following morning, it was raining. Not a downpour, but a steady rain nonetheless. Wee Born, the three-year old filly Ben and Dawn had entered for today, did not like the mud. It would be best to scratch her. There was a race back for her next Friday. But, the race she was in today was only a six-horse field. Ben glanced at his watch. Here came Spears, looking lost, but right on time.

"Good morning," he said.

Ben nodded. "When horses are being walked around the shedrow you'll want to step to the inside. The stall side," he said, adding that last part when Spears seemed confused. "If something scares you, freeze. If you see hooves flying, duck."

"You're kidding. Right?"

"Only about the scaring, freezing part. " Ben smiled. "You are best not to make any sudden moves though, unless it is to duck."

"So what is it you want me to do?"

Tom came around the corner toting his western saddle. "Hot damn, old man. I thought you were kidding when you said you wanted Spears to pony a few."

Spears eyes got big and wide.

Ben chuckled. "Have you met Tom?"

"No, I can't say that I have."

Tom shook his hand and introduced himself. "Tom Girard, pony boy, assistant trainer, friend...servant of the Lord."

"Born again," Ben said.

"Uncle Tom!!" D.R. ran to Tom and wrapped his arms around Tom's leg. "I want to wide."

Tom laughed. "And this is D.R., the little shepherd boy."

Dawn came around the corner, toting Maeve and what appeared to be all of Maeve's earthly possessions. "D.R., come here!" She let Maeve slide down off her hip and set her down in the tack room. D.R. ran to join them. "What did I tell you about running in the shedrow?"

"Good morning," Spears said.

Dawn smiled as best she could with a pacifier clenched in her teeth. "Good morning," she said, and went about getting both children settled in. D.R. climbed onto the couch and turned on the TV. He stood on his tippy-toes to push the video button and then sat down and started singing. "I love you, you love me...." Dawn turned the volume down.

Ben entered the tack room with Spears right behind him. "Where's Randy?" Ben asked.

"He had an emergency." Dawn glanced at Spears. He was a club member; she knew him in passing. D.R. was on his tippy-toes again, reaching for the volume button. Dawn whisked his legs out from under him and he bounced down on the couch, giggling, and then stood on his head.

Spears laughed.

Dawn pretended to scowl. "Please, don't encourage him."

"Coffee?" Ben asked.

Spears nodded, still laughing. Fortunately he took it black like everyone else. He added a little sugar. "Help yourself," Ben said, motioning to a box of donuts. "Don't touch the fried cake. That's little Maeve's."

"Don't touch," Maeve said, in that cute little voice of hers, rocking back and forth in her playpen.

Dawn chuckled. "She's going to grow up thinking a fried cake is a "don't touch" after all the times she's heard it referred to that way."

Spears smiled, rather enjoying this homey little scene. They all sat down and had coffee and a donut.

Tom came up the shedrow astride Red, all decked out in a rain slicker. Dawn handed him his coffee; he took a sip and handed it back. Behind her, Ben was explaining to Spears, "The horses all got a scoop of oats for breakfast. No hay. Not until after training."

Dawn closed the child's gate Randy had built in the tack room; it not only kept the children safely inside the tack room, it was set far enough away from the door in the event a horse would kick out coming around the end of the shedrow.

Dawn walked down to get Born All Together, put the chain part of the lead shank up over her nose, and led her outside into the increasing rain and handed her lead shank to Tom. Tom had already taped her tail to keep if from getting muddy and sticking to her hind legs.

"I'm going to get one of Richard's between her and Whinny." Whinny was Winning Beau's nickname.

Dawn nodded. That would give her time to clean Born All Together's stall and hand walk her before he came back for Whinny.

"Come on," Ben said to Spears. "I watch every horse that goes to the track." Ben popped open an umbrella and the two started their trek to the racetrack. The rain softened the silence of the other trainers, grooms, and owners that they passed. And for that matter, no one recognized Spears. No one even looked at him. He was a "nobody."

"So you say your horse doesn't like the mud?"

Ben nodded. "She won't run a lick in it."

"Are you going to scratch her?"

"No. Joe'll just piss me off when I try. It's only a six-horse field."

Spears nodded. "You are his boss though, you know."

Ben glanced at him. "All the more reason to let him do his job the best he can." There was a steady stream of horses coming and going off the racetrack. "Watch your step."

Spears was just about to step in a pile of fresh horse manure.

When they got to the racetrack, the only area for standing out of the rain was under the tiny eave by the back door of the track kitchen. It was jam-packed. Ben noticed Spears rather disgruntled expression at the situation, unprotected but for the umbrella. "Yep, a Ginny stand would have been nice."

"A what?"

"A Ginny stand. A small grandstand for the grooms and the trainers, the owners, even the track manager for mornings like this and for watching the races from the backside."

Spears smiled apologetically. "I feel like Ebenezer Scrooge seeing Christmases past. I didn't realize."

The rain picked up.

"Yeah, well let's hope we have a future."

The morning was like any other morning at Nottingham Downs. Rain or shine, horses still needed to be trained, bathed, walked, bandaged, vetted. Randy stopped at the barn twice, once to treat a horse and then again in passing to check on the children. Dawn was never far away and always with a watchful eye on them. Ben and Spears went back and forth to the racetrack four times. Wee Born was hand-walked.

Spears found himself in and out of the tack room, coffee, another donut. "Bandages? These?" He held them up. Dawn nodded. Ben and Dawn had the first five stalls of a forty-eight-stall barn. Everywhere Spears looked, there was activity. With it raining as hard as it was now, just about every horse in the barn had to be hand-walked. The shedrow got harder and harder to navigate with all that activity. It was a slippery-sliding, watch-your-step ditch by nine o'clock.

"This is ridiculous," Spears said, when he almost fell for the third time. "Surely there has to be a way to keep the rain from coming in."

"Not really, but better drainage would help," Tom said, while doing up Native Beau Born. "Maybe some roll-down canvas or awnings. Boy, now that would be nice. Can you see it all now, old man?"

Ben gave it some thought.

"What about indoor barns?" Spears asked.

Ben shook his head. "All you get is sick horses that way; too many horses, not enough fresh air."

Randy stopped again at the barn to check in on Dawn and the children. D.R. and Maeve squealed with delight upon seeing him. Spears observed with a smile. The children seemed perfectly content with their play area in the tack room. Johnny, a young man that was Dawn and Ben's favorite jockey, stopped at the barn. Everyone huddled inside.

They all heard the shouts "Loose horse" then the advent of thundering hooves. Tom took a cautious glance out the door. The horse was just coming around the corner. He timed his move perfectly, stepped out just in time to startle the horse. It stopped, slipping and sliding, and just like that, Tom grabbed hold of the lead shank dangling from his halter. Then here came the horse's groom, madder than hell.

"This common son-of-a-bitch," he said, and started shanking the horse.

"Hey, hey, hey," Tom said, stopping him. "Don't make me to have to pray for you."

The man shook his head, still angry, but then had to laugh when Tom added, "You know I will if I have to."

"Don't, please..." the man said, laughing again.

"All right then." Tom patted the horse on the shoulder. "My work here is done." That had everybody laughing. "I'll see you at the kitchen in about ten minutes." He tucked his racing form deep into his back pocket and underneath his jacket to keep it from getting wet. "I'll be in the reading room until then if anyone needs me."

Dawn and Randy gathered up the children, piled into Randy's truck, and rode on ahead to the kitchen. Ben and Spears followed under Ben's umbrella. It was raining even harder now. The track kitchen was bursting at the seams. Tom walked in behind Ben and Spears. Randy had pulled two tables together.

"Have you ever eaten here before?" Ben asked Spears.

He shook his head.

"Then you're in for a real treat."

Spears thought he was joking. There were donuts, bagels, sweet rolls, coffee, milk, juice.... He didn't realize they actually cooked food - food.

"My usual," Tom said.

"Me, too," Ben added.

Spears looked at the menu posted overhead. "Two eggs over easy, toast, and hashed browns."

"Bacon?"

"Sure."

They drew some stares, some glances, but still, no one was talking to Ben. They talked to Tom. "Who's that?" a groom friend of his asked.

"Oh, him?" Tom glanced over his shoulder and flashed one of those "shit-eating" grins of his. "That would be Richard Spears, your racetrack General Manager."

"No kidding?" the man whispered.

"As God is my witness."

Tom, Ben, and Spears got their trays, poured themselves a cup of coffee, and after getting their meals, walked to the back of the room to join Dawn and Randy and the kids. By the time they sat down, every horseman and horsewoman present knew who Spears was and were all staring daggers in their direction.

Ben noticed. "Let the man eat," he said. Several people nodded. No one was leaving.

"This is really tasty," Spears said, with a hardy mouthful.

"Brownie's the best cook there is."

"You mean present company excluded?" Spears said, glancing at Dawn.

She shook her head. "Don't look at me."

"Daddy cooks," D.R. said.

Everyone at the table laughed, as well as some other people sitting nearby, all ears. It was nice having an excuse to laugh. The tension in the room was reminiscent of a big thundercloud on a hot summer afternoon. You knew any minute now, it was going to storm. No sooner had the last person at the table placed their fork down, than the questions started.

"How did the racetrack go bankrupt in the first place?"

"Where did all the money go?"

"How could something like this happen?"

"Who's not doing their job?"

"What's going to happen now?"

"How is it we've never seen you on the backside before?"

"Well...." Spears started to stand up to answer but Ben discreetly nudged him to stay seated. No grandstanding. They were all on the same level at the moment. "I apologize for not being on the backside previously. I had no idea how much fun you all were having." It was meant as a joke, in light of the weather, but no one laughed. "Or how hard you all work," he added, which drew a few nods.

This was not an easy crowd.

"I know you all have a lot of concerns and that's completely understandable."

"Why don't you just answer our questions?"

"Come on, let the man talk," Tom said, holding up his hands.

Spears cast a glance in Tom's direction. "Thank you," set deep in his eyes.

Tom nodded, taking both sides. "I believe the first question was, 'How did the racetrack go bankrupt in the first place?' I'd actually like to know that myself."

Spears concealed a smile. He could see why Tom was so well-liked.

Ben crossed his arms, waiting for the answer as well.

"Well, it's all rather complicated and would take forever, but I can tell you this," Spears began. "A little over two years ago, attendance started to drop."

Everyone nodded.

"Now it's hard to say which came first, the chicken or the egg, but...." He paused, wanting to choose his words carefully so as not to anger the crowd. "But when the pots started going up at Mountaineer, a lot of horsemen started running there. We never really had to compete with Waterford. If a horse couldn't compete here, that's where they went. But with Mountaineer, all of a sudden we did. Now, I don't blame anyone for running where they're going to get the most money, but...."

"Why can't we get the same money here?" one of the trainers asked.

"Well, for one, we didn't have the investment dollars. We were trying to operate off the daily handle. Rudolph was tapped. It was sink or swim, and while we were able to keep afloat, if you will, for a while, in the end...."

"What about *our* investment?" one of Brubaker's owner's asked.

40

"Let me finish," Spears said, looking like the General Manager for the first time since walking into the room. "We can point a lot of fingers here. I personally know of six horses two weeks ago that should have won and didn't. They ran up the shithouse."

Everyone sat silently, even D.R. at the sound of the "bad" word.

"I guess I don't need to tell any of you where those horses placed this past week down at Mountaineer. Am I accusing anybody of "holding" their horses up here? No. Not outright. But it sure is a coincidence they can't hit the board here for five and ten thousand and all ran one-two down there for twelve and fifteen."

There was some uncomfortable shifting of weight and fidgeting in the room.

"And how about racing a horse fit? I've heard that expression a lot over the years. But tell me, do you think that's fair to the betting public?"

Ben smiled. Even he was a little guilty of that.

"Did you ever listen to the bettors as they leave? I have. They think every person on the racetrack is crooked. And you know what? A lot of them are."

Randy glanced around the room. Talk about silencing a crowd. He looked at Dawn; she was taking notes.

"We all know why the betting public comes here. It's to win races. They want to lay their two dollars down, their ten, their twenty, their fifty, and they want to win. Eight out of every ten people bet the favorites. And you know what? If they win, we win. If a horse is favored to win, he should either win or run second approximately seven out of ten times. Do you want to know what the average is here? I won't keep you in suspense. It's not even fifty percent."

Dawn raised her hand, an elegant hand, yielding a lot of power. "How do track conditions play into that percentage?"

Spears looked at her. "Some," he said.

"And post position?"

"Again, some."

Dawn nodded.

"It's all about winning and losing? Losing day in and day out, after a while, is like pounding your head against the wall. What's the point? Then there goes the attendance, there goes the handle, there go the purses. The betting public wants to pick a winner. They want to sit with that racing form and handicap. They want to take an active part. You want to know why they don't come down to the paddock anymore to pick a winner? Because there's no reason to pick the fittest-looking horse in the lot. I stood next to a man yesterday and these are his exact words, 'Yeah, that's if they let him run.' How many of you have heard similar sentiments? How many of you have held a horse? I challenge you all to sit down with the racing form for a half hour between now and post time and see how many winners you pick. And that's with no inside information I might add. Money's tight, the economy is suffering. If the public can't pick a winner, they stop coming. They stop coming, we have no money. We have no money, you don't get paid. None of us get paid."

"There are times when a horse needs a race."

"That's understandable. But statistically that's going to show on their form. They might draw the longshot betting public, but that's it. The bettor knows they're playing a longshot. It's the favorites not winning their share that sours the crowd. It's like playing the lottery. If you know you have one chance in a million of winning big and your number doesn't come up, you weren't that one in a million. Try playing the other games, where one ticket in every ten are supposed to pay off, and you keep buying ten at a time and haven't won in thirty or forty or fifty. Pretty soon you're going to stop playing that game."

One of the women trainers spoke up. "So you're saying this is all our fault?"

"No, I'm not saying that at all. I'm just giving you one of the reasons why the handle is down. The economy plays a big part as well. And public fickleness."

"By that," Dawn said, head down and writing. "You mean there are a lot more choices where a person can wager their money, like the lottery?"

Spears nodded. "Precisely. Thoroughbred racing has lost a lot of its entertainment appeal. We intend to bring it back."

Ben glanced at Dawn and then at Spears. If Spears had a plan on how to bring the entertainment appeal back, he wasn't offering it. "There are many variables that play into the success or failure of a racetrack, or any business this size for that matter. Pointing fingers at who's to blame or who dropped the ball, so to speak, is not the direction to take. It's what we do from here on in that needs our attention." He looked around the room. "Were there any more questions?"

"Yes." A tiny voice came from the back of the room. It was Mim Freemont speaking up, a tiny little woman ex-jockey now trainer who weighed about a hundred pounds soaking wet, and was crusty as one could be. She stood with the help of a cane. "What about the jocks? What about their part in 'holding a horse?'"

Ben answered that one. "Don't you worry, Mim. We'll be heading there next."

The little woman smiled. "Another question, one that I think's on a lot of horsemen's minds. Ben, with all due respect, what makes you think you can run a racetrack?"

Ben chuckled and scratched the back of his neck. "I don't. But I figure I can't fail any worse than Rudolph did. The way I see things, the only direction we can go is up."

Everyone laughed, agreeing.

Dawn laid her pen down, a subtle action that got both Ben and Spears attention. 'Quit while you're ahead,' her body language said. Everyone there seemed agreeable to that. They all had work to do and it was still raining. Dawn and Randy bundled up the children. "I'll be back by two," she told Ben. Their nanny was due home around noon.

"Are you going to try and get something in the paper?" Ben asked, motioning to the notes she tucked into her jacket.

"Yes," she nodded.

Randy hoisted D.R. and Maeve into his arms. "You did good," he told Spears.

Spears thanked him and when they left, turned to Ben and Tom. "The jocks' room?"

"Not yet. We have two more horses to do up and a blacksmith due any minute now for Wee Born."

"Isn't that the one running today?"

Ben opened the door, peered out into the rain and shook his head in disgust. "She won't run a lick."

Spears tucked himself in under the umbrella. "Maybe she'll surprise you."

Ben peered over his glasses at him, a look that said volumes.

Tom laughed. Spears blushed. Ben was a man of few words and Spears was learning that the hard way. Very few horses surprised Ben. He was a hands-on trainer and knew his horses inside and out. Wee Born did not like the mud, end of subject. He was having the blacksmith put stickers on only in hopes of giving her a little more traction to keep her from hurting herself.

The jockeys had been forewarned and on the defense. Small men and women in stature, pound for pound, what they lacked in bulk, they made up for with attitude, guts, and tenacity. Ask any jock his or her opinion on who could give a horse the best ride and ninety-nine out of a hundred will point to themselves. Ben liked that in a jockey. It's what wins races.

He looked around the room.

By the same token, poll a hundred jocks and at least ninety-nine out of the hundred would have to admit to "holding" a horse on occasion, whether by the design of the trainer or amongst themselves to cash a bet.

"What are you accusing us of, Ben?" Juan Garcia, the leading jockey asked.

"I'm not accusing anybody of anything," Ben said, standing his ground. "I'm just telling you how it is. This isn't about the past. This is about how it's going to be from here on in. No more. It will not be tolerated."

Tom stood at Ben's side with his arms crossed as he looked around the room at the guiltiest of the bunch. Then he let his eyes rest upon Annie Griffin, a new female jock on the scene. She was rather cute, maybe even pretty, he thought. When she smiled at him, the way most women do, he subconsciously slid the toothpick dangling in his mouth from one side to the other. The Lord would not be pleased at all with the thoughts running through his mind. He forced himself to look away, but just so she wouldn't feel slighted, he glanced back at the woman and touched the rim of his cowboy hat. Annie Griffin melted.

The next order of business was Wee Born's race. It rained all afternoon, she ended up running fifth, beaten eight lengths, and as Ben had predicted earlier, never ran a lick. Hours, minutes, morning, noon, afternoon, here, there, the day was a blur. Ben sat down in the tack room and sighed. Bad enough to waste a race, but the filly had also nicked herself on the inside of her left hock. It was a pretty good gash. Racing her back in a week was iffy at this point.

Dawn did Wee Born up and smeared goop on her hock, then came into the tack room and sat down across from Ben. He looked beyond tired and she couldn't help but worry. "Are you taking your blood pressure medicine?"

Ben nodded. "Why? Do I look that bad?"

Tom walked in behind her and she shifted her attention. "What's the matter with you?" she asked, from his expression.

"It's that damned Linda Dillon. I feel so sorry for her ponies."

When Dawn nodded in agreement, Tom sat down next to Ben and stretched out his legs.

"Is there anything we can do about it?" Dawn asked.

"You mean as owners?" Ben said. "Like what?"

"I don't know," Tom said. "Kick her sorry ass off the track." Linda Dillon underfed her ponies to keep them from getting high and on top of that, worked them practically to death. And not just her, but about five other pony people on the track as well.

"She'd just take them somewhere else," Ben said. "That won't solve anything."

"Yeah, well at least I won't have to see them anymore. She was just bathing that palomino of hers and honest to God, you could practically hear the metal sweat-scraper scraping its ribs. And every time it flinched, she took to…."

Dawn held up her hand. "Spare me this. Okay?"

Tom fell silent, staring at the floor.

"Why don't you go talk to her," Ben suggested.

"Are you kidding me? That's woman's mean. I saw her rip a wing off a fly once just so she could watch it buzz around on the ground in circles."

"Tom, enough, all right," Dawn insisted. "I mean it."

He nodded. "It's just that as long as it wasn't any of my business, I could almost look the other way. But now…." He glanced from one to the other. "It looks bad too, you know?"

No argument there.

"Another thing I've been thinking. Whatever happened to that guy who used to blow the bugle at the start of the races?" A CD broadcasted over the loud speaker had been used for the last couple of years. "That taped music sounds so cheesy."

Ben nodded. "Wasn't it just a few days ago, when all I had to think about was…."

"Don't even go there, old man. What's the point?"

Ben laughed and looked at Dawn. "What can we do?"

Dawn thought for a moment. "We could hire somebody to be a liaison person."

"A what?" Tom asked.

Dawn chuckled. "A person that patrols the backside, someone designated to specifically address these kinds of issues."

"How do we find this person?" Ben asked.

"Well." Dawn paused, thinking. "I don't know that we want it to be somebody that's already here."

Tom shrugged. "Why not?"

"We don't want them biased."

"Yeah, but if you bring a stranger in here…" Tom said.

Ben nodded. "Why is everything so difficult?"

"But at the same time, they'd have to be a horseman to know what to look out for," Tom insisted.

"Or horsewoman," Dawn said, purposely.

46

Tom grinned. "All right then. How about a good-looking one, a religious one?"

"What about Missy Brinkley?" Ben suggested.

Tom shook his head. He and Missy had a history; a shit-kicking romp-stomping hell of a history.

Dawn looked at both of them. "Is this going to be full-time or part-time? Deciding on that will help narrow it down."

"And what they'll cover and how tough to get," Tom said. "Maybe your Uncle Matt could suggest someone with some muscle."

"Very funny," Dawn said.

The three of them sat there for a moment.

"What about Dusty Burns?" Tom said. "That is, unless you're hell bent on having it be a woman?"

Dawn shrugged. "It doesn't have to be a woman. It just doesn't *not* have to be a woman. I like Dusty Burns. What do you think?" she asked Ben. "He's probably available."

Dusty was a trainer who'd lost all his horses a couple of months back when his owner died. The family sold every one of them right out from under him. Since everyone's business on the racetrack *is* everyone's business thanks to the rumor-mill, they all knew that not only was Dusty devastated with the loss of his friend and employer, he was heartbroken over the loss of the horses.

He'd gone on a binge shortly thereafter and having been there more times than he would care to count, it was Tom who pulled him up out of the gutter, so to speak. "All right, I'll talk to him. What are we thinking as far as pay?"

Ben looked at Dawn, hands held out.

"I don't know," she said. "What do you think?"

Ben hesitated. "I don't want to insult the man, but we're broke."

Tom stood up and adjusted his cowboy hat. "I'll handle it, don't worry about it. I'll play it by ear."

Ben peered over the top of his glasses at him, a look that related a thousand words. "I don't want this all over the racetrack. Okay?"

Tom chuckled. "Oh ye of little faith."

Chapter Six

Ben looked up as the stable guard walked down the shedrow toward the tack room. He didn't like the look on the man's face. "What's the matter?"

"Trouble. There's two cops up at the stable gate."

"And…?"

"They claim that they got a tip that there's a body in barn 14. It came through an anonymous call."

"Barn 14," Ben said, thinking. "That's Billy Martin's barn on the north side."

The guard nodded. "I don't know if it's true. The cops don't either. They just want to take a look. They say they have to follow the lead."

"Well, tell them to go ahead."

"They said they need you with them."

Ben shook his head and walked with the guard to the stable gate. He didn't like Billy Martin, but certainly didn't want to see him dead. The two policemen were standing by their squad car blocking traffic from coming in and going out.

Ben motioned to the drive on the side of the entrance. "Do you think you can pull over there?"

They both said no. "Sorry." One officer stayed at the track gate. The other one walked with Ben to barn 14. It was a long walk.

"Did they say who this body might be?"

The officer shook his head.

Everyone they passed by, gawked. Some looked as if they wanted to say something. Some looked as if they wanted to follow. Some look concerned, some looked smug. Ben pointed his finger at one of the smug ones. "That would be Dave Brubaker," he told the policeman, loud enough for Dave Brubaker to hear.

The officer concealed a smile. Ben and he walked down barn 14 shedrow. All the horses came to the front of their stalls. All their haynets were empty. How many horses did Billy Martin have? Ben glanced back, counting. Twelve.

When they reached the tack room, Ben was reluctant to look inside. He himself had almost died in his own tack room a few years back.

"The informant said the body would be in the, uh...." The officer checked his notes. "The feed room."

It was just beyond the tack room. Ben looked inside and there sat Billy Martin, dead as they come. "I'll be damned," Ben said to himself, and to the officer, "Now what?"

"Procedure, sir." And procedure it was. The officer phoned for the rescue squad.

Apparently someone of authority had to confirm the death. Ben stood by, shaking his head. By now, Tom was at his side. "I dated his daughter once, you know. She was a vegetarian."

When Ben just looked at him, Tom shrugged. "What, I was just stating a fact."

The fire department showed up next. "Do you want to turn those sirens off," Ben said. "You're scaring all the horses. Turn them off! There's no fire. There's no emergency."

More cop cars. More cops. Then the coroner arrived. "Excuse me. Excuse me," he kept saying, as he pushed through the crowd. He viewed the corpse. "Does anyone know this man?"

Ben nodded. "We all do, on some level or other."

"Kin?"

Tom stared. "Kin?"

"Family?"

"He has a daughter. She lives out of state." Tom gazed in at Billy Martin; on a stretcher all bent over and stiff. "Do you mind if I say a prayer?"

One of the cops shrugged. The paramedics and firemen stepped back. "Lord," Tom said, bowing his head. "Billy Martin wasn't the greatest guy in the world. I don't think he was an honest man. But have pity on him. Amen."

He raised his eyes and looked at Ben. "I'm sorry. It was the best I could do." When the body was removed, Tom took it upon himself to fill all Billy Martin's horses' haynets, and topped off their water.

Ben walked over to the secretary's office and had the clerk look up the information on Billy Martin's horses' owners. He sat down at the desk about to phone all three of them, when in walked Tom with Dusty Burns. "I'll take care of that, Ben," Dusty said.

"Wait a minute. Just like that?" Ben stared.

"It's my job, right?"

Ben nodded and handed him the phone. "Thank you." By dinner time, Billy Martin's horses were under the care of three other trainers. Before Ben left for the day, he had a full report from Dusty.

"I moved his truck to the far end of the lot. It's locked. The stalls are stripped. The feed tubs and buckets and stall guards are locked up in the tack room. The feed room is still taped off. I'm going to deal with Linda Dillon tomorrow."

Ben wished him luck.

"Don't worry. I won't let you down."

Ben gave that comment thought as he walked down through the barn area. In the distance, a storm was brewing.

Ben had a restless night's sleep. Aside from the obvious in regards to Billy Martin and the man being dead, something else nagged at him but he couldn't quite put his finger on it. He gazed out the kitchen window, waved to Randy as he drove by in his truck on the way to the racetrack, and then heaved a big sigh. "That's it...That's it." He phoned Dawn. It was not that uncommon to call her at 5:00 in the morning. She had a cell phone with a nice little bell chime that didn't wake the children.

"Bring your notebook with you. We're going to make an announcement."

Dawn cleared her throat. "About what?"

"About the murder."

"Murder?"

"Well, I don't know if it was a murder, but the best defense is a good offense. I'd rather call it a murder before anyone else does."

"Okay, and who are we going to announce this to?"

"The backside. I'll have Dusty do it."

"Dusty?"

"Why not? After all, he is our *liaison* man."

Dawn smiled. "I'll see you in a few minutes."

Tom was always first at the barn. Dawn and Ben usually arrived shortly after him. Tom had the coffee made, horses fed, and Red tacked.

Ben sat down at his desk and glanced at the "overnight" which listed the horses entered for tomorrow. Tom stood looking over his shoulder. "How'd we go from ten and twelve horse fields to six and eight in the blink of an eye? What's going on here? Didn't we ask the horsemen to give us the benefit of the doubt? What are they holding out for?"

Tom crossed his arms and shrugged. "I wonder how that affects the handle?"

"The handle?" Ben had to laugh. "Well don't you sound like front office."

The plus side of the morning: at least people greeted Ben as he walked up to the racetrack. Some had a question or two and he even had some answers for a few. "Ask Tom," he told one. "Check with Dusty," he told another. "Now if you'll excuse me." He walked along, mulling over in his head what he wanted to say about Billy Martin's death.

"Dawn!"

"I'm down here," she called from one of the stalls.

"Come here now and write this up before I forget."

Dawn chuckled. Ben's announcement was brief and to the point: "Nottingham Downs mourns the death of one of our own. We support the criminal investigation into Billy Martin's untimely passing and trust justice will be served." Dawn was impressed. But, Ben wasn't done. "I urge you all now to observe a moment of silence." He paused. "Thank you."

Tom returned then and was given the note to pass on to Dusty. "I just saw him," he said. "He'll be right down." He handed Wee Born to Dawn and dismounted Red.

"Holy shit," Dusty said, entering the tack room. "I just heard Hollywood Park is closing."

51

"What?!" Ben sat down heavy in his chair.

"Yep, it was just on the radio."

Ben propped his head in his hands. "You've got to be kidding me. What's with giving me such bad news?"

Dusty sat down on the cot next to him. "I raced there once, you know. God, it was a nice track."

Tom counted on his fingers. "Okay, in the last ten years, that's Longacres, Sportsman Park, Hialeah and Bay Meadows, not to mention...."

Ben looked at him. He'd heard enough. If racetracks of that caliber could go belly-up, what on earth was going to save them? He observed Dusty as he read the announcement he was to make. The man nodded. "This is good."

"Thank you." Ben shook his head. This was ludicrous. "So, uh...did you have any luck with Linda?"

"Well, yeah, in a way. She told me to get the hell out of her shedrow, and I told her to get the hell off the racetrack."

Ben glanced at Tom. He was smiling, grinning actually.

"I gave her until tomorrow."

Ben stared. This was all going too fast for him.

"I figure she'll head to Mountaineer, so I gave them a call to give 'em a heads up."

Ben nodded. It was about all he could do in response. He motioned to the note. "I figure as soon as training's over would be the best time for that." Dusty agreed.

It was still early in the morning and the Miller barn had three more horses to track. Randy checked in around nine-thirty. "You ready for a break? We need to talk," he said to Dawn.

She climbed into his truck and leaned her head back. She too, hadn't slept well last night. She looked at Randy and smiled. He needed a haircut. When it got this long, it curled over his collar. She combed her fingers through it. "So what's going on?"

"I'm not sure," he said. "But I just got a call from my mom. Apparently Dad's had a heart attack."

"Oh no."

"She said he's stabilized. They may have to do bypass surgery."

"Are you going to go see them?"

He nodded. "I've got two more calls to do and then I'll head out. It'll be easier just to drive than try and book a flight." Randy's parents' farm was a six-hour road trip.

"Do you want me to go with you?"

He shook his head. "Nah, not with everything you have going on here, and the kids."

"The kids will be fine with Carol."

"I know. I love you," he said, kissing her.

"I love you too. Call me."

"I will."

Ben took the news harder than Dawn would have expected. He and Randy's father had spent some time together last year when Randy's parents visited the farm. But aside from that, they hardly knew one another personally. "The man's so young," Ben said. Randy's father was sixty-two years old. "I'm old enough to be *his* father."

Tom had cooked chili for dinner, brought it down to Dawn's, and the three of them were just about to sit down to eat. D.R. and Maeve had played hard all day. Carol had fed them earlier and they were already in bed for the night. "You better not have put hot sauce in that," Dawn said.

Tom frowned. "I did not, but...." He took out a bottle of Tabasco from his pocket. "I'm packing."

Once, Dawn had put a big mouthful of Tom's famous chili in her mouth and couldn't taste food for a week. "Oh, this is good," she said, of today's batch.

Tom shook five blasts of hot sauce onto his. "Well, the announcement went well."

Dawn and Ben agreed.

"Here."

"No thanks," Ben said, when Tom tried passing the Tabasco to him. He motioned to the bread instead, and then the butter.

"Are you trying to clog up your arteries, old man?" Tom said.

Dawn kicked him under the table.

"What?"

Dawn rolled her eyes.

"Listen," Ben said. "I'm an old man, I know it. My days are limited."

Dawn sighed.

"I've been thinking. I'd like to leave a mark. I'd like everyone to know I lived and that I did something with my life."

Tom looked at him. "What, like, raise some of the finest Thoroughbreds Ohio has ever seen?"

Ben smiled. Tom was indeed the best friend a man could have, pain in the ass and all. "No, I'd like to do more'n that."

"Okay." Tom shrugged. "What's the one thing you'd change about your life?"

Ben looked at him. "My life? I'm not talking about my life. What's wrong with you? My life is great. I'm talking about racing."

The three of them laughed and then grew quiet, eating. "I personally would like to do away with the whip," Dawn said. "That's what I'd like to do. I've been giving it a lot of thought."

"It'll never happen," Tom said, with his mouth full.

"You're kidding me." Dawn shook her head. "Do you really believe that? Come on, how much difference can it make?"

"A lot coming down the stretch," Tom said, matter-of-factly. "On the average, it's what separates the winners from the losers."

"I disagree," Dawn said, in that way of hers that always tweaked a sparring nerve in Tom.

"Oh yeah, and how many horses have you ridden to the wire?"

"None," Dawn said. "But if I did I would never use a whip."

"They're called crops," Tom said. "Crop is the *politically correct* term."

54

Ben laughed. "And since when are you politically correct?"

"Since yesterday," Tom said, reaching for the chili ladle. "Wait a minute. Didn't I see you smacking Wee Born just this morning?"

Dawn laughed. "She bit me! It was an eye for an eye. And I didn't hit her with a whip; I smacked her with my hand."

Ben looked at the two of them, as close to a son and daughter as he's ever had. "I don't like a whip either, excuse me, a crop, but I honestly don't see stretch runs without them. How do you keep the horse going when it's tired and wanting to pack it in?"

"Precisely my point," Dawn said. "When they're tired, they shouldn't have to...."

Ben's cell phone rang, interrupting them. He looked at it as if it were alive. "I'll never get used to that damned thing going off."

It was Dusty. Ben handed the phone to Tom.

"She did what?" Tom said, and then a sigh. "Feed them. Just give them hay. I don't know if she grains her horses. We have extra water buckets."

Ben and Dawn correctly surmised the conversation was about Linda Dillon, the pony girl. Tom brought them up to date. "Apparently she called and was turned down for stalls at Mountaineer and left here in a huff, took everything she owned but her ponies. The bitch left them standing in their stalls with a note saying we could all stick the ponies up our...."

"Tom! We get it, okay?" Dawn said.

Ben shook his head. "I never did like that woman."

"Are the ponies all right?" Dawn asked.

Tom nodded. "Dusty said they're okay, or at least they will be. We'll have to get some groceries in them and find them a home."

"How did Dusty hear about this?" Ben feared another scandal on the backside, feared everyone talking about it and him being the last to know.

55

"He didn't. He went to check to make sure she'd left and found the ponies and the note. That's as far as it'll go."

"How do you know that?"

"I just know. I know Dusty. Come on, old man. What did he ever do to you?"

Ben looked off and sighed. "He used to flirt with Meg."

"What? When?"

"A few years back."

"A few years back?" Tom raised an eyebrow. "How many?"

Ben sat for a moment, counting in his head. "Thirty-two. Yes, I know the exact year, because I …."

Tom laughed. "Thirty-two years ago." He looked at Dawn; she was smiling.

"Ben, Meg was a beautiful woman. Men flirt with beautiful women."

There was a knock on the door. Tom got up to answer it and a moment later, returned. "Ben, there's two detectives here to see you."

"What about?"

Tom tugged at his ear, a nervous habit of his when facing the unknown. "They wouldn't say."

Ben motioned for him to show them in and when they entered the room, stood and shook their hands rather formal-like. "What can I do for you?"

"We wanted to let you know about the preliminary report on Billy Martin's death. Apparently he died of suffocation."

Ben sat down. "You mean someone smothered him?"

"Well, we don't know. This is just a preliminary. Apparently there are many ways one can suffocate."

"Oh Jesus," Tom said.

The detectives looked at him.

"Could he have been strangled?"

"No, there are no signs of strangulation."

"Well," Ben said. "Thank you for the uh…." He figured that was it. They were being courteous, there just to give him the news.

"We cannot locate any of his family."

Tom fidgeted. "He has a daughter."

The detectives looked at him. "*Had* a daughter. Apparently she is deceased also."

Tom stared at the floor, an image of the last time he saw Cathy Martin flashing in his mind. She was eating sprouts. "What did she die from?"

"We don't have that information."

"Is there anything you want us to do?" Dawn said.

Both detectives nodded. "Apparently he owed a large debt to a booking agent."

Ben dropped his head. The last thing they needed at the moment was a betting scandal.

"For how much?" Tom asked.

"We are not at liberty to say. But apparently it was for quite a large amount."

"Apparently," Tom said, nodding with authority.

When Dawn's cell phone rang, she excused herself to take the call. It was from Randy with news of his father's condition. By the time she hung up, the detectives were gone.

"Well?" Ben asked.

"He's doing good. Randy said they still don't know about surgery but he's comfortable and in good spirits."

Tom and Ben acknowledged the good news and then Tom motioned to the door. "They want us to pay for Billy's funeral."

Dawn looked at him.

"Burial actually, is the way they put it."

Dawn poured herself another cup of coffee. "I thought they were leading up to wanting us to pay his debts."

"Nope, just the burial," Tom said. "I wonder how much a burial costs."

"That coffee's too weak," Ben said, pointing. "It tastes watered down."

"It's decaf, remember?" Decaf was Ben's doctor's orders and when Ben said after all these years he wasn't about to stop drinking real coffee, Dawn suggested as a show of support that they all switch to decaf. "Watered down coffee" was taking some getting used to for all of them. She took a sip. "I like it."

"Yeah right," Tom said, pinching his nose. "It doesn't even smell good."

Dawn changed the subject. "The article I wrote will come out tomorrow."

"Is it good?" Ben asked.

"I hope so. I'm a little out of practice."

Dusty Burns showed up at the barn first thing in the morning with a copy of the article. "I posted copies in the track kitchen and also the secretary's office."

Dawn poured over it word for word as if she'd never seen it before. It was a short article by most standards, but by the time she finished reading it, she had sweat on her brow. "What's everyone saying about it?"

"They like it! They think it shows a side of them that most people don't see."

"Good point," Ben said, reading it a second time. "Is that how you spell liaison?"

Dawn smiled. "Yes."

"It looks funny."

The morning barn routine proceeded as usual. Three horses were galloped, one hand-walked, one was ponied. By eleven o'clock, Dawn was getting ready to leave. "Where are you going?" Ben asked. "We have a meeting scheduled."

"What? Where? I want to stop by and see Linda and little Alice Marie."

"But we need to decide what we're doing about Billy Martin."

Dawn looked back from the tack room door. "What do you mean? I thought they just wanted us to pay to bury him. Write a check."

Ben smiled. "Come on, Dawn. That's not like you."

Dawn just looked at him for a moment and then with a sigh, walked back and sat down on the cot. "What's the debate?"

"Well, Tom thinks even though no one liked Billy, that he should have a proper funeral. He's up talking to Pastor Mitchell about it now."

"You mean we'd have it here at the track?"

"Yes, a service up in the chapel." The chapel was a small room above the track kitchen that also served as a meeting place for the HBPA.

"What if no one shows?"

Ben looked at her. "Then you and I and Tom and Dusty will be there alone."

Tom walked in the tack room all excited. "Pastor Mitchell had a great idea! A funeral procession for Billy down through the barn area. He said ole' Billy was a son of bitch but that God loved him, and Billy loved his horses. We can have the procession go right past his barn."

"Oh, good grief," Dawn said. "Tell me you're not serious."

"Well, yes. What gave us the idea is Billy's from New Orleans. We think he'd really like a funeral procession, a proper send-off."

Dawn shook her head. "Do I need to remind you that no one liked this man and that as Pastor Mitchell said he was a son of a bitch."

Tom smiled. "Well, actually, those were my words."

"Surprise, surprise," Dawn said, waving her hands.

Tom chuckled. "Dawn, seriously, it is precisely because Billy wasn't liked that we need to do this. We need to show compassion."

"To who? He's dead," Dawn said.

Tom looked at her. "To his memory," he said. "And to the will of God."

Dawn sighed. "When's this all supposed to take place?"

"Well, Dusty's checking on a horse-drawn carriage now."

Dawn bowed her head. "You've got to be kidding me."

Since there was no racing today, Tom headed across town to the address listed on Billy Martin's trainer's license and ~

59

arrived at a vacant lot. He sat there wondering. The house to the right of the vacant lot looked abandoned. The one on the left was boarded up with a charred roof.

"What's going on?" he heard a male voice ask. It startled him. A uniformed cop stared into the open passenger-side window.

"I'm looking for the home of a Billy Martin," Tom said. "This *is* 1428 Benson, right?"

The cop nodded. "There hasn't been a house here in years." He motioned to the trainer's license Tom had in his hand. Tom handed it to him. "Yeah, that's the address all right." He handed it back.

"Well, maybe he just didn't update it," Tom said. "Thank you kindly for your time."

"You're welcome," the cop said, adding, "You're not from around these parts, are you?"

Tom smiled. The cop was having fun with him.

"You best be moving along," he said. "I don't to want get a call saying someone's stolen this fine truck."

Tom tipped his hat, thanking him, and drove away. Instead of going home he drove back to the racetrack and to the secretary's office. Joe Feigler looked up from his desk. "What do you want?"

Tom laughed. "I need you to confirm something for me."

"What?"

Tom was just about to hand him Billy's trainer's license, but had second thoughts about it. Joe wasn't one to keep things to himself. "Uh...I want to know what the arrangement Rupert's tack shop has with the track." It was the first thing he could think of right off the top of his head. He'd been to Rupert's earlier and complained about why Vetwrap was so expensive there.

"What do you mean?"

"Do they pay the track for use of the building they're in?"

"I don't know."

"Well, who would know?"

"Maybe the accountant, but Ben fired him."

Tom laughed. "Okay. All right. Thank you for your time."

"Try upstairs, maybe they'll know."

Upstairs Tom went. There was no one there. As he started back down the stairs, he heard a familiar voice. It was Dusty. He was sitting on one of the steps talking on his cell phone. He motioned to Tom he'd only be a minute. Tom sat down next to him.

"So what's going on?" Tom asked when he hung up. "What are you doing here?"

"Well, I was following you, and then I got this call. Did you know Cathy Martin only died about a month ago?"

"No." Tom shook his head. "Did you know Billy lived in a vacant lot?"

Dusty looked at him and sighed. The two men just sat there for a moment.

"I've been trying to find a place for Linda's ponies," Dusty said.

"Any luck?"

"No, I was going to talk to you and Ben about that. I need to know how much you can pay. They haven't been on grass so we can't just turn 'em out and the only stalls available at the stables I know of are full board."

"Let me check with Ben. We don't have anybody up in the foaling barn right now. Maybe we can get them over there, at least for a few days."

Again, the two just sat there, quiet for a moment. Dusty looked down at his hands; both men deep in their own thoughts. "Surely there has to be someone out there that cared for this man."

Tom sounded just as forlorn. "Surely he had to have a place to call home."

Dusty sighed.

"You don't think he lived in his truck, do you?"

There was only one way to find out. They both drove over to the horsemen's parking lot to take a look. Peering into the windows, it didn't appear as if someone had been living in it; it was rather bare and relatively clean inside. It had a crew cab with a front and back seat and someone could very easily sleep in the back, but there were no blankets, pillows, no extra clothing. No signs of home.

"All right, so maybe I'm reading more into this address thing than meets the eye," Tom said. "I'll try and find out."

"Me too," Dusty said.

"But you know…" Tom said.

Dusty looked at him.

"For some reason, I just keep thinking that he *was* homeless and that in some way even aside from that and all his debts, he needed us." Tom hesitated. "I guess I just don't want anyone talking about him."

"I know. Me too."

Billy Martin's burial planning continued.

Chapter Seven

The six dogs at Ben's farm were all Yellow Labrador Retrievers but for the one Standard Poodle who though appearing rather prissy, was rough and tough and held his own. Randy kept them all up to date on their vaccinations and the poodle got groomed once every six weeks much to his chagrin. For the most part, the dogs lived a free life. If they felt like sleeping all night on the porch, that's what they did. Occasionally they would come inside Ben's house, and he'd shoo them out. They often slept in the barn, a pack all curled up around one another. In the winter they slept in Dawn and Randy's kitchen. And every now and then one would show up missing.

"Which one?" Dawn asked, when Ben phoned.

"I don't know. They all look alike to me."

"Well, it's obviously not Rotty," the poodle nicknamed for the way he bossed the pack around. As for the Labs, Dawn started pointing out their different characteristics. One had a slight limp; that would be "Gimpy." One had a swayed back; that would be "Sloopy."

"Never mind," Ben said. "Here he is." It was "Runt," the smallest of the Retrievers at ninety-five pounds. All accounted for, Ben chased them out of the house and started supper. The pack settled down outside the screen door, waiting for table scraps.

"Don't tell Randy," Ben said, throwing them some. They loved potato peels, leftover pasta too. "Now go on, get." Ben sounded tough, but he loved the dogs and they knew it. They all took off barking and wagging their tails.

It wasn't long before Linda Dillon's horses arrived by van. Tom was right behind them, and following him, Dusty. Ben walked down to the foaling barn and got there just as they'd unloaded the horses. "Jesus," he said.

Tom nodded. "She ought to be shot, or at the very least, banned from ever stepping onto the backside of a racetrack again." The ponies were well-behaved, and ducked their heads when Tom raised his hand for emphasis. Tom led them into the barn side-by-side. One was a Palomino, the other a bay. They each had a foaling stall the size of Montana and sniffed and snorted as they made their way to their hay racks.

"Why is it no one cared?" Tom asked.

Dusty shrugged. "Everybody wanting to mind their own business I guess."

"If she were a guy, I'd kick her ass."

Ben looked at him.

"Don't look at me like that, old man, I'm serious. I don't give a shit."

Ben nodded. Religion and all, Tom was still Tom, particularly when it came to horses. They heard the sound of a diesel engine. It was Randy, returning. He walked in the barn and shook his head. "Linda Dillon's?"

Tom nodded. "The bitch."

Ben brought Randy up to date on what happened to Billy Martin as Randy looked over both ponies. Out of the corner of his eye he saw a little person appear in the doorway.

"Daddy!" D.R. shouted.

Randy laughed. If he lived to be a hundred, he'd never get tired of hearing that. Dawn entered the barn right behind D.R., toting Maeve. D.R. ran into the Palomino's stall and jumped into his daddy's arms. "Horsey! Horsey!" The Palomino raised his head and sniffed the little boy. "Horsey! Horsey!"

Randy gave Dawn a kiss, and kissed little Maeve. She made a funny face and giggled. They all turned and marveled at how enthralled the Palomino was with D.R. It was as if the boy was his long lost friend. He sniffed his arms, his legs, his hair. Amazingly, considering his condition, he was giving up eating his hay to say hello to this tiny little person.

"I wonder if he was a kid's riding horse once upon a time?" Dawn asked.

"Could be," Tom said. It was anybody's guess.

"I have stew cooking and Dawn made cornbread," Ben said. "Dusty, stick around."

"You made cornbread?" Randy asked.

Dawn smiled. "Don't get excited. It was out of a box."

Randy gave both ponies a vitamin injection and everyone, minus the children who were with their nanny, met at Ben's house a little while later. Randy brought them up to date on his father's condition. Surgery was still a possibility, but at the moment, he wasn't agreeing to anything. "He can be so stubborn," Randy said.

Dawn smiled. So could he.

"I had a talk with Spears today," Ben said. "He's going to get some quotes on having a Ginny stand built on the backside."

"Do you think that's wise with the purses so low?" Tom asked. "I mean, even though it is for the horsemen it might just give them something else to complain about. They've been without one forever, so why build one now?"

Ben looked at him. "I spent a lot of time cutting up the vegetables for this stew. Don't be giving me indigestion. Okay?"

"I'm just telling it like it is. Damned good stew by the way," Tom said, adding more pepper. "I'm just wanting you to look at the big picture."

"The big picture...?" Ben laughed. "Who are you?"

Dawn helped herself to more stew. "We could set up a foundation that would pay for it, that way no one can complain."

"A foundation?" Ben looked at her. "What do you mean?"

"You know, money set aside in someone's name to be used for things like this."

Tom's eyes lit up. "We could put it in Billy Martin's name and announce it at the funeral."

"Funeral?" Randy said, reaching for another slice of cornbread. "This isn't out of a box, tell the truth."

Dawn smiled. "I added a little sugar and put some vanilla in it."

When everyone dropped their mouths and stared, everyone except Dusty, who had no idea what the oddity was all about, Dawn laughed. "All right, so maybe there's hope for me yet." She was NOT a cook. She grew up in a house where there were live-in cooks, three of them, and maids, nannies, a full-time landscaper, all of the above.

Randy looked at Tom. "So what about the funeral?"

"Well...." He looked at Dusty.

"We're planning it for the day after tomorrow. We're going to send him off New Orleans' style. He used to race at the Fair Grounds you know."

"Oh?" Randy said, with Dawn looking on.

"Chaplain Mitchell is going to lead the procession."

"Procession?"

"Horse drawn carriage and all," Tom said, with his mouth full.

Randy shook his head.

"We figure, just because he didn't have any friends or family and no money doesn't mean he's not one of us," Dusty said.

"No money?" Randy sat back. "Wait a minute. What's said at this table stays at this table, right?" When Dusty nodded, Randy reached over to shake his hand. It was an old habit of his father's; as good as saying "amen" and represented truth.

"Billy always paid his vet bills with cash," Randy said. "And he would peel it off a wad of money thick enough to choke a horse."

Tom and Dusty looked at one another.

"Recently?" Tom asked.

"I haven't done any work for him for a couple of weeks now, but yes, always."

"So why are we paying for the funeral?" Dawn asked. We, meaning the racetrack.

Ben looked around the table. "Well, that's a good question. What would make the police think he had no money?"

"Well, for one thing," Tom said. "The address listed on his trainer's license is a vacant lot in a ghetto."

Ben stared at him. "What?"

"I went over there today to see if he had any neighbors or friends, someone who cared."

"And?"

"No, not there."

Ben paused. "All right, so what's the game plan?" He wanted to get this over with and talk about actual racetrack business.

Tom motioned for Dusty to take it from here. "Well, there'll be a horse-drawn carriage arriving at ten just after training ends. Billy Martin's body will be brought by a hearse and transferred over, and then the procession will go down through the barn area, over by his barn and then on up to the chapel, maybe a couple of hymns....we're leaving that up to Pastor Mitchell."

"That's it?" Ben shrugged. "I guess that sounds simple enough."

Tom nodded, motioning again for Dusty to continue. "Then after the service, we thought the carriage could make a lap around the racetrack, you know to...."

"No," Ben said. "Definitely not. No way, no how."

Dawn's cell phone rang. She looked at the caller ID. "It's Jackson from the newspaper."

Everyone stared at her as she said hello. "Yes. All right. Okay. Thank you." She hung up and paused. "They want me to do an article on the Billy Martin Funeral. They think it'd be a good follow-up for today's article. They'll be sending over a photography crew." She looked around the table. "How did they find out?"

Tom and Dusty shook their heads; neither had any idea. "Honest," Tom said.

As Ben covered his face with his hands and sighed, Randy couldn't help himself and burst out laughing. "Sorry," he said, when Ben gave him one of his looks. "But you have to admit, it is kind of funny."

"Not in the least," Ben said, pushing his dish away. "Not in the least."

Chapter Eight

The morning was cool, the air crisp with a slight breeze. Dawn and Ben arrived at the barn shortly after Tom, and morning training began. Immersed in what he loved most, for a short time Ben was actually able to forget he owned the racetrack and that he had two meetings scheduled today. One was with Spears and the other with the mutuals manager. "Back-to-back," as they say in the racing business.

Wee Born galloped a mile and a half. Beau Together broke from the gate. "He's getting there." Another time, maybe two and he'd probably get okayed. Ben wasn't sure he was going to run him as a two-year old. He was a big colt and looked just like Beau Born, chestnut with a white blaze and one hind white sock. Born All Together got ponied. She hadn't cleaned up her morning oats, so that was somewhat of a concern. She'd done this before on occasion, but even so, it was something to pay heed to.

This horse was a bit of a worrier. If there was a commotion in the barn, a loose horse, thunder, she showed the most signs of it bothering her. Ben sat with her one night for over two hours when there was fireworks the 4th of July. "There, there," he kept saying. "You're okay. You're okay." The filly liked the sound of his voice. It was the first voice she'd heard when she was born. "Oh, you're a fine one," Ben said. "Just you wait and see."

He was on the way back from watching jockey Juan Garcia gallop Winning Beau when he ran into the racing secretary Joe Feigler. "Oh no, what now," Ben said.

Joe laughed. "I'm trying to fill a race."

"Don't look at me. Running the other day in the mud when I should have scratched cost me."

"The race is perfect for Native Born Beau."

Ben glanced at him. "If the race was perfect for him, he'd already be entered in it."

Joe laughed again. "If I don't fill it, I'm going to come see you again."

"Don't bother," Ben said, waving over his shoulder.

"You're a tough man, Ben Miller. That's why I like you!"

Ben looked back at him, shaking his head, and walked on mumbling to himself. "Now that felt good. Some things don't change. That was just an everyday conversation between a trainer and the racing secretary. That felt real good."

Dawn was handwalking Wee Born and put her back in her stall so she could untack Winning Beau and give her a bath. She was such a sweet horse, never any trouble. "Wise beyond her years," Ben liked to say.

"Where's Tom?"

"He and Dusty took the keys to Billy's truck to go check the registration. He said he'd be right back. He has one more to pony for Tipton." Red stood outside the barn, catnapping.

Tom and Dusty were deep in conversation as they walked through the horsemen's parking lot, the keys jingling in Tom's hand. When they glanced ahead, both men stopped dead in their tracks. Billy Martin's truck was gone.

They went through the reactionary, are you sure it was parked here? Yes, dammit. They both were. Who would take it? How did it get past the guard? Easy. If it had a Horseman's Sticker on it, there was nothing extraordinary about it coming and going, particularly at night and leaving.

"What the hell?"

"Who would even attempt that?"

"Maybe the cops came and got it."

"Maybe it was repo'd."

"Maybe Billy Martin came back from the dead and came and got it. Are you sure he was dead?"

Tom imitated a corpse, eyes rolled back, arms and legs stiff. "Deader than a door nail."

The two of them stood staring at the vacant parking space, and then, just to be sure, both found themselves looking around again. "This is ridiculous," Dusty said, repeating, "Did someone else have a key? Who would take it?"

"I don't know," Tom said. "Since we saw it last yesterday, that's four guards. My guess is it went out at night and that would be Franklin. Ask him about it and you might as well tell the Morning Press. Wrangler might know." Wrangler was the morning guard at that gate.

"I'll try and find out something without asking anyone," Dusty said.

"Okay, let me know. I've gotta get back to the barn."

Dusty went one way, Tom, the other.

"Well?" Ben asked.

Tom shook his head. "You don't want to know, old man." He mounted Red and headed for the Tipton barn. "I'll tell you later."

"Later" was fine with Ben. He had too many other things on his mind. He gathered up his eyeglasses, notepad and pen, and set out for Spears office. Mim Freemont stopped him on the way.

"Ben, is this true, this funeral thing for Billy Martin?"

Ben nodded. "We're going to show him some respect."

"For what? What did he ever do to earn respect?"

Ben hesitated. Good question. "Well, for one, every one of his horses look good, and they run good. Regardless of what we think or thought of Billy, there was some goodness in him somewhere."

Mim, one of the tiniest, toughest, women on earth, looked up at Ben. "Don't you be doing no procession for me when I die, you hear?"

Ben smiled. "Do you want to put that in writing?"

Mim laughed. "If I have to."

Ben shook his head. "Mim, we're just trying to do the right thing. He didn't have anybody, just us."

Mim nodded. "I ain't wearing black, you hear."

"I hear."

Spears looked up when Ben entered his office and started to rise to his feet. Ben waved him off. "Sit."

Spears sat back down and watched as Ben eased himself into a chair across from his desk. "Everybody's talking about this funeral."

"I'll be glad when it's over," Ben said. He scanned his notes. "We drew up a list."

"Here, I'll make a copy of it and we can go over it." No sooner said, Spears buzzed for his secretary. Ben handed her the paper. "Make four copies. Tom and Dusty will be here shortly."

"Would you like some coffee?" she asked.

Ben looked at her. "Real coffee?"

"No, just decaf. I can see if I can....?"

"Never mind, decaf'll do. Thank you."

First on the list was the possibility of night racing one day a week on one of the "dark" days when the harness racetrack wasn't racing. "I don't want to compete with them. They're struggling too."

"I'll look into it." Spears made some notations on the back of the page. Next on the list was, "Bugler?"

"Yeah, what's with the piped in music? How much does that save?"

"I'll check." More notations on the back of the page.

Ben looked at him when he'd finished writing and motioned for him to show him the page. Spears was reluctant to hand it over. Ben insisted.

Spears had written, Night Racing, it'll never happen! Bugler, total waste of time and money!

Ben handed it back. "Let me tell you a little story."

Spears' face reddened all over. "I'm sorry, I just...."

"No, it's my turn," Ben said. "I had this horse once named Tender Tiger. I don't know if you remember him, it could have been before your time, but I tried everything I knew to get this horse to run. He'd train like a stake horse in the morning and come back strong, but in the race, nothing. He'd come back to the barn kicking and squealing. He never ran a lick. His first quarter fractions were always about the same as the last. Flat."

Spears sat back.

"So I started training him harder. I galloped him two, sometimes three miles a day and he thrived on it. Did he run any faster, no, but they started writing two- mile races, and I guess I don't need to tell you where this story's going. First time out at two miles, he was fifteen lengths off the lead at the head of the stretch. Then the announcer says, 'And here comes Tender Tiger.' He win drawing away. The other horses were tired and he was just getting going. He was running *his* race. So the point is, if I'd given up on him we'd have never known just how good he could be. And here, he'd had it in him all along."

Spears hesitated. "With all due respect, Ben, that's a great story, but I don't know how it applies to the situation at the racetrack."

"The racetrack...?" Ben said. "The reference is to you."

Spears nodded and slowly lowered his eyes.

"I don't like playing games," Ben said. "The way I see it, when we make a suggestion, if you don't agree, we have two options. You can tell me why you don't think it's a good idea, or we can give it a try. Not much has worked so far and we have everything to lose. When the doors close here, I'm done. And frankly, although I can't speak for you, I'm not ready to quit. All right?"

"All right."

There was a tap on the door and in came the secretary with Ben's coffee. "Sorry I took so long, but I found some *real* coffee," she said, proudly.

"Aw, geez, thank you," Ben said, and was just about to take a sip when in walked Tom and Dusty. Tom turned all of his attention on the secretary.

"Well, aren't you about the prettiest little filly I've ever seen."

The secretary smiled and shook her head. She was used to compliments, even ones that may or may not be sincere. "Actually, if you were correct in your observation, I'd be referred to as a mare."

Tom followed her out. "What a minute, does that mean you're married?"

"Nope," she said. "Just old enough to know better."

Tom grinned and tipped his cowboy hat. When he walked back into Spears office and sat down, Ben's coffee was now sitting in front of Spears. "I'm on to you, old man," Tom said. And to Spears, "Don't let him have caffeine. I'm warning you, it won't be pretty!"

Ben laughed, and introduced Spears to Dusty. The two men shook hands. "So what did we miss?" Tom asked, both men pulling up chairs.

"Oh, we were just discussing strategy," Ben said. "We're on the same page now," he said, pointing to his notes and looking Spears in the eye.

"We were talking about the possibility of night racing" Spears added. "I think it's a great romantic notion, but…."

Ben smiled. Now that was more like it. "Why do you think that?"

"Well, the red tape for one. If I got started on it today, right now, this very minute, we'd be lucky if we got it okayed and in place by next year this time."

"All right, we'll shoot for next year then. Get the ball rolling."

Spears crossed out his initial comments and wrote the words "Do it – Make it Happen!" in big bold letters on the back of the page. Ben nodded.

"And the bugler?"

"A done deal," Tom said. "Pastor Mitchell lined someone up to play TAPS tomorrow at Billy's funeral and if he's any good...."

"If I might ask," Spears said, "why is a bugler so important?"

"Because it's tradition," Tom said. "It's horseracing! It announces the live action."

"Do you think the people care one way or the other whether it's a *live* bugler or taped music?"

Tom looked at him. "Wait a minute, I'm getting the impression you're the one that canned the guy."

"Well, I may have."

"You either did or you didn't," Tom said.

"All right, I did. And all indicators...."

"Indicated...?"

"Indicated no one even noticed."

Tom looked at him. "Well, I'd like to see that report if you don't mind."

Spears studied Tom's expression. "The man got paid $45,000 a year."

Tom nodded. "No report, huh?"

Spears smiled. "No report."

"I thought so."

Ben motioned for them to move on. Next on the list, another question Tom had. "Does Rupert's tack store pay the racetrack for their space?"

"Yes."

"How much?"

"Well, I'd have to check."

"How about a ballpark figure?"

"Uh...probably around $300 a week."

"Well, no damned wonder their prices are so high. What the hell? We shouldn't have to drive a half hour away to get what we need."

"All right, let's see," Spears said. "That's $45,000 for a bugler plus 38 weeks not charging the tack store $300 a week. How's that going to help us, Tom?"

73

"I'm going to leave that up to you, and while we're at it, go on down the list a little. Whatever happened to a $1.50 hotdog? This is the racetrack for Christ sake. Excuse me," he said, glancing to the heavens. "$3.00 for a hotdog? A hotdog? What makes a hotdog worth $3.00, and don't tell me it's because of the fucking bun or the mustard either. Sorry," another apology to the heavens.

Spears drew a deep breath. "I wish I could say these things are important, but in the grand scheme of things...."

"Listen," Tom said. "The handle's down, it's been going down for a long time. I get that, but what I don't understand is odds are odds. Two to one pays two to one. No math needed. But the problem is no matter what the odds, people stopped coming. They can't afford it. Why do we charge to park? Why do we have to pay to park at a baseball game? The parking lot's ours, the parking lot's theirs! We're charging them to park and we're charging them admission. And we're marking up the food and drink 300-400%. And who gets that money? The horsemen? No! It goes to this building. It's not going to the hotdog guy or he'd be charging less. What's your salary? How much do you make? How much does the average horseman make? I guarantee you...." He held his hands up. "All right, let me step back a minute." He bowed his head and drew a breath to try and calm down. "How did we get to this?"

Spears looked at him and sighed. "Tom, if you knew what we pay in insurance, your head would spin."

"My head's already spinning," Tom said. "I'll be back." He walked out into the hall to a drinking fountain. "Lord," he said, out loud.

The secretary looked up from her desk. "Are you all right? Would you like some water?"

"I'm getting some," he said, taking a long drink. "What's your name?" he asked, wiping his mouth on his sleeve.

"Wendy," she said.

"Well, Wendy...I'm Tom." He shook her hand. "It's nice to meet you." With that he walked back into the office and sat down. "I feel like we're one of those charities where the administration gets all the money and the people still go hungry."

Spears looked at him. "These are things we can work on, Tom."

Tom nodded.

Dusty cleared his throat. "I remember when I was a kid and how I felt coming to the track."

"Those days are over, Dusty," Spears said. "The kids don't care, and we're competing with the casinos."

Ben looked at the list. "What about the whip?"

"What about it?"

"How would we go about doing away with it?"

"Are you serious?"

"It's something to consider."

"It would be suicide. They tried it in England and the jocks refused to ride. If that happens here, then what?"

The four of them just sat there for a moment.

"When God gave us dominion over the animals, I don't think he meant we were supposed to beat them."

"It's not exactly beating them, Tom," Spears said.

Tom looked at him. "Did you ever get whipped as a kid?"

Spears just stared.

"I think I've had enough for one day," Tom said. "If you all will excuse me." He walked out of the office and down the stairs. When he made it outside, he drew a deep breath. "That was too weird," he said, to himself. "I never thought there was anything wrong with it, until just now. God, forgive me."

Ben shook hands with the mutuals manager. The man had drawn up a very detailed report for him. The average mutuals clerk made between $18 and $24 an hour. The benefits package was generous as well. "If you'll be wanting to make any changes, I will contact the union rep and we can...."

"No, that's okay," Ben said. "I've got someone that will go over all this and I guess I'll get back to you."

"Any changes will take time, Mr. Miller."

Ben nodded. He hadn't said anything about changes, but since the man brought it up. "What are we looking at, next year at the earliest?"

"Yes, at least."

Ben figured as much, thinking, that's if we even make it until next year. As he walked back to the barn he had visions of it all empty. He'd seen it empty before. It closed down for four months each year during late fall and winter. It looked desolate then. He could only imagine how it would look shut down completely. He wondered what he'd do with the property. It's not as if this was in the best of neighborhoods. It used to be nice, once upon a time.

He glanced ahead, saw Randy's truck, and figured he'd hitch a ride the rest of the way. Randy waved to him from Gibbon's shedrow. "I'll be right there."

"Take your time," Ben said, relishing the thought of just sitting in the truck for a few minutes, hidden from the world. Someone tapped on the window. He'd rested his head back and had closed his eyes. Had he dozed off? He must have. He rolled down the window reluctantly. There stood Pastor Mitchell.

"I was just headed for your barn to talk to you and I look up and here you are. What luck!"

Ben smiled as best he could. This had to be about Billy Martin. What else?

"I was wondering if I could count on you to say a few words at the service tomorrow."

Ben shook his head. "Ah, geez, I don't think so. I uh...."

"I know how you feel, Ben. A lot of people here feel the same way. For all practical purposes, Billy was a no-count. He wouldn't lift a finger to help anyone."

Ben nodded.

"But as the owner of the racetrack...."

"Oh, so you're going to play that card on me."

Pastor Mitchell smiled. "Seek and ye shall find sayeth the Lord. Come on, Ben, just a few words, that's all."

Ben scratched the back of his neck. "Why don't you get Tom to do it?"

"I tried. In fact I just talked to him. He says he's not worthy to say anything about anyone."

Ben stared ahead and sighed.

"Thanks, Ben."

Randy came out to his truck for some additional supplies and greeted the two of them. "All set for the big event tomorrow?"

Ben shook his head. "Very funny."

"Yes," Pastor Mitchell said. "We're all set."

Tom was tacking Red when Ben returned to the barn. "What's the matter with you?"

"Nothing."

"What are you tacking up for?"

"Ah, I'm going to pony Dave's horse in the first. With Linda gone…."

Ben patted Red on the neck. He was a fine pony. "Is there anything you want to tell me, Tom?"

Tom looked at him. "Yeah, I want to tell you I'm a sorry son of a bitch. I talk out of both sides of my mouth."

"Since when?"

"Since today."

"And the whip thing is what brought this on?"

"That and, I don't know - life. What is life all about anyway? You live, you die, and if you're lucky, you go for a carriage ride."

Ben stared, waiting….

Tom tightened Red's girth and mounted. "I think you've got the wrong partner, Ben."

Ben grabbed hold of Red's rein. "No, I don't think so. Come on, what's going on?"

Tom looked down at him and hesitated. "Someone stole Billy Martin's truck. I don't know what to do about it."

Ben smiled. "That's it?"

"Well, for the most part…and the whip. Damn, Ben, how many times have I watched a horse get whipped?"

"Wait a minute, we're talking about in the race, right? Cause I can't see you ever standing by and watching any horse get whipped."

"It's the same thing. I'm as guilty as anyone. We are all one in God's eyes, Ben. You don't understand. Never mind, I gotta go."

"Tom."

"What?"

"We're going to work on it, all right?"

Tom nodded.

"And uh...." Ben sighed. "Don't be coming down on my best friend like this anymore, okay?"

Tom smiled. "I want to make it right, Ben."

"Me too," Ben said. "But it's going to take time."

When Tom rode away, Ben shook his head and walked into the tack room and sat down. "I'm starting to sound just like the rest of them." Time.

From the first stall, Native Beau Born, B-Bo, nickered. Whether or not that was a vote of confidence or perhaps a little criticism, it brought a much-needed smile to Ben's face. "Let's not forget who feeds you." And takes care of you, Ben thought, and makes sure, as best he can, that nothing bad happens to you. He stared. "How did whipping horses ever get started anyway?"

Chapter Nine

Since Dawn was gone for the afternoon, Ben picked stalls. He couldn't remember the last time he picked stalls. Tom usually did them. As a rule, the only time Tom ever ponied horses anymore for a race was when they were running one. Linda Dillon's absence was being felt in many of the barns. She most always ponied a horse in each race. She'd bring one off the track and pick up another. No wonder her ponies were worn out.

Ben walked up to the track kitchen to watch the second race and sat down with a cup of decaf coffee. He added cream and then a little sugar. It didn't taste half bad. All these firsts; he couldn't remember the last time he put cream or sugar in his coffee, or had a hankering for a piece of pie in the afternoon either.

Rita from behind the counter pointed to the banana cream. "I just made them this morning." Banana cream it was. Ben walked over to the table closest to the TV monitor broadcasting the race and sat down. The horses were loading in the gate.

"And they're off!"

He found himself watching the three horse. It had dropped back off the pace and was running easy six or seven lengths off the lead. He squinted. Enrico was riding him. "He'll win it," he said to himself. He took a bite of pie, gave a thumbs up to Rita, who nodded and smiled and all the while had his eyes on the race. At the head of the stretch, the three horse swung five wide and started coming.

"Come on," Ben said. "Come on."

He had no idea who the horse was, who owned it or trained it. But it was clearly the best horse, on this day, and in this race. It won by two lengths. Ben finished his pie. How many races had he watched in his lifetime? How many winners had he picked? "Or losers?" he said, laughing to himself.

"Is the pie that good?" Rita asked.

"Better," Ben said. He needed this; the race, the pie, a common everyday racetrack moment, life. He scraped up the rest of the piecrust, savoring every last crumb, and walked outside to see the horse pull up. He peered over the shoulder of one of the grooms standing at the rail to see his racing form. The winning horse was Demo Don, owned and trained by Doug Smith. It was the first time this horse had won all year, let alone hit the board in his last eight starts.

"What did he go off at?" Ben couldn't read the tote board from here, but hopefully the young man could.

"8-1"

Ben nodded and started back toward the barn. There would be no way to prove it, but it looked as if they'd been holding the horse and finally let him run. He win so easy. As he approached barn 14, Billy Martin's old barn, he paused and gazed down the shedrow. Someone called his name and he turned.

It was none other than Linda Dillon.

"Where are my ponies?"

Ben just looked at her for a moment. He remembered when she first came onto the scene at the racetrack. If he recalled, she had hopes of being a jockey. She exercised fifteen to twenty head a day. "Worked her ass off," so to speak, and still couldn't make weight. She'd practically starved herself to death and even passed out once coming off the track on a two-year old colt she'd just breezed for the Dugan stable.

"Well?"

Ben took off his hat and scratched the back of his neck. "What ever happened to you?" he asked. "How'd you get to be the way you are today?"

"What? Don't give me a hard time, Ben. I just want to know where my ponies are."

"You no longer have any ponies, Linda. And even if you did, there isn't a racetrack in this country going to let you pony anymore. You don't belong in the horse business. You're what's wrong with the horse business, you and all the trainers that don't care."

"Those ponies are mine, Ben, and I need to sell them."

Ben couldn't believe he was standing here having this conversation. "Sell them to who? You wouldn't get a hundred dollars killer price for either one of them."

"They're my ponies," she repeated emphatically. "They're mine."

Ben walked away. "Take me to court," he said. "Seems to me that note you left with them standing in their stalls with nothing to eat or drink is my Bill of Sale."

"Ben!" She grabbed his arm. "I don't have any money. I don't have any place to go! What am I supposed to do?"

"I don't know," Ben said. "Go find Dusty."

"Dusty won't help me," Linda said, tears welling up in her eyes. "Fuck him."

Ben held up his hands. "I'm done talking to you now, Linda. I want you off the racetrack, okay?"

"Ben, I've got no money." She swiped at her tears and wiped her nose with the back of her hand. "None."

Ben stared at the walking machines between the barns. One was red, one was chipped-paint blue, one was more than likely green once upon a time but was now all rusty colored. The walking path was overgrown. It obviously hadn't been used for a long time.

"Ben?"

He sighed and took out his wallet. He had four twenties and a ten. "Here," he said.

Linda looked at the money in his hand. "I don't want your charity."

"It isn't charity."

"Then what is it?"

"I don't know, just take it. Go get a room and something to eat and think about what you're going to do with your life."

"A room? And tomorrow, then what? This is all I know, Ben!"

"I don't know what you want me to do, Linda. I don't know what you want me to say. You're not my responsibility. This racetrack is. And you're not welcome here anymore."

Linda took the money and had to wipe her nose again, and again. "Ben," she said. "My little girl's in the car."

Ben lowered his eyes to the pavement.

"She's only two."

"And the father?"

"I don't know." She coughed and covered her mouth, trying to stifle her tears.

"Come on," Ben said, thinking she should come to the barn, sit in the tack room for a moment, get a hold of herself. But he had second thoughts instantly. She was a known liar, who knows what she could concoct. He looked around and far off in the distance up by the racetrack saw Tom on Red, coming their way. He appeared to be singing, in a good mood. Ben heaved a heavy sigh and waited.

Tom approached them warily. Linda wiped her eyes as best she could and wouldn't look at him. "What's going on?" he asked.

Ben stood thinking. "Can you go get Spears' secretary."

"Why?"

"Never mind. Linda, go around and I'll have someone meet you at the clubhouse gate."

"Who?"

"I don't know her name."

"Wendy," Tom said, staring Linda down.

"Yes, Wendy. Bring your uh, little friend too," Ben said, and walked away before Linda could object. Tom followed him on Red.

"What's that all about?" Tom asked, dismounting at the barn. "What the fuck is she doing here?"

"Speaking your language," Ben said, handing Tom his cell phone. "Here, show me how to work this thing."

"What number do you want?"

Ben paused. He didn't know the number. "How would I know the number?" He shook his head. "I can't think. There's just too much. I think I'd actually be able to run a racetrack if I didn't have all this other drama to deal with."

"What do you want her to go see that Wendy for?"

"I'll tell you later. Go on over there, get her in, and take her to the clubhouse."

"Her?"

"Linda. Go on, go. You can get there faster than me. I'll take care of Red, go on."

"Do you mind if I take off my chaps?"

"No, but hurry. Here, give them to me. Go! And remember, take that Wendy with you. Don't be with Linda alone."

"You concern me, old man."

"Just go!"

Fortunately the woman was at her desk. Unfortunately, she thought Tom must surely be kidding. "You want me to do what?"

"Actually it's Ben who wants you to do this. I personally don't want anything to do with the woman."

"Because…?"

"It doesn't matter," Tom said. "We need to get going."

Wendy reached for her keys and walked to the elevator with him. She hesitated boarding. "This is just too weird."

"Tell me about it," Tom said. Then realizing she was obviously uncomfortable getting onto the elevator with just the two of them alone, he motioned to the stairs door. "I'll meet you on the bottom floor."

"That's really nice of you," Wendy said. "But the clubhouse entrance is on the second."

Tom smiled. "I'll see you there, then."

"You can ride down with me, I have mace." She showed him.

"That's all right," he said. "I have manners."

Wendy was waiting for him when he got to the second floor. When he touched the rim of his cowboy hat in greeting, she just looked at him for a moment.

"What?" he asked.

"Nothing." She shook her head. "Come on, it's this way."

Tom expected Linda Dillon to be standing at the clubhouse gate entrance, waiting. She was not. He looked across the parking lot to see if anyone was pulling in off the street. Nothing, no one.

"Is this some kind of joke?" Wendy asked.

He looked at her. "Do you see me laughing?"

"Sorry. Who is this person anyway?"

"Oh, just some…." He hesitated. "Someone who…." He motioned. "There she is." She'd parked across the road and was walking to the gate carrying something in her arms, someone, a child. He stared.

His first instinct was to go help her, but then again this was Linda Dillon, someone he despised. Wendy stood at his side, unsure of her part in all this, what to do. When the parking attendant seemed to be "giving Linda a hard time" Tom sighed. "Come on," he said. Wendy walked with him.

Linda looked up with mixed emotions in her eyes as they approached. "It's all right," Tom told the attendant. "Let her in."

The man looked at him. "Who are you?"

Tom showed him his groom's license. Not good enough. "Do you have a pass?" he asked Wendy?

The child in Linda's arms hid her face in the crook of Linda's neck.

"No," Wendy said. "Not on me at least."

"How much?" Tom asked of the attendant.

"Seven dollars."

Tom took out his wallet and paid the man. "Do you want help with that?" Tom asked Linda, of the obviously heavy diaper bag she was lugging as well.

"No," she said, and walked along with them to the clubhouse entrance. "Ben said to meet him here."

"Yeah," Tom said. "I'm your welcoming committee."

Linda Dillon shook her head. "Fuck you."

"That's nice," Tom said. "Wendy, this is Linda. Linda, this is Wendy. And this little one," Tom motioned. "This is…?"

"Maria," Linda said. "My uh…niece."

Tom took the diaper bag from her as they walked along. The child had dark wavy black hair, and the cutest little smile. She kept ducking her eyes behind Linda's shoulder.

Ben was waiting for them at the clubhouse entrance. He'd tried to get a table, but had no money. His name meant nothing to the maitre de. Wendy had little clout as well. Tom had to pay their way. "This is a joke," he said, and motioned to a table by the window.

"I'm saving that one," the maitre de said.

"For who?" Tom asked. "The owner of the racetrack?"

They all sat down; Ben and Linda and the child on one side, Tom and Wendy on the other. The third race was about to go off.

"They're at the post!" the announcer said. The latch sprung!

They all watched the race, Wendy included, one of the few she'd ever seen. It was a nine-horse field. The favorite won. And then here came the maitre de with a highchair.

"I'm sorry, Mr. Miller, terribly sorry. I didn't realize...."

Ben glanced at his name tag. "That's all right, Jeremy. It's all right." This could not have been a more awkward moment for any of them. "So," Ben said, watching Linda get the child settled into the highchair. "I guess we're going to need menus."

"Would you care for anything from the bar?"

Ben shook his head on behalf of all of them. "Water, juice?" He looked at Linda and motioned.

"Her name is Maria. Yes, juice. Apple juice if you have it." She pulled a baby bottle out of the diaper bag and took the protective cover off the nipple.

"Isn't she too old for a bottle?" Tom said.

Linda looked at him. She just looked at him.

"I mean....how old is she?"

"Two."

Wendy smiled. "She's darling."

"Thank you." Linda shrugged. "We're working on a sippy cup, but she doesn't have it down pat yet and I don't want her getting all wet and...." She trailed off.

Ben looked down at the horse being led into the winner's circle. "So," he said, again, for lack of anything better to say.

"I've been ponying that horse all year," Linda said. "I'd have gotten a stake."

"A stake?" Wendy looked puzzled.

"A tip," Tom explained, "for a job well done. Only in Linda's case, since she starves her ponies...."

Linda shook her head. "Judge not, Tom. Isn't that what you preach? Here's another one, how about walking a mile in my shoes."

Tom looked at her and hesitated, about to say something sarcastic, but then just sat back. Ben was getting all red in the face. "You okay?" Tom asked.

Ben nodded. "I just think we need to all calm down and just have ourselves a nice little lunch."

The waiter came with their drinks, and for a moment, they were all entertained with Maria getting her juice. She rocked back and forth in the highchair, hands out and babbling, "Joosh, joosh!"

"Just a minute," Linda said, "Hold on." She poured half water, half juice in the bottle.

Tom stared and shook his head. "You're kidding me, right?"

Linda looked at him, about to fire something right back at him, but glanced at Ben instead. "Apple juice straight is not as good for little kids as people think."

Wendy fidgeted in her chair. "I've heard that. Cutting it with water is a good thing."

"Thank you," Linda said, smiling shyly.

Tom took a good look at the child. She appeared well-taken care of, a little chubby maybe. Her clothes were clean, her hair shiny, she was as cute as can be. "So where's her mom?"

Linda darted her eyes at Ben. He sighed; the truth, it implied.

"She's mine," Linda said. "And no, the father is not from the racetrack."

Tom looked at her.

"It's just me and Maria."

Wendy glanced around the table. "I have two children. They're grown, two boys; Matthew and Gordon. They're both in college."

Silence, but for the conversations all around them at the other tables. "My husband passed away twelve years ago. I know all about being a single mom." Wendy smiled at little Maria.

Tom took out the racing form from his back pocket and opened it to the next race. Someone waved to him from across the room. It was Jimmy Kath. "Any hot tips?" the man asked.

Tom shrugged. "I like the nine horse."

The man motioned, should he go bet?

Tom nodded.

86

The waiter came to take their lunch orders. Wendy ordered a Cobb salad, Ben ordered a lean burger. "Doctor's orders." Tom ordered a Rueben sandwich. "Extra sauce."

"And you, Miss?" The waiter looked at Linda.

She hesitated and glanced at Ben. He nodded slightly. "Tom's treating."

Tom sat back.

"I'll have the spaghetti and meatballs."

"What about for the little one?"

"She'll share mine. I have things for her with me." She had a little container of peas and carrots that appeared as if she might have cooked the food herself. Maria ate it heartily. Tom looked away. The happy little scene was just a bit too much, considering this was Linda Dillon.

Ben relaxed as soon as they started eating. "Linda doesn't want anyone on the track to know about Maria," he said. "All right?"

Wendy found herself nodding along with Tom.

"The thing is we need to find a place for her and her little girl to stay."

"I'm okay," Linda said. "I'll find something."

Ben looked at her. "Do you have somewhere to go? Seriously?"

"No." Linda fed her daughter a tiny piece of meatball. "When I get a job, I can get back into the Thames." The Thames was a low-budget motel where a lot of racetrackers lived during the season. Rates were cheaper by the week. "I can head down to Florida in about a month."

"What's in Florida?" Wendy asked.

"Florida Downs."

Ben's cell phone rang. He answered it and handed it to Tom. It was Dusty. "We're up in the clubhouse. Where are you?"

"Down in the secretary's office."

"Why don't you come up and join us."

"Oh wonderful," Linda said, debating whether to finish eating or just pack up and leave now. "I can't do this."

Ben motioned for her to stay seated. "I don't want any indigestion, so just eat. Okay?" He smiled at little Maria. She wanted some more of the meatball. Linda fed her another piece.

The horses were being loaded into the starting gate. It was a mile race. Ben leaned over to see how many spectators were outside to watch the race, around twenty. He shook his head. At least the clubhouse had a good crowd. Dusty motioned to Ben's table and was shown in. He pulled up a chair and sat down on the end. They all watched the race.

There was a little bumping and shoving amongst the horses at the head of the stretch. The nine horse was three lengths off the lead way out in the middle of the racetrack. Tom's friend Jimmy was rooting the horse on. "Come on!"

The horse started closing ground, shortening the gap.

"Come on!"

Everyone in the clubhouse was shouting for their picks.

"Come on! Come on!"

As they approached the wire, the nine horse was neck and neck with the leader, then nose to nose, and…. It was a photo finish!

"Do you think he won?" Tom's friend asked.

"I don't know. I don't think he got up. If he doesn't get knocked all around at the head of the stretch, he'd have win easy."

Dusty agreed.

Number five won, number nine placed.

Tom shrugged and leaned back.

"That's all right," his friend said. "I backed him up." He'd bet him win, place, and show.

"Good for you!"

"So who do you like in the fifth?"

Tom laughed. "I'm only good for one a day. That's why I'm still a working stiff."

His friend waved and went to cash his tickets. With the excitement of the race over, the unlikely five people sitting at the table fell silent again. Wendy wondered if she should be getting back to work.

"It's a conundrum," she said.

"A what?" Tom laughed.

"A conundrum. I'm away from my desk and sooner or later my boss is going to wonder where I've gone, or where I've been, but *his* boss is sitting right here, so...."

"Saying, enjoy your salad," Ben said. "Would you like some dessert?"

Wendy smiled. "I'd love some, but I'm on a perpetual diet."

Tom looked at her. "Perpetual?"

"Constant."

He shook his head. "I know what perpetual means, perpetual motion. Now conundrum? I admit that was a new one."

Everyone at the table laughed, even Linda, and then little Maria. When they all settled back down, Tom looked at Wendy. "You're not heavy."

"Oh, is that a kind of backside compliment?"

Tom laughed. He liked this woman's sense of humor. "Now Linda here," he said. "She could use a few pounds just like her...." He looked at her, stopping mid-sentence. She *was* thin, too thin. He glanced at her wrists. There was nothing to her. "Now this is a conundrum," he said, and it served them up another laugh.

"This is crazy," Tom said. He motioned for the waiter. "Since I'm paying, can we get a whole cake? I don't know, maybe a chocolate one?" he said, looking around the table. They all nodded. "Yeah, chocolate."

The waiter did the math in his head. A cake was eight slices. There was only five of them and the little one. Cake was $4.95 a slice. He wrote a number down on his order pad and showed it to Tom. $39.60 for a chocolate cake.

Tom drew a breath. "Well, it sure as hell better be good."

The cake was delicious, and the fifth race kept them entertained, but eventually the table fell quiet again. "I think I should at least call Mr. Spears," Wendy said. "He might be worried."

89

Ben nodded. Tom watched her as she placed the call. When she hung up, she had an idea. "We have a room over at the Hilton, two actually. They're for VIP owners that come in for stake races."

"I can't afford...." Linda said, wiping Maria's face with a wet napkin.

"Actually," Wendy said, glancing at Ben. "The racetrack pays for them."

"You're kidding me," Tom said.

Wendy shook her head.

"Let me get this straight," Tom looked at her. "Linda here can't afford a room but the VIP owners who ship in for a stake race who could very well afford it, get a room free?"

"Precisely," Wendy said.

"Well," Ben nodded. "Then that fixes that for the night."

Linda shook her head. "Ben, I'm sorry, but I can't...."

Ben held up his hand. "I have enough on my mind without worrying about you and this little girl out on the street."

Wendy said she'd call and make the arrangements and Ben suggested Linda go with her. This left a whole lot up in the air in regards to the Linda Dillon situation, but that was okay as far as Ben was concerned. He'd had enough for one day. Not to mention, Billy Martin's funeral was tomorrow.

"Any more surprises?" he asked, when the women and child were gone.

"Nope," Tom said. "None that I know of."

Dusty hesitated. "Well, there is one thing. That's why I was trying to track you down," he said to Tom. "Now, it's not the end of the world, but...."

Ben braced himself for the news.

"Billy Martin wasn't a Christian."

"Well, that's no surprise," Ben said. "So?"

"So Pastor Mitchell said he needs to be saved first."

"There is no saving him," Ben said. "What are you talking about? He's dead."

"A mere technicality, Pastor Mitchell says."

"Meaning?" Tom asked.

"He says as a congregation, we need to forgive him and ask God for forgiveness on his behalf. He said it would only take a minute or two."

Tom and Ben sat back. "A minute or two?" Ben said.

"He's printing out the program now."

Ben looked at him.

"He said you already agreed to say a few words at the service."

Ben shook his head in utter disbelief. He feared where this was headed.

"He wants you to lead the forgiveness."

Ben shook his head. "What's wrong with Tom doing it?"

"Pastor Mitchell says it's important for you to do it."

"Pastor Mitchell can kiss my ass," Ben said.

Dusty chuckled. "He said to tell you that you're not just doing this for Billy Martin, but that you are doing this for mankind. He said to tell you it's God's way."

Chapter Ten

Dawn was in the main barn at the farm, grooming All Together when Ben arrived home. She smiled at him. All Together was huge, as broodmares go, and her belly was ticklish. Ben sat down on the bench outside the feed room.

"Are you okay?" Dawn asked. She and Tom were always asking him that.

"Actually," he said, "I'm not feeling so great."

"You look okay. Why, what's wrong?"

"I don't know. I'm feeling....never mind, I don't know."

"What did you eat today?"

She and Tom were always asking him that too. "Well, I had a piece of pie and a burger and two pieces of chocolate cake. Not much else."

"Well, that's probably why. You can't eat like that."

"Did you make something for dinner?"

91

"No, Randy's going to bring us Chinese." As Dawn brushed All Together's front legs, she recalled again the injury that ended the mare's career and almost her life. She'd long forgiven Randy and Ben for keeping the details of the surgery and recovery from her, grateful the horse had survived. But she would never forget.

"Do you want some stir-fry?"

"Not unless it's going to have some meat in it," Ben said.

"What about Tom? Do you think he'll want something?"

"I don't know," Ben said. "He and Dusty are working on the 'final details' of Billy Martin's funeral tomorrow."

Dawn looked at him. "Did you think of anything good to say about him?"

"No, but I guess I don't have to anymore. Seems I'm supposed to read some kind of 'forgiveness' speech instead."

Dawn brushed All Together's mane. It was so pretty, all silvery and long. On the track, they'd always kept it short. "I love you," she said softly, and the mare nodded as if she understood. She and Dawn had this bond. She loved Beau Born; he was her first horse love. But now that he was used for breeding, he wasn't as loveable. He was still Beau, but with his mind on other things.

Dawn picked out All Together's feet, all four from the left side, just like at the racetrack. Done. "You're such a pretty girl." She still favored her right front leg. Randy said she always would. But it didn't hurt her; she showed no signs of pain. It was just old scar tissue and stiffness. She could still run and played just like a sound horse. The limp was pronounced only at a walk. Dawn put the mare back into her stall and walked over and sat down next to Ben.

"So, what kind of afternoon did you have?"

"Well." Ben brought her up to date and gave her all the details, even the part about everyone needing to forgive Billy Martin.

"I don't have anything to forgive him for, I didn't even know him," Dawn said. "Does this mean I don't have to go?"

"No." Ben smiled. "Actually, I'm more concerned about what to do about Linda Dillon."

Dawn had to admit, that bothered her too.

"But she's not my responsibility. My responsibility is to the horses."

"Still...."

"Ah, you know me and little kids."

Dawn smiled and wrapped her arm around his. "You're the best grandpa in the world."

Ben patted her hand. "I just wish I knew what to do."

Dawn paused. "Well, for the moment, I say we call Randy and order you something good to eat."

The dogs rushed in and jumped all over them. "Quit, quit," Ben kept saying. "Enough."

"Watch," Dawn said. "Let me show you what I taught them." She clapped her hands to get their attention. "Rotty, Rotty listen." She clapped her hands again. "Okay, everyone sit."

They all sat; that was nothing new. "Okay, everyone wave bye-bye." She waved her hand up and down. "Bye-bye."

All six dogs raised their paws.

"Wave bye-bye."

When they all flapped their paws up and down, Ben laughed.

"D.R and I worked with them this afternoon. Rotty was the first to get it." She imitated D.R. picking up the dog's foot up and waving it. "Good boy, good boy." Then, at the sound of a truck pulling up the driveway, all the dogs took off running out to greet Tom. He fussed over them and walked to the barn.

"Things just keep getter better," he said.

"What do you mean?" Dawn and Ben both asked.

"Billy's truck."

"Yes?"

"It wasn't his."

"Who's was it?"

Tom shook his head. "We'll never know."

Chapter Eleven

It was a glorious morning; the sun was shining, the sky was blue. The birds were chirping. It couldn't have been prettier, couldn't have been nicer. Radios were playing happy music in the barns. Horses were coming and going to the racetrack. The aroma of Absorbine mingled with the smell of manure, alfalfa hay and wheat straw. Coffee....

And then just like that, the air changed. A truck and trailer arrived at the front gate. The horse aboard, whinnied. A van hauling a carriage followed, and a moment later a hearse pulled in off the main road. Billy Martin had arrived.

Tom and Dusty walked down to greet the drivers. Pastor Mitchell joined them. Dusty had informed just about every person on the backside about the service and also walked through each barn this morning to remind everyone. As planned, the horse-drawn carriage procession was to start precisely at 10:00. The camera crew from the local news station took their places.

"Do we walk in front of the carriage or behind it?" Tom asked.

"Behind it," the coachman said. He was dressed in black. The carriage was black. The horse was black. The horse's tack was black. When they had the carriage in place, the two men accompanying the hearse placed Billy Martin's coffin onto the back of the open carriage. The bugler arrived with two other musicians; a saxophone player, a drummer, and a singer. They also were dressed in black, complete with black fedoras.

"We figured since you guys have gone to all this trouble this man must be someone special. You get the four of us for the price of one. We're digging this!"

Tom nodded and glanced down the road between the barns. Not a soul in sight. At five minutes to ten, Dawn, Randy, and Ben walked down to join them. Ben heaved a sigh at the sight of the carriage. The musicians were warming up.

"Oh Danny Boy...?" Pastor Mitchell said.

"It's got to be a song I know all the words to," the singer replied.

"Do you know any hymns?"

"I'm Buddhist," the man said.

Pastor Mitchell nodded.

"Do we really want to do this?" Ben asked.

"Yes," Pastor Mitchell said. He handed Ben his script.

"It's ten o'clock," Dusty said.

The driver of the horse-drawn carriage clicked to the horse and the procession began. Pastor Mitchell, Dusty, and Tom fell in behind the band. Randy, Dawn, and Ben followed them. When the bugler, saxophone player and drummer started playing Danny Boy and the young man began to sing the words of the song in a most beautiful tenor voice, what seemed ridiculous just moments before…turned into somber awareness.

~ ~ "Oh, Danny boy, the pipes, the pipes are calling" ~ ~ "From glen to glen, and down the mountainside" ~ ~

Tears welled up in Dawn's eyes. This was Billy Martin's last ride. As they passed down between the first two barns, one person stepped out from under the shedrow.

~ ~ "The summer's gone, and all the flowers are dying" ~

Two grooms from the second barn started walking behind Ben. He nodded to them. "Thank you."

Three more people from the next barn joined them.

Ben gazed ahead, where Mim stood at the end of her shedrow supporting her weight with her cane. He reached out his hand, and she gripped it tightly.

~ ~ "Tis you, 'tis you must go and I must bide." ~ ~

More and more people joined in, the camera crew flashing photos and rolling video.

~ ~ "But come ye back when summer's in the meadow ~ ~ ~ Or when the valley's hushed and white with snow." ~ ~ ~

Tom bit at his trembling bottom lip as they approached Billy Martin's barn, the horse-drawn carriage slowing to a stop. ~ ~ "Tis I'll be here in sunshine or in shadow" ~ ~

Over a hundred horsemen and women stood outside Barn 14, hats off and heads bowed.

~ ~ ~ "Oh Danny boy, oh Danny boy, I love you so" ~ ~ ~

After a long pause, where sniffling sounded and tears flowed, Pastor Mitchell stepped forward and opened his bible. "From the eighth chapter of Romans, verses thirty-eight and thirty-nine. 'For I am persuaded that neither death nor life, nor angels nor principalities nor powers, nor things present nor things to come, nor height nor depth, nor any other created thing, shall be able to separate us from the love of God which is in Christ Jesus our Lord.'"

Billy Martin's barren shedrow and twelve empty stalls loomed behind him, the straps on the walking machine swaying back and forth in the breeze. The carriage horse pawed the ground. One, two, three, four times.

"God giveth and God taketh," said Pastor Mitchell. "We are on earth but for a short time, for Jesus said, 'I go and prepare a place before you.' He is with you now and forever. Shall we pray. Father, we come to you today with a heavy heart. We know you are a just God. We know you are a caring God. We ask for you to hear our prayers. Amen."

Pastor Mitchell stepped aside. "Ben," he said.

Ben turned to face the people and found himself shaking his head, humbled. So many people, so many tears. "Thank you," he said, nodding, his eyes blurry as he looked at his script. "We all knew Billy Martin. We saw him every day. We saw him here in the barns. We saw him up at the racetrack, in the track kitchen, in the secretary's office." Ben paused, reading ahead to himself. "But we never saw him at home. We really don't even know if he had a home." He hesitated and had to clear his throat.

Tom smiled at him through his tears.

"But God willing, Billy Martin's going home today."

Several people said, "Amen."

"If it's possible to ask for forgiveness for a fellow man, we ask you to forgive Billy Martin for any transgressions. He loved his horses…."

Just about everyone there nodded.

"And he loved this racetrack. Please take him home."

"Praise the Lord," Tom said.

Ben stepped back in place and heaved a big sigh. Tom gripped his shoulder.

Pastor Mitchell smiled. "And now we'd like to make an announcement. Dusty."

Dusty stepped forward. "A foundation has been formed in Billy Martin's name and the first order of business will be to erect a monument of sorts on the backside here at Nottingham Downs in his honor." He smiled at some of the expressions and held up his hand. "Starting tomorrow, a Ginny stand will be constructed just beyond the track kitchen."

Everyone clapped.

"A state of the art Ginny stand, complete with bleachers, monitors, heat, and glass front." When everyone clapped even louder, Dusty stepped back, clapping right along with them.

"Tom," Pastor Mitchell said.

Tom stared down at the ground for a moment and then stepped forward. "I think the last few days here at Nottingham Downs may very well have been the most challenging we have ever faced. But I'm hopeful. I'm hoping with God's grace, we'll be here next year this time, and that we'll all still be a family. We don't always have to like the person down the shedrow or in the next barn, but we do have to stick together." He looked at the coffin in the horse-drawn carriage. He looked at it long and hard. "Good-bye, Billy Martin. May we meet again someday...and may there be racehorses in heaven."

Pastor Mitchell nodded and paused, collective tears appearing everywhere in the crowd. "We think Billy would like to go to the racetrack one more time. I think we should all walk up with him. 'Going to heaven's gate could be frightening for some. Who really knows what happens when the latch is sprung. Let's all walk with Billy so he's not alone, for as we stand here today, his future is unknown.'"

The carriage turned and the procession started the long walk to the racetrack. Horses from some of the barns whinnied to the carriage horse leading the way. He called back to each one of them. When they approached the far turn at the racetrack, the bugler, standing well behind the crowd, began to play TAPS.

97

As they stood at the gap leading onto the racetrack, the very threshold where thousands upon thousands of Thoroughbreds had crossed, Mim bent down gingerly and picked up a handful of dirt. With tears in her eyes, she walked over and placed it on Billy Martin's coffin. "Rest in peace, Billy," she said. "You can go home now."

Chapter Twelve

Ben sat in the tack room studying the racing form and couldn't remember ever being this tired in the middle of the day. If Tom weren't stretched out on the cot, sound asleep and snoring, he'd take a nap himself.

"I'm sure there's something I should be doing," Ben said to himself.

"Like what?" Tom asked.

Ben chuckled. He'd forgotten how much of a light sleeper Tom could be. Equally amazing was how he would start snoring even before he dozed off and would snore non-stop until he woke up. "Shouldn't I be running a racetrack?"

"No," Tom said, turning onto his other side and burrowing down. "That's what you have 'people' for."

Ben laughed. "Who'd have ever thought I'd have people."

"What time is it?" Tom asked.

"Three-thirty."

"Wake me up in ten minutes." He had a horse to pony in the eighth race.

"I told you I would," Ben said.

"I'm just making sure."

From all accounts the Billy Martin funeral procession send-off was a success. Ben was happy to see Joe Feigler in attendance, not to mention Spears. Dusty did a good job. "You too, Tom."

"Okay," he said, to whatever Ben mentioned.

Randy pulled up next to the barn and came into the tack room with a syringe in his hand. "Who gets the B-12?"

"Wee Born," Tom said, still half-asleep. "Who's asking?"

Ben shook his head.

"Did Dawn leave?"

"Can you shut the fuck up," Tom said. "I'm trying to sleep here."

Randy laughed.

"She left a little while ago. She said she was going home to write up the article about Billy Martin."

Randy looked at Ben. "I have to tell you, that was quite a tribute."

"Thank you," Tom said.

Ben and Randy laughed.

Dawn hit "Send" on the article file and sat back. She'd had to shorten it since she was over the word limit and sat wondering about the film crew that showed up this morning with the newspaper photographer. She wondered if this was common practice now. She'd been away too long. And since when did I get so wordy? She'd always been such a succinct writer. Now she couldn't seem to say enough. "That's what writing that novel did to me. I'm ruined." She chuckled.

She'd phoned her Uncle Matt earlier and was surprised she hadn't heard back from him yet. If he couldn't come up with anything on Billy Martin's truck, nobody could. Maybe, as Tom said, they'd never know. She went to check on D.R. and Maeve. Their nanny, Carol, had just put them down for a nap. Dawn tiptoed out of the room, motioned to Carol that she'd be outside, and walked down to the foaling barn to check on Linda Dillon's ponies.

Randy had said they were in no danger; they were thin, but not quite emaciated. Still, she worried about them. They were both standing in their stalls, eating hay. The Palomino raised his head to look at her. The bay just darted his eyes at the stall door. She wondered which horse was used the most, and why the different reactions to people.

She smiled. "Yes, I hear you," Ben, she said in her mind. "There are no two horses alike." She opened the stall door of the Palomino and went in and petted his neck. She ran her hands over his thinly covered ribs. "Poor thing."

How was this treatment of these ponies allowed to go on? With a big western saddle and numerous saddle blankets, she supposed the horse might appear okay to the majority of people. Not horsemen though. We're all guilty for not stepping in.

She thought of what Ben said about Linda Dillon's little girl, "As cute as a button and so smart." How could a woman who obviously took such good care of her child, treat her horses like this? Her bread and butter, their livelihood. Tom said Linda Dillon was skinny too.

She thought about Tom and Ben's pony Red; how tough he was, how strong, how solid. He was kind, but he was also a horse who wouldn't stand for being pushed around. Was that by nature? Or was it because he'd always been so well cared for? She looked in at the bay pony. He was watching her every move as if he expected her to explode at any second. He looked ready to duck for cover. She wondered how old the ponies were.

She thought about a pony she had as a child. A real pony, not a horse called a pony because it was used for "ponying" horses at the racetrack. It was a Shetland pony and ornery as could be. She loved that pony and cried for days when it died of old age. "Apparently I never did handle death well," she said to herself, recalling the day her father and mother died in a plane crash.

She remembered holding her breath, holding it until she couldn't hold it any longer, wanting it all to go away, wanting to die herself. But then she had to breathe. There were things to do, the funerals. She wondered if she hadn't had to bury them, if she had nothing to live for, could she have just held her breath until....

Glenda entered the barn. "Oh, thank God it's you, Dawn," she said. "I saw the stall door open, and...." Glenda and her husband George used to train at the racetrack, but never had any luck at it. They had a fairly good claimer now and then, but that was it. They were both good horsemen, just couldn't make any money at it. When Ben offered them the job here, they both agreed in an instant. George was a mountain of a man and Glenda big boned and lean. They made the perfect couple. "If it was Linda Dillon, I was going to pitch the bitch."

Dawn smiled. "No, but I was just standing here wondering, among other things, how she could do this and sleep nights?"

"Well, she used to have a drug problem. I don't think anymore, but...."

"I don't get it. What happens to people on the racetrack? Drugs, booze, infidelity."

"Dawn!" Glenda laughed. "It's everywhere! You just haven't been to enough places."

"Good point," Dawn said. She'd lived a privileged life, but a sheltered life.

"How'd it go this morning?"

"Amazingly," Dawn said, scratching the Palomino behind its ears. "There wasn't a dry eye in the place."

Glenda shook her head. She knew Billy Martin fairly well. She'd had no desire to attend.

"It's going to be on Channel 8 at six o'clock."

"You're kidding," Glenda said. "Sorry."

Dawn smiled. Glenda and George lived in a small house two farms up that Ben bought several years back. If and when the middle farm went on the market, it would give them an additional seventy-five acres and they'd be able to grow their own hay. As it was now, they leased the land, and the old man that lived there, T-Bone they called him, rode roughshod over the haying process. Randy's father came in last year to help them hay, and he and T-Bone went round and round about "proper rowing." On more than one occasion that week, Glenda had to play go-between.

Ben had to admit during one rather heated discussion that he personally had never grown his own hay. He always bought it in. He was a horse trainer, not a farmer. "Then stay out of this," they both told him. And Glenda agreed with them. Glenda loved hay season, loved falling into bed at night, exhausted. She loved foaling season, she loved putting in a

101

vegetable garden, a big one, with harvest enough for all of them.

Dawn liked Glenda. They had twenty some years difference between them, but their love of horses bridged the gap. "We're going to have pizza at Ben's. I'm going to make a salad."

"I'll bake a cake."

"Chocolate- chocolate," Dawn asked, imitating D.R.'s voice.

Glenda smiled. "With real whipped cream on the side."

Ben's farmhouse was big yet practical: hardwood floors, solid furniture, few frills. His wife Meg had been a no-muss, no-fuss kind of gal. Little had changed since she'd passed away. Ben liked things just the way they were. His only concession was a huge L-shaped recliner couch in the living room, a gift from Dawn and Randy. He said the "damned thing" always put him to sleep, but he liked the looks of it. It was brown leather and "didn't stand out."

It could seat a lot of people too, and kids. They all gathered for the six o'clock news. Randy brought the pizza; Dawn brought the salad, Glenda the cake, and Carol – the children. She had her own granddaughter for the evening, so that made three youngsters. She sat them at their little table and cut up their food. D.R. wanted cake.

"Eat your pizza and salad first," Carol said.

The other adults had their eyes glued to the television. Tom sprinkled red-pepper flakes onto his pizza and for good measure, some on his salad too. "I invited Wendy to stop by," he said.

"Wendy?" Randy said, all looking at Tom.

"Wendy from the office."

"You mean like a date?"

"No, just to watch the news. What do you mean, a date? What the fuck?"

"Tom!" Dawn motioned to the children's table.

"Sorry. But you know what, I can have a woman friend. It doesn't have to be a date."

"Since when?" Randy said.

"Besides, she's not even my type."

"Oh, what type's that?" Glenda asked. "Wait a minute, didn't we date once?"

Tom laughed. "No."

"Oh thank God," she said.

There was a knock on the door.

Tom looked around the room. "Does somebody else want to get that?"

"Holy crap," Randy said, getting up. "And you're shy now too?"

Wendy had come straight from the office, obviously still dressed for work. Perhaps she thought she'd still be working. She seemed a little out of her comfort zone as well. She looked for a place to sit.

Glenda moved over. "Hurry, get your food. It's about to come on."

"And now we go to Nottingham Downs where one of their own was laid to rest today."

Glenda sighed.

George nudged her in the ribs. "Shhhh...."

Those that were in attendance at the funeral procession relived the moment; the sight of the horse drawn carriage, the slow and methodical sound of the horse's hooves, the tenor softly singing Danny boy, the horsemen and women walking behind the carriage, the gathering at Billy Martin's barn, his shedrow. The camera zoomed in on an empty stall. They showed Mim bending down, using her cane for support as she picked up a handful of dirt, placing it on the coffin....

Glenda, George, Carol, and Wendy, seeing it for the first time, sat in awe. The camera zoomed in on the bugler playing TAPS, that beautiful, mournful, haunting sound. Heads were bowed, tears flowing. "Ashes to ashes, dust to dust." The story ended with a still-life close-up of the horse-drawn carriage looking out over the racetrack.

"Stay tuned for your local weather."

103

Everyone sat back.

"It always comes down to weather," Randy said, wiping his eyes.

"Daddy cry! Daddy cry!" D.R. said, running across the room. "Don't cry, Daddy!"

Randy picked him up. "These are happy tears, D.R. I'm just happy this is all over now."

Everyone laughed, wiping their eyes as well.

Wendy looked around the room. "I thought no one liked this man."

"I know," Glenda said, blowing her nose. "I know."

Dawn introduced herself to Wendy and then introduced her to Randy, Glenda, George, and Carol. "And this here is Louisa, Carol's granddaughter, and these two are mine and Randy's. This is D.R. and this is Maeve. D.R., don't cross your eyes."

Tom laughed. "I taught him that."

Wendy shook her head along with everyone else. Dessert was next. "Ooh," she said, when Glenda placed a big dollop of homemade whipped cream on top of her serving. She was about to refuse, since she'd already blown her diet once this week.

"You'll never eat chocolate cake any one way after this," Randy said.

Tom handed the plate to Wendy. "It'll be 'perpetual' from this day forth."

Wendy smiled. "Thank you."

A little socializing seemed in order, so that's what they did. They sat and talked about the weather, they talked about the kids, they talked about horses, and eventually they talked about the racetrack.

"I've been wondering," Tom said.

"Oh no." Randy laughed.

"No, now listen, hear me out. The bugler, by the way, he'll be there Saturday for the first race."

"What's he going to get paid?" Ben asked, recalling their conversation with Spears.

"I don't know. Dusty's working on it. He said the guy's willing to work cheap if we promote him in some way. He said he's trying to get 'gigs' for his band."

"Maybe we can put a little blurb about him in the program," Dawn suggested. "They're really good."

"I wonder how much that would cost?" Ben said.

"Very little," Wendy said. "We design our own programs."

"See," Tom said, hand out and smiling. "Done."

Wendy leaned forward. "That's if they can submit something camera-ready."

"Okay," Tom said. "We'll make it happen."

Ben and Dawn nodded. "I wonder...." Dawn said.

Wendy looked at her.

"Would there be a way to run that Dusty Martin clip on the grandstand monitors tomorrow. I'm sure I can get a copy of it."

"I'll find out and let you know. Advertising has fallen off, so there might be space."

"Two or three times during the afternoon if we can," Dawn said. "That way we catch everybody."

"Which reminds me," Tom said. "Have we given any more thought to two Daily Doubles?"

"I think it's a good idea," Ben said, everyone nodding.

"So how do we get work on that going?"

They all looked at Wendy. "I'll uh...check into it. Can I have something to write on?" Ben handed her a note pad.

"And moving the post time to two instead of one."

"Won't you miss the lunch crowd that way?" Glenda asked.

"Lunch crowd?" Tom looked at her.

"You know, the people that rush in there on their lunch hour and bet the daily double."

"Hmmm," Tom said. He turned to Ben.

Ben paused. "Is there a way to know what times most people show up?"

105

Wendy nodded. "Yes." She wrote that down too. "I'll let you know."

Tom sat looking at her. "Are you a horse person?"

She shook her head.

"Well then how'd you get the job?" he asked.

"I applied."

"You mean, like through an employment agency or something?"

"Yes. Precisely. Five years ago."

"And you didn't have to know anything about horses? You didn't have to even like horses?"

She shook her head. "No. Sorry. My degree is in business. I'm an administrative assistant."

Tom sat back, shaking his head. "Now that's just wrong."

Wendy glanced at her purse and the door. "Uh…."

"Come on," Tom said. "I'm going to introduce you to some of the finest Thoroughbreds you will ever lay eyes on."

Randy stood. "I've got to go too. I've got one more call today."

"Do you want me to go with you?" Dawn asked.

"Sure," he said. They each picked up a child and followed Carol and Louisa out the door to their house.

"Come on," Tom said. "I'm serious." He glanced at Wendy's high heels.

Glenda helped straighten up, rinsed the dishes, and she and George were soon gone as well. Ben was happy to have some peace and quiet. It had been a long day. "A long day for everyone," he said out loud to himself. "But they're all younger than me." He sat down on the recliner end of the couch, leaned it back, and closed his eyes.

He could hear Meg's voice far off in the distance. "Sleep tight, Mr. Miller."

"I'm not going to bed, I'm just resting," he said, and a moment later, "Good night, Meg."

106

Chapter Thirteen

Tom and Wendy walked along the pasture fence in the warm night air. "This is a beautiful farm," Wendy said. "I'm sorry I don't know horses."

Tom glanced at her. "Horses are *all* I know. I know little else, so I guess we're even." When he smiled at her, she looked away. "That one right there," he said. "She's in foal. It'll be her first."

"Does she mind being out here by herself?"

"No, actually she doesn't like being in the barn. She prefers the great outdoors."

Wendy looked at him. "How do you know that?"

"Well," he said, resting his arm on the fence rail, watching the mare. "When you turn her out, she runs like the wind. She kicks up her heels, she bucks and she plays."

"I've read where it's said Thoroughbreds are bred to run. Is that true?"

"Yes," Tom said. "More than any other breed, and I've seen 'em all."

"So she just says, leave me out here, I like it?"

Tom chuckled. "Just about. When it comes time to bring her in - I'll be bringing her in shortly - you gotta bribe her. She'll stand there, right where she's at now, and just look at you. Now All Together, Dawn's mare, she's just the opposite. She'll run and play, and graze, but after a while, you'll look out and she'll be standing at the gate wanting back in."

"How do you explain that?"

"I don't know," he said. "It's the wonder of horses." They walked on. "Actually she was raised outside. She didn't even have a halter on her till she was three."

"You're kidding. Is that wise?"

"Well, no, not really. But that's a whole other story. And then when she broke down."

"Oh no."

"No, it's all right, she's fine. In fact, there she is." She was in the first stall in the main barn. "She's had two foals already and working on her third."

"I can see that," Wendy said.

All Together was huge.

"They seem to get bigger, quicker, with each foal," Tom said.

"Like women," Wendy said.

Tom looked at her and shook his head. "You're really hung up on this weight thing, aren't you?"

"All my life," she said, looking in at All Together. "I'll bet she doesn't care."

"No," Tom said. "They don't have those kinds of issues." He walked on. "And this here is Back in Time. She's Wee Born's dam."

"Pretty." Wendy followed along.

"This one is Raging Wand. She's Winning Beau's dam."

"They're all so pretty."

"And this is Native Fire, she's Native Born Beau's dam. She was in foal to Beau Born and at an estate auction. The two-year olds are all out back. Hop on," he said, of the four wheeler parked there.

Wendy climbed up, not an easy task in heels, and sat back.

"You ready?"

She nodded, holding onto the bar on the side.

Tom drove slowly down through the barn and out toward the back pastures. "We have three two-year olds. Beau Together's at the track. The other two need to do a little more growing first."

"They look pretty big to me."

"Their knees are still open."

Wendy stared.

"Inside," Tom said. "Their bones."

Wendy nodded.

"And the babies are just up this way."

"Are they out all night?"

"Oh yeah. It's the best thing for them."

There were five of them of assorted colors, two bays, two chestnuts, one gray. "How old are they?"

"They're yearlings." Tom said, driving on. "The weanlings, weaned and not yet a year old," he explained, "there just up here a ways."

It was dark out, but with a full moon. "Are they out all night too?"

"Yes. They have two old broodmares with them to keep them in line."

"Are they safe out here at night? They're so young."

Tom pointed to one of the old broodmares. "I wouldn't mess with her if my life depended on it. She screams like a fucking pig. Sorry." He tipped his hat back and they watched the weanlings, little replicas of racehorses, grazing lazily under the watchful eye of the broodmares. "It's a perfect world," Tom said.

"What if they never had to run?" Wendy asked.

Tom looked at her. "Then they would never know what it was like to be a racehorse. I think given the chance, they want to run."

Wendy nodded. The little gray one laid down, stretched out, and heaved a big sigh. "I think I'd like to be a racehorse," Wendy said. "Some place like here at least."

Tom smiled. "Me too. But wait, you ain't seen nothing yet." He drove on to the stallion barn, stopped the four-wheeler, and opened the six-foot gate. "Come on," he said, offering her his hand.

Wendy climbed down, and then jumped mile-high when Beau Born let out a stud-horse whinny that echoed off the barn walls!

Tom laughed. "I should have warned you about that. Sorry."

"It's okay," she said, following him into the barn. He latched the gate behind him. Beau was in a stall that had a small paddock off the back. "It's safer at night for him this way, not to mention any unsuspecting mare within smelling distance."

Wendy looked in at Beau Born and shook her head, breathless as she said, "Oh my God, he's beautiful."

Beau let out another whinny, eyes on the barn gate, looking, watching, waiting, hoping. "Not today, big guy," Tom said, and nudged her along. The sight of a stallion in anticipation wasn't one to everyone's liking. "Now this here is Hurry Sandy. She's still of foaling age, but sterile."

"Aw."

"No, she's all right. Don't be sad for her. She's got it made. No responsibilities, no worries. Her job's just to keep Beau company. We tried a goat, but...."

"So that's all she gets to do? Keep him company?"

Tom looked at her. "No, she gets turned out. They get turned out together. Beau loves her. He follows her around like a puppy and she tolerates him. It's a perfect arrangement."

Wendy laughed.

Tom patted Hurry Sandy on the neck. "It's a sad reality for most stud horses. Once they're of breeding age they don't usually get turned out with other horses, and they're herd animals. Right around the age of two, they're separated. Too much testosterone."

He glanced back in at Beau to make sure he was "presentable" and they walked back by his stall. "I think Hurry Sandy has made him a gentleman."

Wendy smiled. "A good woman."

"Something like that I guess."

Off in the distance, they heard dogs barking. "Oh no," Tom said. Here came all six dogs, five Yellow Labrador Retrievers and a Black Standard Poodle, jumping, barking and slobbering. "Brace yourself! Incoming!"

It was a free-for-all. It was as if the dogs were saying, "New Person! New Person! Mine! Mine! Mine!" Wendy enjoyed all the attention, learned all their names; "Dawber, Gimpy, Piccolo, Sloopy, Runt, and Rotty."

"They're all litter mates, all except for Rotty here. Who put this bow in your hair?" Tom took it off and gave it to Rotty to chew and tear apart. "We all hand-raised them. The bitch died shortly after birth and the owner didn't want the

110

pups. She said they would remind her of their mom…oh well, anyway, we all nursed them with little bottles, round the clock, every two hours. Course every two hours meant five different every two hours each. It's hard to part with them after all that, so we kept them."

Wendy smiled. The dogs had settled down pretty much, except for the two playing tug of war with Rotty and his ribbon. "What about Rotty?"

"Oh, him. Randy brought him home one day too. He was a stray, abandoned. He doesn't know he's a poodle, he likes it outside."

"How old are they?"

Tom had to think. "Oh, around five. Rotty's around three."

Wendy smiled. "What's over there?" She'd pointed to the foaling barn.

"Well, I have to check on them anyway. Come on." When they entered the barn, all six dogs followed along. The ponies looked up. The Palomino nickered.

"Hello," Tom replied.

Wendy stared in disbelief.

"They've had it rough," Tom said, from her expression.

"What happened to them?" It didn't take a horseperson to see the horses were thin and ragged.

"Neglect and being worked too hard." Tom glanced at the notations written on the blackboard. Last time they were hayed was two hours ago. "They should have cleaned up by now." They each had hay left.

"If they're so hungry, why aren't they eating?"

"Well, for one, they're exhausted." He shrugged. "They're drinking lots of water, so that's good." He topped off their water buckets. "I'll come back out around eleven and see how they're doing. They can't have too much all at once."

Wendy nodded. "I can't believe someone would do this to a horse. What kind of person does that?"

Tom hesitated and decided to spare her the truth. "I don't know."

Wendy looked at him. "You're a good man, Tom Girard."

111

He smiled, glancing at her. "I'm an alcoholic."

"Recovering," Wendy said. "You're a recovering alcoholic."

Tom looked at her.

"Linda Dillon told me. I asked her about you."

Tom nodded. Leave it to Linda.

"She also said you were a womanizer."

Tom sighed.

"I told her you had good manners."

"I'll bet she had fun with that." Tom laughed.

"No. She said it was true. But I already knew that. Thank you."

"Come on," Tom said. "I'll walk you to your car."

All six dogs trailed along.

"You might want to wear more sensible shoes next time."

"I'll try and remember," Wendy said.

Chapter Fourteen

Juan Garcia came to the barn to gallop Native Born Beau; nicknamed B-Bo by Tom. Ben had him targeted for the feature race on Saturday. Dawn gave Juan a leg-up and stood watching as Tom and Red ponied B-Bo up to the racetrack. He was dancing and bucking. Ben had left a few minutes earlier wanting to be in good position to watch them "breeze."

B-Bo would act up quite often on the backside, showing off, but as a rule, was usually all business once he hit the racetrack. He grabbed hold of the bit and started snorting and pawing when Tom held him up to let a horse pass. "I hope you're tied on," Tom said to Juan.

"He no run any faster than I ride."

Tom laughed.

Ben stood within hearing distance. "Half a mile, that's it," he said.

Juan grinned, posting and flapping the reins. "You say mile? I no speak-ezy Inglish!"

112

Ben shook his head and laughed. Juan spoke perfect English. Besides, Tom had a good hold on B-Bo. He wasn't going anywhere. They let two more horses pass and then jogged onto the racetrack. Ben picked up the clocker's phone, called in Native Born Beau's name, half mile, and walked down to 7/8ths pole. He never worked a horse to the wire, always a furlong after the wire. He didn't want a horse to get into the habit of pulling himself up at the finish line.

B-Bo kicked at a horse on the outside rail. Red pinned his ears, digging into the ground. "All right, it's party time." Tom clicked to Red and the two horses broke into a canter. After a good long warm-up, he glanced over his shoulder, all clear, and eased B-Bo down toward the rail. "You got him?"

When Juan nodded, Tom let them go. For some, a horse breaking out of the starting gate was most exciting. For Tom, it was moments like this. To see all that horsepower just kick into gear. "Amazing," he said, and cantered Red up and out of the way, positioning himself to help pull them up.

B-Bo breezed the first quarter in 23.6 and the half in 47.8 then galloped strong for another furlong. Tom was waiting out in the middle of the track on the backside at that point, and pulled them up easy. B-Bo was used to the routine. He was used to Red.

"He looked good," Tom said. "How's he feel?"

"Strong! He so strong!"

Ben liked hearing that. He followed them back to the barn. Brubaker walked out from under his shedrow to talk to him. "I just heard something disturbing."

Ben sighed. So much for his good mood.

"Someone up at the kitchen said the purses are dropping."

Ben shook his head and walked on. "That's news to me."

"Is it true?"

Ben stopped. "First off, Dave, I just said that's news to me. Second, if you want to tell me who you heard this from, I'll follow up on it."

Dave just stood there.

"That's what I thought," Ben said, and walked on. At the barn, he made sure B-Bo was okay, looked him over, and headed for the secretary's office. "They won't know," Tom said. "Check upstairs."

Wendy wasn't at her desk and Spears' door was closed. Ben rapped on it. "Come in," Spears said. He was on the phone. Ben sat down to wait, not in the mood to wait, and promptly stood up to leave.

Spears hung up the phone quickly. "What can I do for you, Ben?"

"First of all," Ben said. "You can leave your door open. What's the point of having it closed?"

Spears sat back. "Quiet. Privacy."

Ben heaved a sigh. "There's a rumor on the racetrack that purses are dropping. Is that true?"

"No, not yet at least."

Ben looked at the man. "Do any have any idea how this rumor got started?"

"No," Spears said. "I'd had a conversation with Frank Dillon, but that was days ago. I had no idea where we were headed then."

Frank Dillon? Ben tried placing the name. He was one of Brubaker's owners, a heavy hitter. Ben motioned to the papers on his desk. "If you have a minute…?"

Spears nodded.

"Let's go on down to the secretary's office. I want to nip this in the bud."

Spears walked to the elevator with him.

"And no more of this, okay?"

"As I said, Ben, that was before…."

Ben held up his hand and glanced at him. "Get rid of the tie."

Spears time in the secretary's office was well-spent. Joe Feigler was trying to fill two races. This was all new to him. "So if a race doesn't fill…?"

"We're up shit creek without a paddle," Joe said.

"I don't get it," Spears said. "The condition looks good to me." Non-winners of three this year for $4500. "How many horses do we have here that fits this condition?"

"A good guess would be about fifty, maybe sixty."

114

"And they're not entering because…?

"Because they might have just run. Maybe they don't like the way we write races. Or maybe they're holding out to see what happens to the purses."

Spears had already dispelled that rumor.

"Yeah, but they don't know that."

"Make an announcement."

Dusty entered the secretary's office and looked around for Ben. He was sitting at the table behind Joe. Dusty walked over and sat down next to him. To say all eyes were now on the two of them was an understatement. Dusty chuckled and shook his head. "No one else died. Go away."

It lightened the mood, somewhat.

He leaned in close to Ben. "I just heard that Gibbons applied for stalls at Mountaineer."

"How'd you hear that?"

"My daughter works there, remember?"

Ben nodded. He'd forgotten. There was no reason to remember. He looked across the room. Gibbons was standing right there. Should he approach him?

Dusty read his mind. "No."

Ben nudged Spears. He turned.

"We're raising the pots across the board, a thousand dollars."

"Every race?"

"Claimers. Allowance and starters, two thousand."

"Are you sure?"

"Positive."

Spears held out his hands. Did Ben want him to announce that now? He motioned to Joe. Did he want Joe to announce it? "Starting when?"

"Today?"

Ben sat there, mind scrambling. Raising the pots one and two thousand dollars wouldn't match the pots at Mountaineer, but when you figured in the cost of shipping and the risks of trailering a horse , maybe the horsemen would think twice. He reached for a piece of paper, scribbled something, and handed the note to Spears.

115

"Listen up," Spears said. "And this is not a rumor. Starting today, purses are going up a thousand dollars in all claiming races and two thousand dollars for starter allowance and allowance."

"You hear that?" Feigler said.

Some cheered, some stood quiet, obviously skeptical. They all looked at Ben and he nodded. Jeannie Simpson, the track's leading female trainer walked up and placed an entry. Gibbons followed.

"Joe, you'll need to make an announcement for the backside."

Joe picked up the microphone and handed it to Spears. He'd rather take entries. Spears hesitated, hit the *on* button and repeated the same announcement, complete with, "Listen up."

Ben smiled. Spears had broken out in a sweat and was peeling off his jacket. With no tie or jacket, he almost looked like one of them. Dusty had another issue to discuss with Ben. "It can wait. I'll see you over at the barn."

Dawn was on her cell phone with her Uncle Matt as Ben walked down the shedrow, listening and shaking her head. When she hung up, she relayed the news to Ben. "Six years ago, Billy Martin had a truck registered in his name. It was sold for $1 to a, and I quote, a John Doe Salvage Yard. His address at the time was the same one Tom mentioned. He has not owned a vehicle since. He has not paid taxes. Uncle Matt said for all practical purposes, he ceased to exist at that time."

Ben sat down in the tack room and glanced at the coffee pot. "Who drank all the coffee?"

"Pastor Mitchell," Dawn said. "He was here looking for you. Do you want me to make another pot?"

Ben shook his head. "What'd he want?"

"He wouldn't say. Then again, I didn't ask." She smiled. "I didn't want to know. Also, Wendy was here. She came over to find out how long you want to put Linda Dillon up at the hotel?"

Ben buried his face in his hands. "I forgot about that."

"She said she suggested that maybe social services could help and Linda all but had a coronary. I gave her your cell

116

number so she doesn't have to walk all the way over here again."

"I hate talking on that thing."

"Yes I know, Ben. But you're going to have to."

He looked at her. "I just upped all the purses; a thousand for claiming, two thousand for allowance races and starters."

"Do we have the money?"

Ben shrugged. "I'm not sure. I'll have to find out."

Dawn studied his expression. She could read him like a book. "We haven't messed up yet."

Ben smiled. "Did you get the tape of the funeral?"

"Yes, I gave it to Wendy."

Ben nodded.

"I'm heading over there now to see the spectators' reactions to it. I'll be back in a few minutes. It's scheduled to run the first time in about ten minutes."

"Where's Tom?"

"He's up talking to Rupert."

Ben sighed. "We're probably giving away more money even as we speak."

Chapter Fifteen

Dawn bought a hot chocolate and positioned herself near one of the main monitors. It was flashing up-to-the-minute race results from other racetracks around the country. Few people were paying attention. At ten minutes to post time the monitors displayed the newscast. "And now we go to Nottingham Downs where one of their own was laid to rest."

Dawn noticed several people look up.

"Billy Martin, one of the leading trainers at Nottingham Downs...."

At the sound of the song Danny Boy, more people stopped what they were doing and paid attention. "Look at that," a man said, pointing to the horse-drawn carriage and procession.

Dawn walked toward the next monitor. Several people watching the broadcast there quickly turned into quite a few. The clip only played for a minute and a half, but most everyone that had stopped to watch, watched the entire segment.

"That's so sad," a woman standing next to her said.

Dawn nodded and glanced ahead. A small group had gathered at just about every monitor along the main corridor. A few seconds later, everyone was back to what they were doing initially. "But for that brief moment," she told Ben and Tom back at the barn. "They stopped and listened. They cared."

"Wish we could get them over here on the backside so they get to see who we all are, what we all go through every day," Tom said.

Ben looked at him. "Spears says liability is a huge expense, remember?"

"Yes, what if we just do virtual tours?" Dawn suggested.

"What?"

"Videos. I can do it. Heaven knows I've done enough videos of the kids."

"And what, play one once a week?" Tom asked.

"I don't know. Why not one every day? Just the like the one today. It doesn't have to be as long. We don't want them to be annoying. We want them to be entertaining."

"Like what?" Ben asked.

Tom popped a toothpick in his mouth, thinking. "Well, we wouldn't want to feature a horse that's about to race; we all know how superstitious we all can be with a horse in."

"What about just everyday things, a horse getting bathed, a horse going to the spit barn, a horse retiring, a horse on their way to the track in the morning. We could videotape all these things," Dawn suggested.

"Does that mean another employee?"

"No, I'll do it," Dawn said. "At least until we decide if it has any appeal."

Ben scratched the back of his neck. "I guess it's worth a try. Maybe if they see what goes on over here at the backside every day, they'll appreciate the racehorses more."

"Right," Dawn said, "and nothing negative."

"Which reminds me," Ben said. "I saw Dusty earlier and he let on that there's something he needs to talk to me about. What do you suppose it is?"

Tom sighed. "He thinks we've got a couple of illegal grooms in barn 9."

"Do we?"

"I don't know. I've never seen the guys before."

"Well, how'd he get wind of it?"

"I don't know. He'll be here in a few minutes. You can ask him."

Dawn picked stalls while they waited. Tom topped off water buckets. B-Bo was all wound up, playing in his stall. When Dawn hurried out from under the webbing, Tom chuckled. "Ah, does that bring back memories." Years ago during Dawn's first week at the track, Fancy Pat pinned her in the stall. Tom sidetracked the mare, gave Dawn a hand, and pulled her out of the stall with such force she ended up landing in the muddy ditch the other side of the shedrow. "I saved your life."

"Don't remind me," Dawn said. "That mare hated me."

"That mare hated herself."

"Whatever happened to her?"

"Last I heard she was raising Quarter Horse babies."

"Oh, I'll bet they're fun."

Dusty walked down the shedrow and into the tack room. Dawn and Tom followed. "Well?"

"They're gone."

"Is that a good thing?" Ben asked.

"I guess," Dusty said. "I mentioned I'd be back to talk them and they left - lock, stock, and barrel."

Ben shook his head. "Well, between you running people off and Tom and me giving money away, we're rewriting the book on how to succeed." It wasn't exactly funny, but they all laughed.

119

When Ben's phone rang, he handed it to Dawn.

"Ben!" she said. "Come on, you have to start using this phone."

"Take it. I don't want to talk to anybody."

Dawn sighed. "Hello."

"Dawn?"

"Yes."

"This is Wendy. I wanted to let Ben know that Linda left."

"What?"

"She's not in the hotel suite anymore and all her things are gone."

"Thank you. I'll tell him." Before Dawn could hang up, Tom motioned for the phone.

"Hey, this is Tom. I'm making chili tonight if you want to come over."

Wendy chuckled. "Oh, you sweet talker. How could I resist?"

Tom laughed. "We're going to eat around seven."

Ben wasn't pleased with the news that Linda was gone, and for that matter, neither was Tom. "Now where would she go? What is wrong with that woman?"

Dawn sighed. "She's afraid."

"Of what?"

"Probably losing her child." Dawn took out her cell phone and hit auto dial. "Uncle Matt. I need another favor." She gave him Linda Dillon's name and approximate age, mid-thirties. "We have reason to believe she is leaving the state," she said, and listened. "I did, didn't I?" She chuckled.

"What?" Tom asked, when she hung up.

"He said I sounded like one of Charlie's Angels."

Dusty smiled. "Actually you did."

Not five minutes later, Dawn's Uncle Matt phoned back. "She just gassed up in China Town."

"China Town?"

"It's about five miles from the racetrack."

"Okay, so she's at least still in the area?"

"Do you want her cell phone number?"

"Yes, please," she said. Having this information so soon came as no surprise to her, but certainly Tom and Ben were impressed. "Hello," Dawn said, when Linda answered her phone. "Don't hang up. This is Dawn Iredell from the racetrack."

"What do you want?"

"I uh....what do I want?" She looked at Tom, Ben, and Dusty. Their faces were blank. "I'm uh, wanting to purchase your ponies. I'll give you five hundred dollars each."

Silence.

"Cash."

Silence still....

"I'll meet you at the gas station in China Town."

"Are you following me?"

"No. I can be there in about fifteen minutes."

"You're coming alone, right?"

"Yes. I'll see you in a few minutes."

"Why are you doing this?" Ben asked, when she hung up.

"I don't know. I guess I don't want her to have any right to the ponies." She hesitated, digging out her debit card. "And more importantly, I don't want her to be afraid of losing her daughter."

"Do you want me to go with you?" Ben asked.

"No, I told her I'd come alone." She started out the tack room door. "I'm going home from there. I'll see you all later."

"Do you know where China Town is?" Tom asked.

"No, but I have my GPS."

"I don't trust those things," Ben said.

"Well, I have my Onstar too. See you later."

Less than ten minutes later, Dawn pulled in next to Linda Dillon's car. She was sitting behind the wheel with her little girl Maria in a car seat next to her. Dawn got out and walked around to the driver's side and first gave her a blank piece of paper. "Write out a Bill of Sale," she said, and waited then gave her the money. "Where are you headed?"

"What does it matter?"

"Well," Dawn said. "I might be able to help you get a job if I know where you're going."

Linda stared at the road, shaking her head.

"I'm serious, Linda. Will you call me?" She tore off a corner of the Bill of Sale and wrote down her phone number.

"I have it," Linda said, pointing to her phone.

"Then call me, okay. No excuses." Dawn smiled at little Maria.

"Why are you doing this?" Linda asked. "Why are you helping me? I know what you think of me."

"What I think of you doesn't matter. Hold on," she said, and went back to her car for D.R.s car seat. "It belongs in the back seat, facing the rear," she said, opening the door and buckling it in. "Here, give her to me."

Linda hesitated. "You're going to take her away from me, aren't you?"

"No," Dawn said. "I promise. Just give her to me."

Linda unsnapped the harness on Maria's car seat and handed her to Dawn. "What's nice about this car seat is you can still see her," Dawn said. "Keep it on this side."

Linda thanked her and sat with tears welling up in her eyes as Dawn gave little Maria a hug. "Take care of your mommy," Dawn said. "She loves you."

Linda nodded. "Thank you."

According to the Bill of Sale the ponies' names were Poncho and Biscuit. "Poncho is the Palomino, Biscuit is the bay. Poncho is six-years old and Biscuit is eight."

Glenda smiled. "What are you going to do with them?"

"I don't know," Dawn said. "The children are too young to ride. But Poncho did really seem to like D.R." No sooner said, she figured the reason why: Linda's child. "I think the first order of business is to continue letting them rest and to fatten them up and get them nice and healthy. Randy says maybe tomorrow they can have a little grass."

"Sounds like a plan."

Dawn smiled.

"Do you want Harold to pull their shoes?" The farm blacksmith.

Dawn hesitated. This was the first time she'd ever owned a horse, horses, all by herself. It was her decision, her call. "It looks like they were just done recently. Let's let the feet grow a little before we pull them."

She got a soft brush and comb, gently brushed Poncho and combed his mane, picked his feet. She put Furacin on his saddle sores. Then she groomed Biscuit. This was a whole new experience, grooming horses this thin. She felt loving, brushing them, and yet sad. She found herself humming the song, "In the Arms of an Angel." Poncho liked the sound of her voice. Biscuit liked her soft hands. When she brushed his face, he closed his eyes ever so slowly and sighed.

She tried not to think of Linda Dillon and how she could treat these animals the way she did. She tried to only think of the positive; they were safe now. "Spent all your time waiting, for that second chance," she sang softly. "For a break that would make it okay. There's always some reason to feel not good enough. And it's hard at the end of the day."

Randy walked into the barn and stood watching her, listening.

"May you find some comfort here..." she sang, in the quietest of voices, the softest of touch.

Randy loved listening to her sing, loved when she sang lullabies to Maeve and D.R., loved listening to her singing now. She started out of the stall and looked at him. She had big tears in her eyes. "They're home," she said.

"I know. I heard." He smiled and wrapped her in his arms. "I love you, Dawn."

"I love you too."

Chapter Sixteen

They all sat around the table trying to decide if Tom had added a new spice to his infamous chili. He denied it at first. "But if I did," he said, "it would only be something to make it healthier."

"Healthier?" Randy looked at him.

"Yes, healthier. I was reading today, in the uh, reading room and I came across this very informative article."

Randy laughed, as did Ben, Dawn, and Dusty. Wendy didn't pick up on the humor, not at first. She didn't realize Tom usually didn't talk in such an academic way, not to mention, the "reading room" being the men's room at the racetrack.

"What did the article say?" Randy asked.

"Well, being a doctor, you should know. Certain medicines, actually most of them, are derived from herbs and spices."

"Derived?" Randy smiled. It was then that Wendy laughed. Tom was obviously talking this way for her benefit, the conundrum thing.

"Yes," Tom said. "Derived."

"So this new spice you may or may not have used is a derivative of...?"

Tom helped himself to another bowl full. "It's turmeric; one of the healthiest spices on God's green earth."

"Ooh, I taste it now that you mentioned it," Dawn said. "I like that it's not a hot spice." She glanced at Wendy. "There's only pepper in this house. Pepper and salt, that's it. Red pepper, pepper flakes, ground black pepper, white pepper, jalapeño, habanera."

Wendy smiled. "I think I also taste paprika."

Tom looked at her. "You do? You're kidding me. I added that too. I heated it first in olive oil. It's supposed to add a mild sweet pepper taste and it's healthy as well."

Ben shoveled it in. "Why all the concern about health all of a sudden? This isn't about me, is it? Did one of you talk to my doctor?"

"No," Tom said, "This is actually about people in general." He went and got the article. "See, it says here that if a person is not getting the proper nutrients, they will want to keep eating. But, if their needs are met they eat less, naturally. They don't have to worry about eating too much, or..." he said, "not enough."

124

"Okay," Wendy said. "Now I think you're talking about me. Did you talk to my nutritionist?"

Everyone laughed, and then as usual, talk went back to revolving around the racetrack. "Did you see where Some Sam was eased today? I think he's done." Dusty said.

"He's a nice horse," Ben shook his head. "That's a shame."

"Grand-looking too," Tom said.

Randy nodded. Some Sam's trainer was one of his clients. "Fortunately for him, he's being retired relatively sound. He'll be fine," he said, which was precisely what he'd told Bud Dickson, the horse's trainer today. "He'll just need a little rest for a couple of months and he'll be good to go for his next career."

"That would make a great video to play in the grandstand," Dawn said. "His going home, retired, a happy event."

"Do you want me to talk to Bud about it?" Dusty asked Dawn.

"Thank you. That would be great."

"You'd better talk to him first thing in the morning," Randy said. "I think they're shipping him out tomorrow."

Dusty nodded. "What happened to him?"

"I'd rather not say," Randy said. "Wendy here hasn't passed the sworn-secrecy muster yet?"

Wendy smiled. "What do I have to do?"

"Sign your name in blood on parchment paper," Randy said.

Everyone laughed, Wendy included. "By the way," she said, reaching for her notepad. "I have interesting stats to share. Approximately sixty percent of the people attending the races arrive before the first race. About thirty-five percent come between the second and fifth races. The remaining approximately five percent come through the free turn-style after the seventh."

Tom sat back. "Okay, so attendance doesn't really seem to have much to do with admission. If free admission is after the seventh race and only five percent show up then...."

"But," Wendy said. "At least half the wagering dollars go to the perfectas, trifectas, and exactas. So, forty to fifty percent of the total money gets bet after the second race."

"So what are you saying?" Ben asked.

"I don't know," Wendy said.

Tom shook his head. "So we don't know what any of that means?"

"No," Wendy said. "But it *is* interesting, you have to admit."

Dawn smiled.

"Even more interesting," Wendy said. "Even though there is no real way of tallying this, it appears to the naked eye that at least half of the crowd leaves before the last race."

"Well," Randy said. "Maybe they lose early on and leave because they're broke."

"Or," Ben said. "They leave to go to work, second shift."

Tom sat mulling this over. "You know, I think we might be on to something."

"What? This happens at all sporting events," Dusty said. "When the team's losing, the fans bail. In this case, if the fans themselves are losing...."

"How can we give them better odds?" Ben asked.

Tom looked at Wendy. "Wait a minute, are you saying the daily double has no appeal?"

"No, I didn't say that. I don't know. Don't shoot the messenger, okay? On a more positive note, I got the ad from the band. They call themselves the 'Dew Lotts.'"

"The Dew Lotts?" Tom said.

Dusty made a face. "What the hell kind of name is that?"

"Well, I was curious too, so I asked. Seems they can't remember who actually came up with it, but they all like it, so...." Wendy took a sip of her water. "We'll be running an ad for them tomorrow on the last page of the program, inside flap. And then we'll run it again in the Friday program on the inside front flap. It's a nice ad."

Everyone was pleased to hear that, an accomplishment.

It was a pleasant evening, miles and miles away from the worries of the racetrack, figuratively and literally. When

Wendy offered to help with dishes, Ben declined the offer. "Meg never liked other women in her kitchen," he said. "She's gone now, but that rule still stands."

Wendy smiled. "I'll see you all tomorrow."

"What?" Tom said. "You're leaving?"

"Yes, I have plans to see a movie tonight with a friend."

Tom stared. A friend? What kind of friend, he wondered.

"Good night," she said.

"Good night."

Dusty spoke with Some Sam's trainer first thing in the morning and got an okay to video the horse leaving the racetrack. The van was to arrive around ten-thirty after the track closed for training. "Now that's a good rule," Tom said. "No shipping in and out during training hours. There's already enough activity going on at that time." It felt good to have something they didn't need to fix or address. "The track surface too, thank God." It had been redone four years ago and seemed to get better each year.

Dawn had charged the battery on her video recorder last night but checked it again anyway. Dusty showed up at the barn with yesterday's racing form. "In case you want to narrate it."

Dawn hadn't thought of that. "Rookie," she said, of herself. She jotted down the horse's sire and dam's name and his earnings record. "Okay, let's go. I'll film, you narrate."

Dusty stared wide-eyed. "Me?"

Some Sam was a large thick-bodied shiny black Thoroughbred. With his legs all done up in white shipping bandages, he looked regal. The van sat at the end of the shedrow, diesel engine idling, loading ramp down. The horse's groom led Some Sam toward the video camera. The young man was all business but for a lone tear trickling down his cheek.

"I'm going to miss him," he said.

Dawn nudged Dusty.

127

"Some Sam was sired by Nasty Sam," Dusty said, "whose lineage can be traced all the way back to Nasrullah. He gets his size and tenacious temperament from his dam Queen Ribot, who still holds the track record at Detroit Downs for a mile and a sixteenth."

Dawn glanced at him. That wasn't on the notes. She kept filming.

"Some Sam is being retired from racing to a promising career as a show horse." Now he consulted the notes. "In his eighty-nine lifetime starts, Some Sam had twelve wins, nine seconds, and fourteen thirds. His lifetime earnings as a racehorse is two hundred and ninety two thousand dollars."

The groom led Some Sam up the ramp and backed him into the crossties. Some Sam pawed and whinnied. "Look out, show world." Dusty said. "The big man's coming."

Dawn looked at Dusty and shook her head marveling as the two of them stepped back and watched the van pull away. "How did you know all that?"

He looked at her and shrugged.

"Oh no," she said. "Was he one of your horses?"

Dusty nodded. "I'd had him since he was a three-year old."

"I'm so sorry," Dawn said.

Chapter Seventeen

When all the horses in the Miller barn were done up and the shedrow raked, Dawn scanned the video and headed over to the grandstand to deliver it to Wendy. Ben had entered B-Bo for Saturday and walked over with her to see if the race had filled.

"I can't be here today to see how this video is received," Dawn said. "I'm taking the kids over and spending the afternoon with Linda and Alice Marie."

"I'll watch it."

When they got to the grandstand, Ben headed for the secretary's office and Dawn, the general offices. She took the stairs. Wendy was at her desk and appeared distressed. "What's the matter?" Dawn asked.

"I don't know. Did you ever have a really strong feeling that something bad was about to happen?"

Dawn smiled. "All the time. I think women are just programmed that way. We're afraid to coast. We have to always be pedaling, looking ahead and looking back over our shoulders."

"I like that."

"Is this feeling work-related? Home-related? Kid-related?"

"I don't know."

"When did it happen? Just now? On the way to work? Was there a close call in traffic?"

Wendy had to think and while she sat there pondering for a few seconds, Dawn glanced ahead. Her eyes were drawn to a tiny red light on a book shelf behind Wendy's desk. "What is that?"

Wendy turned and stared. "I don't know."

Dawn walked around behind the desk. "Has it always been there?"

At that moment, the elevator doors opened and Spears stepped off. "Good morning, ladies," he said, all smiles.

Both women returned the greeting, both pointed to the little red light. "What is that?" Dawn asked.

Spears stepped close to look. "Um…." He glanced at Wendy. "Has it always been there?"

"That's what I just asked," Dawn said.

"Maybe it has something to do with the computers?" Spears suggested.

Dawn moved her hand back and forth in front of it, touched the tip. It was warm, not hot, and operating from a single thin wire. "Do you have a pair of scissors?" she asked Wendy.

"It's electrical," Spears said.

"All right," Dawn said. "Do you have rubber scissors?"

129

"Let me call maintenance," Spears suggested. "Maybe it's a thermostat of some sort."

Dawn looked at Wendy and shook her head. "I'm getting that same weird feeling."

Wendy nodded.

"I'll get maintenance and let you know," Spears said.

"That's all right, I'll wait," Dawn said. She tried moving the book shelf. It was bolted to the wall. Spears walked on to his office to place the call and Dawn pulled up a chair next to Wendy. "Here's the video. It's thirty-six seconds and I think it's really good. I didn't know this beforehand, but Dusty used to train Some Sam. He lost him when his owner died and the man's kids sold all the horses. I think his familiarity with the horse is obvious."

Wendy played the video, both studying the tiny screen. "Very nice," Wendy said. "It's touching, tugs at your heart, but doesn't want to make you cry. And the horse is so pretty."

"Then it's a wrap?" Dawn asked.

"I'll get it going," Wendy said.

Spears came out of his office. "Someone will be right up."

Dawn nodded and decided to look around. "Hmmm," she said, at the closed door with Rudolph Swingline's nameplate still on it. "Something else for maintenance to do." She turned the handle; the door was locked. "Do you have the key?"

Wendy shook her head. Both turned to Spears. "I'm assuming Ben has it," he said.

"Ben?" Dawn took out her cell phone and was pleasantly surprised when Ben answered it on the fifth ring.

"Hello."

He sounded so gruff, and at the same time, a voice brimming with dread. "Ben, it's Dawn. If you had looked at caller ID, you'd know that."

"I hate this phone," he said.

Dawn chuckled. "Do you have a key to Swingline's old office?"

"Me? Why would I have it?"

"Oh, just checking. Never mind."

Ben gladly hung up the phone.

"He doesn't have it," Dawn said.

"I'll be right back," Wendy said, video clip in hand.

Dawn sat down to wait. Two maintenance men showed up a few minutes later. "First thing," she said. "I need to know what this little red light is."

One of the men looked at it; the other man just looked at her. "Are you a trainer?"

"Assistant," she said. "Wait, don't," she told the man as he was about to tug on the wire. "Do you have a master key to the offices?"

"All but that one there," the man said, pointing to Swingline's door.

Spears joined them. "You mean you have a key to mine?"

The man nodded, showing him.

"Hmph."

"How much trouble would it be to remove the door?" Dawn asked.

"Considering it's locked," the one man said, "quite a bit." The other man agreed.

"Well then," Dawn said. "Excuse me a minute." She walked away to make a phone call and glanced back. "Don't touch that."

"Do you want us to come back?" the one man asked Spears.

"No," Dawn said, answering for him. "Stay put. Uncle Matt." She relayed the situation. "Twenty minutes? Okay."

The two men looked at Spears. He nodded, motioning to Dawn. "She's the uh...."

"The owner's daughter," Dawn said.

The two men sat down to wait. When the elevator doors opened shortly thereafter, a very distinguished-looking man stepped off. "Dawnetta," he said, in greeting.

"Antonio." Dawn first showed him the wire, which he assessed with a furtive glance, then the door. He took out a Corinthian leather pouch, removed a precision tool and opened the lock. He followed an imaginary path with his eyes, up the wall, across the ceiling, into the office and behind a mahogany étagère.

131

"Apparently it's just a sound system," he said, but there was something about the way he looked at Dawn when he said that, that made her think otherwise.

"Thank you." She dismissed the two maintenance men, waited, and when they'd gone, her suspicions were confirmed

"I'll get someone up here right away to take care of this," Antonio said.

"It's surveillance?"

Antonio nodded ever so slightly.

"Is there any way of knowing how long it's been there?" Dawn asked.

Antonio glanced at Spears standing at her side, but looked at Dawn in answering. "We'll know."

Another nod, a bow of sorts, and Antonio was gone. Wendy returned a few minutes later and was brought up to date. Dawn did most of the talking, as Spears was practically speechless, his complexion pale.

Dawn looked at him. "Are you all right?"

"No. This is distressing."

They all stared at the little red light. "I can't believe I wouldn't have seen it before?" Wendy said.

"Well, we'll find out. We'll just have to wait."

"You can go ahead and go," Spears said.

"No, that's all right," Dawn said.

She walked over to the little red light and leaned in close. "Hello."

Wendy laughed, a nervous laugh, but a laugh nonetheless. "I doubt this is supposed to be funny, but…."

"And this is my best side," Dawn said, turning to the right.

"You have no bad side," Wendy said. She thought Dawn was absolutely beautiful. She was tall and thin, long auburn hair, no make-up. She'd never seen her in anything other than barn clothes, but imagined she had a wardrobe to die for.

When the elevator doors opened, Dawn turned and smiled. It was Tom.

"What are you doing?" he asked Dawn. She looked as if she was talking to the bookcase. "It's a bug," she whispered. "Maybe a camera."

Tom stared. "Oh!" he whispered back. He looked at Wendy. "Shall we moon them?"

Wendy laughed. Even Spears chuckled.

"Uncle Matt's sending someone over."

When the elevator doors opened again a short while later, three men disembarked, each carrying a black satchel. Dawn pointed to the little red light and stepped back out of the way.

"We're going to go ahead and sweep the floor," one of the men said, implying they should all leave.

Tom raised an eyebrow and looked at Spears. "Uh, I was going to ask Wendy if she wanted to go to lunch. Maybe the three of us can go get something. The clubhouse is open."

"Good idea," Dawn said. "I'll see you later." She took the stairs. Tom, Wendy and Spears took the elevator. Spears said he needed to get something from his office, but changed his mind when all three of Uncle Matt's men looked pointedly at him.

"Never mind, it can wait."

There were only a few patrons in the clubhouse, since it was so early. Tom motioned to a window table overlooking the finish line. Spears sat across from Wendy. Tom pulled a chair around and sat on the end so he could look straight out at the racetrack.

It was a pretty day. The sun was shining, the sky a light blue with puffy white clouds. No chance of rain. Tom had ponied six horses this morning and smelled a little like a horse. The waitress didn't seem to mind.

"What'll it be?"

Tom smiled that trademark Marlboro Man smile of his. "I'll have a tall glass of water, no ice."

Wendy ordered water as well. Spears ordered a rum and coke.

"Well, isn't that interesting," Tom said. "That was my drink of choice for years. Then one day, I gave up Coke."

Spears looked at him. "You drink Rum straight?"

"I did," Tom said, leaning back so the waitress could place their drinks down. "Well, that was fast."

"Thursdays are slow," she said.

Tom wondered why? Something else to think about it. Big John Myers came in the door to the clubhouse with one of his owners and the owner's wife. Tom waved to him.

"Do you know all the trainers on the racetrack?" Spears asked.

"Just about," Tom said. "And the grooms, exercise riders, jocks." Speaking of jocks, Richard Jackson entered the clubhouse and walked over and sat down at the Myers' table. He had two more days of his suspension and he'd be riding again. Myers had two horses in today and both had a good chance of winning.

When Tom pointed an accusing finger at the young man, he smiled back. Both their actions said volumes. Think twice next time. Next to come through the doorway was Janie Pritchard. Tom loved this old woman, and given that Janie didn't have much use for most people, the fact that she cared for him as well, also said volumes.

She limped her way over and kissed him on the cheek. "Janie," he said. "This is Richard and this is Wendy."

Janie nodded and turned her attention back to Tom. "Do you think you could give me a hand in the morning? That Forego colt of mine won't stand worth a shit for the blacksmith."

"What time?"

"Oh, around ten-thirty."

"I'll be there."

Spears took a sip of his drink, watching the old woman as she limped away. "Should she still be training?" he asked, when she was out of hearing distance.

"As opposed to...?"

Spears took another sip of his drink.

Tom looked at Wendy. "So, how was your movie?"

Spears sat staring out at the racetrack, thinking, Richard Spears is my name, not "Richard." What kind of cowboy-hick introduction was that?

"We didn't go," Wendy said. "We were too late."

Spears glanced from one to the other, puzzled by their familiarity with one another.

"How is it you don't know anyone here?" Tom asked the man. "Don't you eat lunch here?"

"Not usually. I have food sent up to my office."

"Well, I think it'd be a good idea for you to hang out here a little more often, get to know people."

The tractor operator harrowing the racetrack rode by casually looking up at the grandstand, spotted Tom sitting there and gestured to him. Tom pretended to duck, so as not be seen, and both he and the man laughed.

Spears looked at him.

"He's a heathen," Tom said. "But I'm working on him."

"Exactly what religion are you?" Spears asked, having heard of Tom's proselytizing.

"Christian," Tom said, adding for Wendy's benefit, "An *ecumenical* Christian."

Wendy smiled.

"The road is long, with many a winding turn," Tom sang, and then a litany of, "What's up ahead, may only be around the bend. I've been everywhere, man, I've been everywhere."

"Quit," Wendy said, laughing.

"He ain't heavy, he's my brother," Tom sang, he and Wendy laughing together now, as well as everyone at the Myers' table. "Do wah diddy-diddy, dum diddy do."

Spears excused himself at that point, went to the men's room, and dialed Ben's cell phone number. Ben answered, thinking it was Dawn again, and sounded rather pleasant.

"Ben, this is Richard Spears."

"Oh boy," Ben said.

Spears smiled. He was learning, you didn't have to wonder what Ben was thinking or the mood he was in. It was always obvious. "Did Dawn fill you in on what's going on?"

"Yes," Ben said; a man of few words.

135

"So, I was wondering about Tom."

"What about him?"

"I'd like to know how he figures into all of this."

"What do you mean? Hold on," Ben said. He covered the phone to reply to something Joe Feigler just asked him, and disconnected Spears.

Spears called right back.

"Sorry," Ben said. "If I never had to use this damned phone again it would be too soon."

Spears chuckled.

"So what is this about Tom?"

"Well, I'm just wondering. I know he works for you. I'm just not sure what his capacity is."

Ben hesitated. "His capacity? Let me think. Well, he's my best friend."

"Yes. He's a groom and he does your ponying, and...?"

"And, that's it. What else do you want?"

"Nothing, I was just wondering. I just don't know how to take him."

"Well, you can take him at his word," Ben said, still not understanding where this was headed or why.

"All right. Thank you."

"But don't forget," Ben said, as Spears was about to hang up. "When I die, he'll own half the racetrack and be your boss. You might want to keep that in mind." Click.

Chapter Eighteen

Dawn whiled away the afternoon with her cousin Linda and new baby Alice Marie as if she hadn't a care whatsoever. She never once mentioned the racetrack, never once referred to any other world other than motherhood and family. Never once did she even hint that there might be chaos going on in her life.

Linda and Dawn were both looking forward to their Aunt Maeve's visit next week. It had been at least four months since

136

they'd last seen her. They forever boasted that she was their favorite aunt, but in actuality she was their only aunt. Aunt Maeve often reminded them of this fact and they would always say that it didn't matter. "If we had a hundred aunts, you'd still be our favorite."

Meanwhile, across town, Ben had staked out some of the racing monitors throughout Nottingham Downs grandstand and was pleased that the people watched when the Some Sam video played. Many even made comments on it.

"I bet on him yesterday," one man said to several others standing with him. "I lost my ten dollars, but I'm happy to see he's okay."

"I always wondered what happened to them when they don't race anymore."

Good enough, Ben thought, and walked on. The idea is to get the fans to care about the horses and the horsemen. This was a good start. Wendy caught up with him as he was headed for the exit closest to the barn area.

"They liked it," she said, breathless.

Ben nodded. "Good. Maybe if people see what goes on in a racehorse's life, they'll care more."

Wendy agreed. "Mr. Miller, can I ask you a question?"

"Sure. What is it?"

"Well." She hesitated.

Ben shifted his weight and sighed. "I'm not a mind reader."

"I know. It's just that...never mind."

"Never mind what?"

Wendy hesitated again. "It's about Tom."

Ben figured as much. "What about him?"

"Well, see, that's just it. I don't even know what I want to ask. I just...."

Ben motioned to a bench and walked over and sat down. Wendy sat down next to him. For a moment the two of them just sat there.

"Dawn's nice," Wendy said, breaking the silence.

Ben nodded.

"And Randy seems very nice."

Ben nodded again.

"Glenda and George seem very nice too. You have a beautiful farm."

Ben smiled, wanting to move this along. "And then there's Tom. Is that what you're saying?"

Wendy laughed nervously. "No, he's nice too. That's not what I mean."

Ben's cell phone rang. He stared at it. "Who is it?" he asked, handing it to Wendy.

She opened the lid and looked. "It's Tom."

"Oh God, now he's calling me too." Wendy smiled when he took the phone. "Hello."

"I'm up at Rupert's Tack Shop. I need you to tell him that if he doesn't drop his prices, he can pack up and leave."

"What's his problem?"

"Well, I told him that we won't be charging him rent anymore for the store space and he says he's suspicious."

"Of what?"

"Getting kicked out, someone else coming in. He thinks we're going to set up shop ourselves."

"What? In our spare time?" Ben said.

"Here, do you want to talk to him?"

"No, I'll be right there." Ben hung up and sighed. First things first. He handed the phone to Wendy, absent-mindedly, then chuckled and took it back. The damned phone was his. He looked at it as if it was a bomb. "I hate this thing. It's unnatural. Look at it. It's no bigger than a...." It rang again.

He showed it to Wendy. "Who is this?"

"It's an 800 number. Don't answer it." She pressed the off button and then turned it back on. "If you give me your account info I'll try and get those blocked for you."

"Thank you. That would be good." He looked at her. If she had questions to ask about Tom she'd better get around to asking them. When he stood up to leave, she hesitated still. "Come on," he said, implying she walk with him and think along the way.

"Do you know if they found any more surveillance cameras?" Wendy asked.

138

"Nope."

"Do you think Tom would know?"

"I doubt it."

"Dawn?"

"Probably not."

"Has Tom ever been married?"

Ben looked at her and shook his head.

"Engaged?"

"Not that I know of?"

"In love?"

"I think that's something you're going to have to ask him."

Tom was just up ahead standing outside Rupert's Tack Shop. He marveled at Wendy walking along with Ben doing the best she could in high heels on a gravel parking lot. First things first: "Rupert says he can't lower prices until he makes up for the money he's already paid the racetrack for this month." Second, "If you come inside, pretty lady, I'd like to introduce you to a pair of boots."

Wendy smiled. "I have boots."

"With a walking heel?"

"Well, no…."

Ben went inside. Wendy and Tom followed.

"The problem is, Ben, I mark everything up a certain percentage in order to cover my rent."

"But we're waving your rent, so what's the problem?"

"I just paid it."

"When?"

"Um, just like a week ago."

"All right, so…." Ben looked at Tom and then at Wendy.

She hesitated. "I can confirm that and we can issue you a check for the difference."

Ben nodded. "And meanwhile…."

Rupert shook his head. "But I mark everything up differently. It's not going to be that easy."

Tom turned. He'd been looking at a pair of Ariat women's paddock boots; tan, soft. "Ahhh, the smell of leather," he said.

Wendy chuckled, distracted for a moment.

"Wait a minute, I don't get it," Tom said. "What do you mean you mark things up differently?"

"Well, that's because you don't understand merchandising," Rupert said.

Tom looked at him. "I sure as hell understand the buying end of it."

"I'm sorry, Tom, I didn't mean any…."

"It's all right. Let's just get back to pricing." They'd been going round and round and Tom had had his fill. "How do you decide what percentage you mark things up, if everything's different? Why not just mark everything up the same across the board?"

"Because like I was telling you, certain items sell better."

"So you mark them up more or less?"

"It depends."

Tom drew a breath and sighed.

Ben sat down.

"Actually, Tom," Wendy said, looking at the boots herself now. "That's a standard practice."

"I don't give a shit. It sucks," Tom said. "It's the items we need all the time, so they get marked up the most."

"Yes," she said.

"Well, that has to change." Tom said, "Here, at least."

"Oh, and you're going to tell me how to run my business now?" Rupert said.

"Come on, this isn't right," Tom insisted. "We're trying to make it better for the horsemen."

"Yeah, and I'm one of the horsemen. I'm trying to make a living too, Tom."

"By overpricing things? We're making it so you can fix that? Why can't you understand?"

"Why can't *you* understand? It's like you're turning into some kind of communist."

"A communist?"

"Yeah, trying to tell everyone what to do."

"Everyone?"

140

Ben held up his hands. "Enough, okay. We're all on the same side here."

Tom looked at Wendy and shook his head. "What are you doing?" She was glancing all around the store.

"I'm looking for a place to try these boots on."

"Over here," Rupert said. "If I had more room...."

Tom laughed. "Now you want more room."

Rupert laughed as well and turned his attention to fitting Wendy with a pair of boots.

"Now see, this is what I'm talking about," Tom said, holding up a roll of Vetwrap. "I want to come in here and pay the same price I pay at Wilson's."

"Wilson orders in for the trotters, not just us, not to mention all the riding horse and show people. It's all about volume, Tom," Rupert said. "By the way, Miss, who are you?"

"I'm Wendy Wilson, Richard Spears' administrative assistant."

"Oh," Rupert said.

"Nice to meet you," Wendy said.

"You too." He looked accusingly at Tom and Ben. Forewarned would have been nice.

"So how do we solve this?" Ben asked.

Rupert motioned for Wendy to walk up the tiny aisle way. "How do they feel?"

"Well, they feel comfortable, but my feet are kind of moving around in them."

"That's because you have nylons on. With socks, they should fit perfect."

Wendy walked back and sat down.

"How much are they?"

"Well, if I give you the horsemen's discount they're $110 plus tax."

Tom looked at him. "You only sell to horsemen. You don't have anyone walking in off the street."

"Still, it sounds good," Rupert said. "Everyone likes a discount. You really don't know *anything* about sales, do you?"

141

Ben sighed. Not this again. "I'll tell you what. If you need help getting the pricing done, we'll send somebody over. We want the best prices possible, starting today." He held up his hand. "And we'll look into getting you a bigger space."

"That's only if the prices are good," Tom added.

Rupert motioned to the boots. "$100 plus tax."

"I'll take them," Wendy said.

Tom walked with Wendy to the grandstand. Ben walked to the barn. "You'll want to put some neatsfoot oil on those, Tom said, referring to the boots. "The outside, just the leather."

Wendy nodded. "I'll have to get some."

"Come by the farm, I'll do them. Don't spray any of that waterproofing on them either."

Wendy smiled. Now seemed as good a time as any to ask, "Tom, have you ever been in love?"

He grinned at her and tipped his hat. "That depends on your definition of love, pretty lady? If real feelings don't count, I've been in love probably a hundred times."

Bill Burton approached them in passing on the way to his barn. "Hey, Tom."

"Bill."

"Did you hear?"

"What?"

"I'll talk to you later," Wendy said, walking on.

"The farm, tonight? Seven, dinner?" Tom called after her.

"Sure."

"Bring your notebook. We have lots to talk about."

For whatever reason, Ben decided to visit the announcer's booth. Bud Gipson looked at him and smiled. He was just about to call the eighth race. Ben sat down out of the way. He knew Bud fairly well, had been to the announcer's booth several times over the years, and loved the view. The booth sat on the top of the grandstand on a floor all by itself. There wasn't a better vantage point of the racetrack anywhere.

It never ceased to amaze Ben how the announcers memorized the names of the horses in each race. Bud had his own system which he shared once with Ben, names to numbers, then the jockey colors.

"Not the color of the horses?"

"No."

"And they're off!"

Ben watched the race; it was 6 furlongs. Down the backside Bud used binoculars and then switched to his glasses on a band, like goggles, for the stretch run. The horses' names blended into one another's....

"Ben?"

He looked up.

"Are you okay?"

"Am I smiling?"

"Yes."

"Then I'm okay."

Bud laughed and sat down next to him.

"Apparently I dozed off," Ben said.

"That's a first," Bud said, "me putting someone to sleep with the call of a race."

"It was like a lullaby." Ben smiled. "Music to my ears."

Bud looked at him. "How are things going?"

"Well." Ben yawned. "I think everything'll be all right, once we get through all the rough spots."

Bud laughed.

"Someday," Ben added.

"So what can I do for you?" Bud asked.

"I was wondering when you stopped announcing minutes before the race and saying 'don't get shut out?' I miss that."

"About two years ago. Simulcasting. They didn't want to chance me talking over a race running."

Ben nodded. "They?"

Bud held his hands out. "They, the powers that be, Spears...."

Ben stood up to leave. "I think we need to figure out a way to do both."

"You're saying...?"

"I'll let you know." Ben started out the door and hesitated. "You do a good job, Bud. It's good having you here."

"Thank you."

When Ben boarded the elevator, he figured he might as well stop on the way down and check in with "management." Wendy was nowhere to be seen but Spears was at his desk, door open, on the phone. Ben walked past that office and into Swingline's old office. Everything was nice and neat and quiet. The room had a far-far-away feel to it. No wonder Swingline lost touch, Ben thought. No windows, no view of the racetrack. No nothing.

He walked into the private bathroom, used it, and walked back out into the hall. Spears was still on the phone and still no Wendy, so he walked down the hall in the opposite direction, checking things out. Spears met up with him as he was exiting what appeared to be a conference room, a large table in the center with a dozen or so chairs around it.

"Hi, Ben," Spears said.

Ben nodded. "How is everything?"

"Well, I got the ball rolling for one night a week racing next year. Time will tell on that one."

"That's good." Ben studied the man's eyes. "Do you have any idea who might be behind the surveillance video?"

"Probably Rudolph. He was paranoid as hell."

"Do you mean about his safety?"

"No, about someone trying to steal the racetrack from him."

Ben stared down the hall.

"He was always checking up on people."

Ben continued to stare down the hall.

"I don't know how he thought someone was going to steal the track from him, but...."

Ben nodded. He'd heard enough. "What's on this floor, just these offices?"

"That, and storage."

"What are we storing?"

"I'm not sure. I've actually never been in the storage room."

Ben smiled. "Well then, that makes two of us. Come on. Where's Wendy?" he asked, passing her desk.

"I don't know. I think she's been slacking off lately. That's not like her."

"Well, we've been keeping her busy," Ben said.

Spears nodded.

No sooner said, Wendy stepped off the elevator. "Ben, I have a great idea."

The two men turned.

"Now hear me out," she said, rather breathlessly. "Did you know that after the seventh race, betting slows down to the point that at least half of the mutual clerks are just sitting there. That's it, that's all they're doing."

Spears held up a hand. "You don't want to go there, Wendy."

"Why not?" Ben asked.

"The union."

Ben nodded. "When do we renegotiate their contract?"

Spears looked at Wendy. Evidently he didn't know. "January," she said.

"Okay." Ben paused. "We'll do some thinking on it and throw it on top of the fix it for next year pile."

Wendy smiled. "The thing is, if you cut their hours, they lose their benefits."

Ben looked at her.

"But, if you cut their hours and let them keep their benefits, or find them something else to do instead of just sitting there, they can't cry foul."

Ben smiled. "Where did you find her?" he asked Spears.

Spears shrugged. "She came from another planet."

"Venus," she said, chuckling. She grabbed her purse from her desk drawer and looked at Ben. "I'll see you at the farm around seven. Good-night, Mr. Spears."

"Good night." He walked with Ben down the hall. "What's at the farm at seven?"

"A gathering of the minds," Ben said. "Anytime you'd like to join us, come on over."

Spears glanced over his shoulder at the elevator doors, closing. "I think I will."

Chapter Nineteen

Dinner at Ben's turned out to be lasagna from Luciano's. Dawn had picked up two family-sized orders and a huge Italian salad smothered in shredded mozzarella cheese, black olives, pepperoncinis, and onion.

Randy passed the bread and then the butter. "I have two more calls to do, so if there's anything I need to know, you'd better tell me now."

"Well," Ben said, looking around the table at those assembled; Dawn, Randy, Tom, Wendy, Glenda and George. The children, all tuckered out from their afternoon visit with their Aunt Linda and new baby, were at home with their nanny, having already eaten and getting ready for bed. "I made an interesting observation today."

"Oh?" Dawn said.

"The third floor of the grandstand is totally unnecessary."

Wendy looked at him. The third floor was where her office space, Spears', and "Ben's" offices were located.

"It's not even a full floor."

"It's not?" Tom asked.

"No. It's only goes about halfway."

Randy added jelly to his buttered bread, a habit he got into when D.R. was learning to eat on his own. "You know, now that you mention it, how would the clubhouse be two stories high otherwise?" The clubhouse occupied half of the second floor. The other side was indoor stadium seats. Once upon a time, the stadium seats were open-air. That changed about twenty years ago.

"So," Ben said, hesitating as he looked at Tom, who was looking at Wendy, who was looking warily at the portion sizes of lasagna in the pan. Tom cut one in half, served it to her and shook his head.

"You eat like a bird."

"Yeah, like a swan," she said, and everyone observed the way Tom smiled and looked at her. He passed her the salad. This was a table of good doers; even Dawn after having two children had no weight issues. Glenda was the only one that might be considered a little overweight by some, but she was all muscle. They all loved to eat. Eating was their passion.

"So?" Randy said.

"Well, so I'm thinking…."

The dogs started barking and in the midst of all their racket, there was a knock on the door. Tom got up to answer it. It was Spears. Tom just looked at him for a second.

"Who is it?" Ben called from the table.

"It's the boss man," Tom said, showing Spears in.

Wendy looked up, rather surprised to see him there.

Ben smiled. "Have a seat. You hungry?"

Glenda moved over to make room for him next to George. Wendy motioned to the kitchen, if he wanted to wash up. He washed his hands and joined them. Ben introduced him to Glenda and George. "I think you know everyone else."

Spears nodded. "Nice to meet you."

Tom passed him the lasagna. He helped himself to a portion and glanced to see what everyone was drinking. "Water," Tom said, as if reading his mind. "Coffee with dessert."

"Dessert?" Wendy said.

"Cassada cake," Dawn replied.

Wendy sighed.

"It's tradition. We can't eat lasagna without it," Dawn added.

Wendy smiled, thinking, maybe if I do an extra half hour on the treadmill tonight….

"So," Ben said. "To bring you up to date, I was saying how I don't think the third floor is necessary."

Spears looked at him, mouth full, and literally stopped chewing.

"I don't know how much it costs to heat and air condition that floor, and the lights, the cleaning, the maintenance."

Spears swallowed his food whole. "Where will we go? What are you planning, Ben?"

"I'm thinking about the second floor, or that big empty area down by the secretary's office. What's that used for anyway?"

"Um…." Tom said.

No one knew.

"So, I'm thinking we might make a tradeoff here to help us pay for the bugler and cover the lack of Rupert's rent."

Wendy poured Spears a glass of water and handed it to him. He took a long drink. "Are we talking about this year, next year?" he asked.

"This year, this week," Ben said. "Tomorrow."

Wendy came to Spears' rescue. "The computers would have to be moved. They're all networked."

"I say we check it out tomorrow and see what works best." Ben looked at Wendy. "Will you handle that?"

She hesitated, deferring to Spears with a glance. "Yes, but I do think…."

"Good," Ben said. "Next order of business?"

"Tomorrow's video," Dawn said. "I'm thinking about taping a two-year old getting okayed out of the gate."

Tom shook his head. "You'd better wait till we take Bo-T back up. God forbid something happen unrelated and…."

"Good point," Dawn said.

"How about a video of the secretary's office in the morning?"

"Would we have to get everyone's permission?"

"Probably."

"What else then?"

Dawn looked at Randy. "How about if you come and examine one of the horses?"

Both he and Tom said, "Jinx" at the same time. Not a good idea.

"Why are horsemen so superstitious?" Dawn asked.

"Because it's a game of luck," Ben said.

Dawn nodded. "Pass the salad, please."

Glenda handed it to her. "What about a video of Beau?"

Ben shrugged.

Spears looked at him. "You mean Native Beau Born?"

"No, *the* Beau. Beau Born," Glenda said. "The sire."

"Where is he?"

"Here," Wendy said.

Spears sat back. "Okay, and is there any superstition to that?"

Ben laughed. "No, breeding season is months away and he's already booked full."

"It would have to be in the barn, since it's getting dark outside," Dawn said. "Where's Dusty? He did such a great job narrating Some Sam's video this morning."

"He'll be here soon. He had a little situation to take care of first."

"At the track?" Ben asked.

Tom nodded. "Which reminds me." He looked at Randy. "How do the vets decide what to charge?"

Randy looked at him and smiled. "Rupert said you'd be knocking on my door too."

Tom shook his head. "That son of a bitch. I have never met anyone so hard-headed in my life."

Randy laughed. "Actually I can only speak for myself, for my hospital. But we have a standard mark-up process."

"Do you charge the same for an injection on the farm as you do the racetrack?" Tom asked.

"No, but we don't charge farm calls on the racetrack either. We charge by procedure."

"So what you're saying is you only charge more on the racetrack to make up for that?"

"That, and what traffic will bear," Randy said. "Tom, it's a business. It's about making a profit, paying your own bills. If you had a vet going around charging less than the others, that might get him a few customers initially but the majority are going to wonder why. Why is he discounting or undercutting? Plus, I have to stay on top of things in racehorse treatment. The racetrack business is different than being a

149

farm vet. Things change every week, every day. It's a business from all aspects. No one races for free."

Tom sighed. "Let me ask you this. Do you think the high cost of veterinary medicine has anything to do with the success or failure of horse racing?"

Randy started to answer.

"Not the care, the success?" Tom emphasized.

Randy sat back. "If a person is going to own a racehorse and succeed, they're going to have to give that horse the best, the best trainer, the best care, the best rider, the best veterinarian. And if they can't afford that, they don't belong in the business. They don't call it the Sports of Kings for nothing. I'll go you one better," Randy said. "That's what's wrong with the business. You have people that think because they train a cheap claimer that they can cut corners. No. That's so far from the truth it's a bold-face lie."

The two men sat looking at one another, all the rest glancing from one to the next.

"Every horse," Randy said, "deserves the best shot. They're putting their life on the line every time they race, every time they go to that track to gallop. They're giving it their best. We owe it to them to do the same, or don't race, get out of the business. God, I hate it when a trainer says, 'Well, let's wait and see.' Try walking away from that when you know what that horse needs."

Tom smiled. "Now see, that's why I love you, Randy. You care. Come here and give me a hug."

Randy laughed. "No thanks, I gotta go."

"No dessert?" Dawn asked.

"Oh." Randy hesitated. "I'll take it with me"

Dusty arrived as Randy was leaving. Randy didn't like the look on his face; it spelled trouble. "Dawn'll fill me in later," he said, on the way to his vet truck.

Dusty sighed and went inside.

"Well?" Tom said, passing him a clean plate and silverware.

Dusty sat down and dished out a helping of lasagna. Wendy passed him the salad and bread. Dawn poured him a glass of water. He looked around the table. "Dave Brubaker is shipping out tomorrow."

"What?"Ben said. "Did he say why?"

"He says he sees the writing on the wall. That Nottingham Downs will not be in operation next year, and that he needs to establish himself elsewhere."

Ben stared.

"How many horses does he have?" Spears asked.

"Nine," Dusty said.

Spears shrugged, as if to say, okay, nine's not that bad.

"Nine allowance and top claimers," Tom said.

Spears sat back.

"Is there any talking him out of it?" Dawn asked.

Dusty shook his head. "He says it's a done deal. His owners are in agreement."

Ben crossed his arms. "What would make him do something like this?"

"Well," Dusty said. "Let's not forget he shipped out a month early last year, so this isn't exactly new behavior. Still...." This was three months before the end of the season.

"I've a mind to tell him he can't come back," Ben said. "Ever."

Dawn smiled. "Let's wait until next year to tell him when he wants to ship in. It'll have more impact that way."

Ben looked across the table at her; seems like her comment right there might have been the first real inkling that she was on board with this racetrack-ownership business. "Eat up, Dusty," he said. "We're all waiting on some Cassada cake."

The meeting continued over dessert. "Do you remember years ago when they used to give out barn awards?" Ben said.

George smiled. "Glenda and I won it once."

She nodded. "That was just a couple of years ago. Why'd they stop?"

"Money," Spears said.

"Come on. A hundred dollars a month?"

"It adds up."

151

"But the barns looked really good, for the most part at least," George said.

"But it didn't affect the betting and the handle."

"Fuck that word, I don't like it," Tom said.

Everyone laughed.

"I say we get one going again," Ben said. "We only have three months, so we'll probably have to offer a weekly prize so they have more of a shot at winning."

"Now we're talking even more money," Spears said.

"Yes," Dawn said, "but maybe we could tie it into securing their barns next year. Practically everyone ends up in the same barns anyway, or at least wants to. This way they'll know for sure."

Wendy reached for her note pad.

"Why does it matter?" Spears asked.

"Well, for one," Tom said, "it's a sense of pride. If we care and they care...."

Spears nodded, thinking of his office.

"When does construction on the Ginny stand start?" Dawn asked.

"Monday," Spears said. "There was a delay on the material. It'll be delivered Sunday evening after racing. We're going with something prefab so the construction noise doesn't upset the horses for too long a time."

Everyone looked at him, mouths dropped

"Mim Freemont cornered me in the secretary's office that morning we were down there. She said she wanted to make sure I properly understood the situation." He smiled. "I understand."

Ben chuckled. "There might be hope for you yet."

Chapter Twenty

Randy drove to the Corby Smith dressage barn and went inside. Once a week he stopped to check on the fifteen horses in Corby's care. She was the consummate professional, was always there waiting for him, and sported an illustrious reputation as an award-winning dressage rider, trainer, and judge. She could see things in the way a horse moved that bordered on fourth, even fifth dimensional. Nothing slipped by her. And yet, her own horse, Mickey McGuiness, a 17 hand Irish Warmblood gelding, aged sixteen, eluded her sensibilities. Day in and day out, she saw him as he once was, determined that he still could be, and refused to acknowledge or even consider his obvious decline.

"He's eating much better today," she told Randy.

Randy glanced in at Mickey's almost full feed tub. There was nothing wrong with the horse; his age did not seem to be a factor. He was actually quite healthy. He just didn't have any spunk left.

"No impulsion," to put it in Corby's words. She'd tried different saddles, different saddle pads, different bits, she'd covered all her "training" bases.

Each week Randy examined him he hoped he'd find something, anything. Teeth were good, legs sound, good digestion, bright eyed. He reminded him of his father. He listened to the beat of his heart for the umpteenth time, strong as an ox's. "Well, we'll just keep an eye on him," Randy said, the usual.

He thought of Linda Dillon's two ponies, Dawn's ponies now actually...such different lives. He watched Mickey walk over to his feed tub, nibble, and walk away. "See," Corby said. "Didn't I tell you?"

Randy smiled. They'd already discussed the horse's diet. He was getting fed a quality grain, and lots of it, spread out in five meals throughout the day. Corby had tried different feeds over the past year, always easing Mickey into it gently. She'd done everything right. He got fed a good timothy hay mix, free choice. He preferred hay over his grain. Randy had suggested she cut his grain back, but that was never going to happen. For all the good she did with her horses, she was set in her ways. A good solid dressage horse needed lots of grain in her opinion, and that's all there was to it. Randy once suggested he be retired.

153

"Retired?"

From her reaction, one would have sworn he'd uttered a blasphemous obscenity. Mickey McGuiness was a Grand Prix dressage horse "in his prime."

"How about just turning him out for a couple of months?" Randy also suggested.

"Turn him out? He'll hurt himself and then what?"

Back to square one. Randy checked the other horses in the barn; Corby had a detailed list, and soon he was on his way to the next call. It was his final appointment of the day, a standing visit at this farm each week at approximately this time, barring an emergency.

Shifting Gears Thoroughbred Rescue Farm was landlocked; a mere ten acres, only fourteen stalls and full to capacity. The pastures looked more like dirt paddocks, they were so eaten down. Ohio climate dictates shelter, particularly for a Thoroughbred not used to living out in the elements twenty-four hours a day, seven days a week. The volunteer staff built run-in sheds in each pasture, donations afforded an automatic watering system, but the electric bill was too high, so they were back to watering with hoses. Randy knew every detail, every volunteer. He knew the proprietors; two women in their late 40's, one was "a rugged as hell" and the other "a bleeding-heart liberal." One was a warrior, the other one, a worrier.

"What do we have tonight?" Randy asked, entering the barn.

"Well," Veronica, the worrier, said. "That bow on the Georgio filly seems bigger to me." They walked down to the horse's stall. Randy examined it.

"It looks good, it's nice and tight."

Veronica nodded. "It looks bigger though."

Randy shook his head.

Karen, the epitome of sunshine, came around the corner. "Hi, Doc!"

Randy smiled. "How're you doing, Karen?"

"Okay. We think we have a home for Squeegee."

Randy chuckled. She had nicknames for each horse. Squeegee was named Squeegee because he'd come in with a heavy winter coat and after a bath to rid him of all the caked-on manure, he took forever to dry. Karen took a squeegee to him when a sweat scraper wasn't doing the trick. He was at least two hundred pounds underweight back then, but was looking great now.

"He's such a sweet horse. If this girl doesn't treat him right, I think I'll strangle her," Veronica said.

"Don't let people hear you say that," Randy said.

"Well, it's true."

"Still...."

Randy checked the rest of the horses needing attention. Two had just come off the track, one with a hairline fracture of the coffin bone in his left hind hoof. Randy was pleased he was putting weight on that foot. The other horse had pulled a suspensory ligament in his right front. He'd been iffy the first week here, off his feed, listless, depressed. It was touch and go. Randy had made numerous trips to the farm on his behalf, once in the middle of the night when he was down and wouldn't get up. He was doing much better now. He wasn't much to look at, tall and gangly, and had a wide-eyed frightened expression. Chances are he was going to be hard to Re-home.

Randy gave a talk once at the local hunt club about "Rescue, Rehab, and Rehoming." It was a pet peeve of his, this latest trend of referring to all Thoroughbreds coming off the track as Rescues. "In my opinion if a sound horse from the racetrack can no longer race for whatever the reason, too slow, too skittish, no longer competitive, that horse needs a new home. They are a Rehoming prospect. If a horse is sore or injured, he or she will need to be Rehabbed first and then Rehomed. The term Rescue applies only to a small percentage of all horses; horses that are facing death or in harm's way." He chose his words carefully, "The horses that are neglected or mistreated, malnourished or abandoned."

"A small percentage?"

"Yes," Randy said. "Mind you, I can only speak for the Thoroughbred racing industry, which is my specialty."

"Have you ever insisted a horse be put down?"

"I have."

"And?"

"The horse was put down."

"What about the ones that break down in plain sight but don't necessarily have to be put down?"

"Well," Randy said. "Those are the candidates for Rehab and Rehoming."

"And not the killers?"

"Ma'am," Randy said. "In all due respect, I hear where you're coming from but I'm in the business to heal injuries and to save horses. I would no sooner want to see one go to a killer sale than you would, maybe even more so." Randy looked around the room at that point. "Are there any more questions?"

"Yes," a man sitting way in the back said. "Is there any truth to the old farmer's wisdom about putting copper in a mare's water bucket to keep her from going into heat?"

Randy looked at him and smiled. "My father swears by it."

Karen and Veronica walked with Randy to his truck. He filled their arms with supplies. "You're a godsend, Randy," Karen said. "I don't know what we'd do without you. How are we ever going to repay you or find a way to thank you?"

"You don't have to. What you two accomplish for these horses is thanks enough."

Beau Born pricked his ears when he saw the entourage approaching. He looked first at Ben, then Tom, then George, then Dawn, and then all the rest and let out a stallion whinny. He looked past all of them then, looking, looking, and looking, and they all laughed. If horses could talk, "Where are the mares?" he'd be saying.

Ben had a framed copy of Beau's past performances and the plan was for Dusty to refer to his race record and breeding as Dawn taped the video. Beau was used to being photographed and on video. He was used to striking a pose.

"He is so beautiful," Wendy said, seeing him again only for the second time.

For the most part, it was George who handled Beau now. Dawn started videoing as George put on Beau's nameplate halter and lead shank. She zoomed in as Dusty narrated, "Beau Born is the leading Thoroughbred sire in Ohio. He raced fifteen times in two and half years and has a lifetime earnings of $870,000." Beau tossed his head up and down, and bucked and squealed as George led him out of his stall.

Aside from mares, what Beau liked best was peppermints. Tom unwrapped one he had in his pocket, fed it to him, and patted him lovingly on the forehead, video rolling. George led Beau down to the end of the barn and as he stood looking out into the night, Dawn zoomed in again to capture the look in his eyes.

"The eyes of a champion," Dusty said, looking over her shoulder. "Beau Born."

At that exact moment, hearing his name, Beau turned his head and looked right into the camera and nickered. Dawn focused on him another second or two, then heaved a sigh. "And that's a wrap," she said.

"Wow!" Wendy and Glenda both said together.

"I know," Dawn shook her head. "I got goosebumps."

They all stepped out of the way so George could lead Beau back to his stall, then all hovered over the tiny video screen. Ben looked in at Beau and marveled, "You old showoff."

There was a full moon out, lighting the way as they all parted. Dawn walked up to her house, by way of the foaling barn to check on the ponies. They were both munching hay. Ben walked back to his house. Glenda and George climbed into their truck, Dusty his, and left.

Tom shut off the lights and secured the stallion gate. "Did you bring your boots?" he asked Wendy.

She nodded. "They're in my car."

"Why don't you go get them and we'll oil them," he said. "I'll meet you in the main barn." The two of them started off in different directions, but then Tom found himself hesitating as he watched her walk away in the moonlight.

"What?" she asked, glancing back over her shoulder.

"Nothing, it's just the moon and...." He smiled, blushed actually, not that she could see that in the dark. "You look like an angel."

Wendy stood gazing at him in the night and surprisingly for her, she didn't feel self-conscious. She didn't feel a need to come up with a catchy response. She just stood gazing at him. But then, oh my God, she thought, I'm falling in love with a cowboy, a real-life cowboy. My boys will die. And then....falling in love? Come on, she said in her mind. You're not a school girl. You're forty-eight years old. Get a grip.

Tom was wrestling with emotions of his own and was the first to turn and walk away. This was all new to him, caring about someone as a person, a woman as a woman, and not a...when Wendy walked into the barn, boots in hand, he looked at her and shook his head.

"I'm sorry," he said.

"For what?"

"For being the man I was all my life. I don't know where to begin with you."

She smiled. "Well, why don't we start with oiling my boots."

Tom laughed. While he worked on her boots, the outsides only, never any on the heel or sole, using lots of neatsfoot oil, Wendy walked around the tack room. She looked at all the bridles, the various bits, the saddles. "Who rides here?" she asked.

"Well," Tom said, glancing at her. "Up until a few years ago, I started all the babies."

"Started?"

"I don't like the term, broke. I never did."

"So why aren't you starting them anymore?"

"I'm getting too old."

"Oh?" She knew for a fact he was fifty-one years old from the listing on his groom's license. "You still pony though."

"I don't think I'll ever quit that. I love being out there on the racetrack when the races are run. I love the mornings. I love the action."

Wendy looked at him. "How long have you been on the racetrack?"

"Oh, since I was about thirteen. I drove my parents crazy skipping school and sneaking over to the track. They threw a huge party when I graduated. They didn't think it would ever happen."

"Did you go to college?"

Tom shook his head and smiled. "Not unless you count the school of hard knocks. I've certainly had my share of those learning experiences." He finished one boot and started on the other.

"Were you ever a jockey?"

"No. I would have liked to have been, but as jocks go, even back then I was the wrong size."

"So you just ponied horses?"

"No, actually the first ten or fifteen years, I was an exercise boy. Somewhere along the line I got my trainer's license and did okay from what people tell me."

"What do you mean?"

"Booze. It clouded my memory."

"What made you stop drinking?"

Tom looked at her. "A drunk driver. Me. I almost killed someone, a little boy."

"Is this boy okay?"

Tom nodded. "Thank God" he said, and paused. "Jesus, how many times have I said that thank God?"

Randy pulled up next to the barn, got out of his truck, and walked inside. Tom welcomed the diversion. "Is everything okay?" Randy asked. Lights on in the barn at this time of night was not the norm.

"Yeah," Tom said, motioning to the task at hand.

Wendy smiled. "He's doing a very good job."

Randy chuckled. "He's a perfectionist to a fault." He glanced in at All Together, a habit. She pinned her ears. She never did forgive him for all the treatment she endured in healing her leg injury. "I love you too," he said, when she turned her backside to him.

Tom glanced up as Randy sat down on the bench just inside the tack room.

"Dawn got a great video of Beau."

Randy nodded and yawned. It was nice, just sitting, the sounds of the horses munching hay, sighing. "I just came from Shifting Gears."

"How is everything there?"

"Oh, full." Randy yawned again. "I don't know how those women do it."

"Shifting gears?" Wendy said.

Tom finished up the second boot and set is aside. "It's a Thoroughbred Rescue, Rehab, and Re-home farm. They go above and beyond."

"Are there a lot that need rescued?"

"One is more than I care to see," Randy said. "They get their share, but they have success stories too."

Tom nodded. "I told Karen I'd come get on that Ricochet mare when she's ready. She's going to be tough first couple of times under saddle."

"Be tied on," Randy said. The mare had a reputation on the racetrack for rearing and was ruled off for flipping in the paddock.

Tom nodded.

"Well, I'm going to call it a day. Good night, you two."

"Good night, Randy."

Wendy picked up her boots. "Are they good to go?"

"Let them dry overnight. You should probably wear them tomorrow to get them formed to your feet while the leather is still soft."

Wendy smiled. "Maybe I'll sleep in them."

Tom laughed. "I've done that." He walked with her to her car. "I'll see you tomorrow," he said, closing her door when she got in behind the wheel. He hesitated. "It's nice getting to know you, Wendy."

"You too," she said. "I'll see you tomorrow."

Chapter Twenty-One

It was a busy morning, a rainy morning, a crazy morning. A full moon hovered high above the dark swirling clouds. "Now that's just not normal," Tom said, astride Red standing just outside the shedrow, decked out in a slicker, plastic cover on his hard hat, and waiting for B-Bo. "Come on, Dawn! Let's go!"

B-Bo would not take the bit, which could and would, be another bad omen, had this not been a consistent habit of his. She stuck her finger in the soft area between his teeth, pressed, tickled. Sometimes it worked. Not today. She heard Tom and Red slosh-sloshing their way down the shedrow. "Sometime today would be nice," Tom said.

Dawn gave him a look and tried again, pressed and tickled the opposite side of B-Bo's gum. He opened his mouth. Not all the way, but enough. Juan Garcia stood in the doorway of the tack room, waiting. When Tom turned Red back around, Juan stopped a groom hotwalking a horse coming around the corner. Dawn led B-Bo down the shedrow, handed him to Tom, gave Juan a leg up, and stepped back out of the way.

"I could be home dry and warm *writing* a racetrack novel," Dawn yelled after them.

Tom looked back at her, the rain dripping in streams off his hard hat, and started singing, "Ain't nothing like the real thing, baby, nothing like the real thing...."

Ben had walked up to the racetrack about ten minutes earlier and was holed up in the kitchen peering out the steamy window pane. "I'm too old for this," he said to himself. When he spotted Tom on Red leading B-Bo down through the barn area his face lit up. The rain was supposed to stop later this

161

morning and not rain again until late Sunday. Being a closer, B-Bo liked an off racetrack. If the weatherman was right for a change, the track would be in ideal condition.

At the moment, the track was sloppy but hard on the bottom, not torn up yet. It was early. B-Bo was done up in all fours, rundown patches adhered. His tail was tied up so as not to get muddy, standard racetrack practice. He was dancing and prancing.

Ben walked outside and over to the tiny overhang on the back of the track kitchen. Juan gave him a thumbs up. Ben nodded and glanced at the swirling dark clouds, the moon. There were some that didn't believe in the practice of breezing a horse the day before a race. But Ben was "old school," particularly with a colt as big and strong as B-Bo. He'd laid the groundwork with B-Bo and he was fit enough to run two races back-to-back. This breeze was just to put him on his toes and get him focused.

B-Bo knew the routine and was all business. As Tom ponied him around to the backside, he got more and more on the muscle with each stride. The plan was to breeze $3/16^{ths}$ of a mile down the lane. As they approached the far turn Ben stepped out from under the eaves into the downpour, watched as Tom turned them loose, watched as Juan dropped him down on the rail, watched as B-Bo ate up the racetrack and galloped out strong.

The clocker's phone rang. Ben picked it up.

"B-Bo, was that a work, Ben?"

"Nope, just putting a little air in him."

"Impressive," the clocker said. "Glad I didn't have to report you to the owner for not calling in the work. I hear he's a real son of a bitch."

Ben laughed.

Dawn had B-Bo's stall done, had Wee Born ready to pony, and did a trade-off of the two horses with Juan's help. "I be back in half hour," Juan said, ducking immediately into B-Bo's stall to take a pee.

Dawn hosed B-Bo's chest, legs and stomach, scraped him off, and threw a cooler sheet on him. She had a bucket of fresh water hanging on the hook up by the tack room and after walking him a lap around the shedrow, let him have a drink. He smacked his lips, splashing her.

"As if I'm not wet enough," she said. She walked him around and around the shedrow, stopping each time to let him drink if he wanted, and put him in his stall about twenty minutes later when she saw Tom coming back with Wee Born.

"You have to tack Whinny." Whinny was Winning Beau's nickname.

Dawn took Wee Born over to hose her off. She was covered in mud from head to toe. "How is that possible?" The filly rubbed up against her. "Oh Lord." Now Dawn had mud all over her.

Tom dismounted Red and the pony walked down the shedrow and into his stall. Tom grabbed the tack for Winning Beau, did her legs up and tail, saddled her, and then walked down to help Dawn scrape off Wee Born. "What time's Juan coming back?"

Dawn pushed up her soggy sleeve to look at her watch. "About ten minutes."

Tom put a cooler on Wee Born and wiped off her face with a towel.

"I'll get her stall real quick," Dawn said, handing him the lead shank. "Here." She hurried and did the filly's stall, made a big pile in the center, then switched and took Wee Born next time around so Tom could haul out the piled manure and straw with a pitchfork. In a hurry, doing it this way and not with a muck basket worked well, but it was way too heavy for Dawn to lift, so Tom always did it. As he was heading out to the manure bin, Wendy came walking down between the two barns. He looked at her. "It's a shitty job, but someone has to do it."

She chuckled. He looked like he was in costume, covered from head to toe in slicker, plastic pants, and plastic covered hard hat.

"Look at you in them boots," he said. "Looking good, woman!"

Wendy laughed. Business suit, socks up to her knees, boots and all. "Is Dawn here?"

He nodded, motioned to the barn, and then motioned for her to look out. Dawn was walking Wee Born around the end of the shedrow and the filly was all wound up.

"Loose horse!" someone yelled from a barn away.

Dawn hurried and led Wee Born into her stall to wait. At Tom's urging, Wendy rushed into the tack room. Tom went out into the road, looked one way then the other in the rain and saw the horse coming. He and two other grooms corralled the horse between the barn and the building that housed the restrooms.

"Easy, easy...whoa...whoa...." Tom got a hold of the horse's lead shank and turned him over to one of the grooms. "We got him!" he yelled to Dawn above the din of the rain pelting the roof. Dawn led Wee Born out of her stall and continued walking her, Wendy waited in the safety of the tack room amidst all the activity. Tom finished Wee Born's stall, bed it, filled her haynet, dumped her water bucket, filled it with fresh water, and motioned the stall was ready.

Juan ducked under the eaves of the shedrow, no gutters, drip-drip, and shook off the rain. He glanced in the tack room. "Morning."

Wendy smiled. "Good morning." Tom finished tacking Whinny, led her out of the stall, handed the reins to Juan and whistled for Red. He moseyed out of his stall and down the shedrow. Tom gave Juan a leg up, then mounted Red, took hold of the filly's rein and off they went to the track. He glanced back at Wendy when she peeked out from around the edge of the tack room door.

"What time are we looking at doing the offices thing?"

"Twelve-fifteen."

"I'll see you then!"

Wendy sucked back into the tack room when she saw Dawn leading Wee Born around the corner a final time, waited until she'd put the horse in its stall, and walked down to talk to her. "I thought I'd come get the video and save you the trip. I knew with it raining...."

164

"Thank you," Dawn said. "It's on the shelf above Ben's desk. It came out really good. I put it to music."

Wendy took off toward the tack room, slipping and sliding as she dodged other horses and hotwalkers, and Dawn hurried down to do Winning Beau's stall. With a little luck, she'd have it done before they got back and a moment or two to sit down and have a cup of coffee.

It didn't happen.

With all the sounds of the heavy rain on the roof and still operating off the high of breezing, B-Bo got all wound up in his stall and broke out in a sweat. Dawn blanketed him with a clean, dry sheet and started walking him around the shedrow again. With the downpour and no use of walking machines, by now it was a convoy of horses being cooled out under the shedrow. By the time Tom and Juan got back to the barn with Whinny, B-Bo had calmed down a little, but not enough to put him away. Dawn kept walking him, Tom took care of Whinny, and it started raining harder.

"Fuck this!" Tom said.

Dawn looked back over her shoulder at him. He was two horses behind her. "My sentiments exactly," she said. "Kinda sorta."

Tom laughed.

Another two laps and Dawn put B-Bo back into his stall, kept the cooler on him, and watched him for a moment. When he started eating hay out of his hay net, she slish-sloshed her way to the tack room, hugging the stall fronts to stay out of the horses and hotwalkers way.

She poured herself a cup of coffee, finally, and it was cold. "Damned timer." She tossed the rest of the coffee out into the rain, made another pot, and walked down to check on Red. Tom came back around with Whinny. "Do you want him un-tacked?"she asked. Red had eating with his bridle on down to a science. He was happily munching hay.

"Here, I'll do it. Take Whinny. She just needs a couple more turns."

Red got dried off and a good rubdown. His stall had already been cleaned, fresh water, hay, so all was well with

165

him. As mornings go, aside from the rain, he'd had it easy. "What time's Johnny coming by?"

"Nine," Dawn said. "Is Ben staying up at the kitchen?"

"No, he walked over to the secretary's office for something."

"In this rain?

Tom nodded, hauling Red's soggy saddle down the shedrow. It weighed a ton. "We need to get that old man a golf cart."

"He won't drive it." Dawn stood staring at the coffee pot, it was still dripping. The aroma was intoxicating. "Come on, come on." After an agonizing wait, she poured them both a cup.

Tom sat down on the cot. "What did Wendy want?"

"The video," Dawn said, sitting down next to him. She studied his profile as he sipped the piping hot coffee. Next to Randy, Tom was about the best-looking man she'd ever seen, in a rugged, hard-life cowboy kind of way. And deep down, he one of the sweetest, kindest men she'd ever known. "You really like her, don't you?"

Tom looked at her and smiled. "Well, see that's just it. I honestly don't know what it's really like to like a woman."

"What? Excuse me."

"Don't look at me like that. You don't count." They both laughed. "But I do enjoy being with her, though it's kind of usual with her being my age and that we actually talk."

"True," Dawn said. He'd always gone for younger women and probably did very little talking. "This is called a relationship, Tom. Welcome to the real world."

Tom glanced at her and smiled. "Maybe I'm just getting old."

She smoothed his wet hair back. "I'd like to think maybe you're just growing up."

"Isn't that the same thing?"

"If you say so," Dawn said, smiling.

Tom finished his coffee and walked down to tack Born All Together - nicknamed Batgirl for all the times as a two-year old when she acted like she thought she could fly. Johnny was due any minute.

Chapter Twenty-Two

Ben walked into the secretary's office and shook off the rain. He had on a full raincoat, rain hat, goulashes over his boots, waterproof gloves, and still felt chilled to the bone. He sneezed, blew his nose, and sneezed again.

He was curious to see if Brubaker had pulled all his horses' papers. He glanced around the room, unsure of whom he wanted to ask. He needn't worry. Joe Feigler looked up from taking entries and announced to the world. "There'll be very little competition for Native Beau Born in tomorrow's feature, now with Brubaker gone."

Ben sighed. It had been a nine-horse field, with Brubaker having two horses in as an entry. Down to seven. "There's no such thing as a sure winner," Ben said, and shook his head. Talk about talking trash, he said to himself. I sound like the owner of the track, talking down my own horse. He motioned to the Stewards' office and walked past the counter. There were three racetrack Stewards, judges so to speak, at Nottingham Downs. Two of them were hired by the racetrack, one appointed by the state.

All three looked up when Ben entered the room. "Good morning, Ben!"

"Good morning! I'm checking to see which one of you is planning to build an ark and if I need to make a reservation?"

The men laughed.

"Actually," Ben said, "I'm just checking in." He'd known all three men for years. "Everything all right?"

The three men nodded.

"Well then." Ben smiled. "Keep up the good work."

All three men nodded again, all three men said, "Thank you."

Ben looked back before leaving. "By the way," he said. "Just so you know…I don't hold any grudges." He looked into the eyes of each man. "I believe the decision you made against me was wrong, but I respect that you were following rules. I want you to know that."

When Ben stepped outside it was still raining but showing signs of letting up. Off in the distance there was a glimmer of clear blue sky. As he walked to the gap by the track, he relived that day of the ruling. It was his one and only violation ever on the racetrack, and for all practical purposes, not his fault.

The day of the race, Tom Cajun, a horse he'd claimed for Gloria, was the favorite but had to be scratched by the track veterinarian late when Ben noticed a swollen area on Cajun's neck. The horse was also showing signs of lethargy. Turns out, someone got to him, trying to throw the race by tranquilizing him. It was not Ben nor anyone associated with Ben's stable. But the horse was in Ben's care, hence the ruling and fine.

He chuckled, thinking about Gloria. The woman wooed him for months, but Ben was "un-wooable" as he put it. He fixed her up with the gate guard, Charlie, and the rest is history. The two of them married and moved to Florida after a couple of years. They became family and visited at least two to three times every year and stayed in Randy and Dawn's guest room. It worked out good, them staying there. Ben had plenty of room, but there were no women allowed in Meg's kitchen. No.

Tom Cajun was thankfully fine and went on to win six more races until his retirement as a six-year old. He's a riding horse now. That day though, Gloria cried her heart out. Ben had to make her leave the barn and go home. She didn't want to leave Cajun's side, was afraid someone was going to come back and….

Ben walked along, thinking. The track Stewards had a thankless job and generally weren't thought of very kindly by the people they were charged with overseeing. The rules of racing, from ownership to groom, pony boy to jockey and trainer to entry clerk in the racing secretary's office, no one escaped their constant monitoring. Every race run and every license applied for needed their approval. They were the officials of racing and did not take their job lightly. Rules are rules and they were there to enforce them.

"Hey, Ben," said a trainer in passing.

"Morning." Ben walked on. Were people getting friendly again or was it his imagination? He glanced ahead and saw Tom leading Batgirl onto the racetrack. Johnny was adjusting his goggles. Ben stopped and leaned against the rail, figuring he might as well just watch them gallop from here. He drew a breath and sighed. All this walking back and forth was either going to kill him or get him ready for an old-man marathon.

Tom walked down to stand with him; both stepped back when Johnny jogged Batgirl on the outside rail, splashing mud and slop everywhere. "Take her nice and easy," Ben said.

Johnny nodded. He was one of the leading jockeys at Nottingham Downs. Batgirl was one of his favorite horses. Circumstances years ago, led to his riding Beau Born to a win in the horse's last race. He loved Beau Born and he loved this filly. She was Beau Born's daughter.

Johnny turned Batgirl around. They stood for a second, both jockey and horse taking in the activity all around them. Then Johnny clicked to the filly. She jogged off, broke into a canter, and then galloped strong. She was a sensible horse. She got that from Beau Born; sensible, but competitive. Even as a youngster she would always have to be first at everything. You'd best put her out in the pasture first or she'd pitch a fit. She always had to be first when it came time to bring them back in too. And she loved to run!

When a horse galloped up next to her, she dug in her heels and Johnny had to fight to keep her from turning the other horse's sudden presence into a horse race. She got that from her dam, All Together, a mare that always had to have her way, and her say.

She pulled up "sensibly" and jogged back around. Johnny dismounted her up by the gap and Tom led her down through the barn area. Ben walked along behind them, talking to Johnny. "How'd she feel?"

"Great! She feels great! She gets stronger every time I get on her."

Ben waved him on. Johnny had several more horses to gallop this morning. Ben appreciated the effort put in by his regularly named riders, their "vested interest" as he liked to put it when someone asked why he liked riders over exercise boys. It's not that he didn't use exercise riders, he did. He just felt that once his horses were racing and fit, the relationship between horse and rider was very important to being successful. Now when it came to starting his babies out at the farm or beginning their career at the track or getting them fit, exercise boys were invaluable because of their patience and strength. He was old school.

Dawn helped Tom bath Batgirl, scraped her off and put a sheet on her and was about to start walking her. Tom said he'd do it. "I'm a little stiff."

Dawn looked at him. The Tom of old would have followed that up with something obscene for sure, but not today. He just walked off, leading Batgirl, and singing, "What a friend we have in Jesus." Dawn knew the song by heart. He sang it all the time. "All our sins and grief to bear...."

She wrung out the sponge, gathered bucket, towel and sweat scraper, saw Ben coming down between the barns and waited. He smiled. "You won't believe who I just ran into."

"Who?"

"Do you remember Cracker Jack Henderson?"

Dawn had to think. "No, I don't think so."

"Well, he's in town for a few days. I invited him for dinner."

Dawn hesitated, still trying to place the man. "I'll see what Randy's schedule is. Maybe we can grill something."

Beau Together, the two-year old nicknamed Bo-T, was the last horse for the day. He was scheduled to walk, as he'd galloped yesterday and the day before. By the time Tom cooled out Batgirl, Dawn had been walking Bo-T for about fifteen minutes. Tom did his stall, hung his hay net, scrubbed his water bucket and filled it with fresh water. He was one of those horses that dunked his hay and rinsed his mouth a lot while eating. All was well with his teeth, it was just his habit.

"You're all set," he told Dawn. "I'm going up to Janie Pritchard's barn and hold one of her horses for the blacksmith."

She continued walking Bo-T for another fifteen minutes, then put him away, and had a lukewarm cup of coffee. "Damned timer." Again. By the time Tom returned, she had Wee Born and Whinny done up and groomed. Wee Born always had her front legs done up, and Whinny, all fours.

Bo-T didn't need done up. Tom painted his shins with an iodine mixture, standard practice to try and ward off his shin-bucking. He brushed him off and picked the mud out of his feet. "You got half the shedrow in your hooves," he teased.

Tom went down to do B-Bo next, and Dawn did Batgirl. She loved all the horses, but if she had to pick a favorite of the horses they had at the track, it would be Batgirl. Though chestnut and not grey, she had her dam's mannerisms and looks, had her lovey-dovey affectionate side.

"Stand still," Dawn said. She also had All Together's arrogance. Dawn brushed her until all her hair was laying flat and shiny, did her up in all fours, and met Tom coming down the shedrow, having just finished B-Bo - his favorite.

"He's a man's horse," he insisted.

Dawn agreed. Beau was easier to handle on the racetrack. He passed some of his temperament on, but B-Bo's dam was a challenge to handle, and so was B-Bo. "The key," Ben always said, when referring to B-Bo, "Is to meet his energy level with training, head on."

When it came time to meet with Spears over at the grandstand about the offices, Dawn went along reluctantly and whining, "I'm wet, I'm tired - I want to go home."

Wendy was at her desk, Spears his. When the man looked up and sighed, Ben laughed. "Bear with me," he said. "I just want to check things out, that's all. Wendy."

Wendy didn't look as resistant to possible change, but seemed supportive of what Spears was going through and rose from her chair with trepidation. Tom smiled. "Do I know you, pretty lady?"

She blushed.

"I'm chilled to the bone," Dawn said, walking alongside Tom and Wendy.

Tom put his arm around her. "That's 'cause you need a little meat on your bones." No sooner said he wished he hadn't said that, but it was too late. It was said and done. Lord, help me, he thought. I have never been so tongue-tied in my life. He looked at Wendy. "Is now a good time to tell you that I love you?"

Wendy laughed. "No."

Tom winked at her. "I didn't think so."

The five of them took the elevator down to the second floor. Dusty was waiting for them, soaked and chilled to the bone as well. The six of them strode down the hall as if they were about to board a space shuttle.

Dusty had already surveyed any open space. "You're in for a surprise. Once upon a time," he said, opening a door, "there was a magical room for only those who believed."

The room wasn't huge by most standards, but it was larger than Spears' office upstairs, and it was entirely empty but for some hideous dark maroon drapes blanketing two walls, floor to ceiling. "What was this?" Ben asked.

"Near as anyone can figure, it was a private uh....play room of sorts for an owner way back. Are you ready?" Dusty motioned for Tom to give him a hand. The drapes were heavy and no longer slid open on the curtain rod. They both pulled back a side.

Dawn stepped closer. "You've got to be kidding me."

Spears eyes lit up. "Is this one of those see-through mirrors?" The full length of the wall was glass, but odd looking glass, smokey, silvery.

"What's next to us?" Tom asked, trying to see, and seeing nothing. "It has to be the clubhouse, right?"

Wendy touched the glass with her fingertip, left an impression and then rubbed a tiny area. "You can see the racetrack," she said, peering through the tiny looking-glass hole.

Everyone rubbed their own little area, everyone but Spears that is. He looked through the opening Wendy had made.

"Okay," Tom said. "So this has to be to the near side of the clubhouse. "I'm going to go look. Wave so I know where you are." He went down the stairs, out through the secretary's office and into the open area in front of the grandstand.

At first he couldn't figure out where they were, the grandstand was all glass. He followed the line of club seats, dining tables, more club seats...stared and stared, and then saw a narrow black vertical line of what looked like a solid wall. He waved. Nothing....no response, no one.

Everyone was waving at him, again, everyone but Spears, who was walking around the room, sizing it up. Dawn wiped a larger area with her wet sleeve, larger and larger, and Tom, peering and peering, finally saw her and waved. "I see you!" he yelled, and to Wendy, "I see you too! Listen!"

They couldn't hear him, but could practically read his lips, and laughed. Whatever he was saying was sure to be funny. He headed back upstairs. "You're not going to believe this," he said, holding his hands slightly apart. "It looks like an area this wide. And black, like it's a wall."

"So it's not a mirror?" Spears said. "It's a see-through both ways?"

Tom nodded.

Ben stood looking out the large window area Dawn had cleaned. "We'll need to get somebody to clean all of this and get rid of these drapes. Then we'll take another look."

"I'll contact maintenance," Wendy said.

Ben nodded and turned to Dusty. "Are there any other rooms on this floor?"

"A men's room and a ladies room, four stalls each."

"No private executive bathroom?" Spears asked.

Everyone looked at him. "No," Dusty said. "But there is a private bathroom downstairs."

"Where?" Spears asked.

"Come on, I'll show you."

Ben's cell phone rang. He handed it to Dawn. Dawn shook her head. "Hello."

"Hello, may I speak to Ben Miller?"

"Who is this?"

"Customer Service with TLC Telecommunications."

"TLC Telecommunications?"

Wendy turned. "I'll take it. It's about Ben's new 'user friendly' phone."

Dawn handed her the phone gladly.

"Maybe you need one of those earphone thingies," Tom suggested as they all walked to the elevator.

Ben looked at him.

"It was just a thought," Tom said, pretending to be serious.

"I'll meet you all downstairs," Wendy said, turning her back and still talking to the phone rep. "Yes, larger. No bells and whistles, just plain old talking, plain ringer, programmable contacts and volume adjustment, unlimited local and long distance."

When she hung up, she walked down the flight of stairs and at the bottom, listened for the sound of the group's voices. Nothing, not a sound. They'd picked a fine time to be quiet. She'd always taken the elevator, so using that as a guide and knowing the secretary's and Stewards' offices were down the long corridor to the right, she took a left. She found all five of them standing, looking into a private bathroom.

"Since I'm here," Tom said. "I wonder when it was cleaned last?"

Spears looked at him, eyes wide, wondering precisely the same thing.

"Just kidding, just kidding," Tom said. "I can hold it." When he crossed his legs, Dawn pushed at him, laughing.

"Show us the rest of the rooms," Ben said to Dusty.

"Well, they're small, but...."

"Isn't there an office that connects to the restroom?" Spears asked. They were going pretty far down the hall.

Tom looked at him. "I think I'm going to have to do some serious praying for you. A shitter's a shitter, what's the big deal?"

Spears shrugged. "I guess I just have a hang-up about cleanliness."

"That's all right," Tom said, "I have enough hang-ups to sink a ship. Man overboard!"

Everyone laughed.

There were three empty offices in a row, small, no windows. "From what I understand, once upon a time, each Steward had their own office," Dusty said. The offices still had old desks and file cabinets.

"It looks like a dungeon," Spears said.

Ben had to agree. "I wouldn't want to spend any amount of time in here." All three offices were the same. "So the offices just sit here, empty. Do we heat them?" He turned the light switch on, the room lit up. He checked the thermostat. "Well, at least it's set at fifty."

Dawn looked in one of the file cabinets, the desk drawers. Empty.

"They're all empty," Dusty said. "I checked all three rooms. Apparently the state Steward had his own bathroom." They walked down to the third office so Dusty could show them the bathroom. It was nothing more than the size of a closet with a stained white sink and toilet.

Spears shuddered."Wonderful."

"Well, this has been fun," Tom said.

"There's one more room," Dusty said. "I saved the best for last." They all followed him back out into the hall and down the corridor to the right. "It sits directly behind the secretary's office. You'll have to look past all the boxes."

He opened a door to a large room, probably 40' x 60'. It had wood-paneled walls, and served as storage for all the racetrack records over the years; a racing form for each and every day, a program, the overnights, accounting records.

"Is there a reason to keep all of this?" Ben asked.

Spears wondered the same thing. "I don't know, I'm not sure."

175

"It's a nice size," Dawn said.

Tom looked around. "Yeah, but where's the bathroom?"

They all laughed.

"Okay," Ben said. "Let's give this some thought. I don't really need an office, so...."

"Yes you do, Ben," Spears said. "Trust me. Even if you don't think so now, as the owner you will come to realize it's a must."

Ben sighed. "Where can we all go sit and talk? I really don't want to go back upstairs."

They all walked to the secretary's office. This time of day it was generally deserted, aside from the racing secretary, assistant, and several other employees. Ben waved to them, then motioned to the table, implying they'd be occupying it and the group sat down.

"You're not expecting me to bring you guys coffee or anything are you?" Joe Feigler said. "If so, it's going to be a long wait. We're still trying to fill the last two races."

"See," Spears said, of the interruption, the distraction. "This is what I'm talking about."

Ben looked at him. "And this is what *I'm* talking about. If we hadn't just walked in here would you know they were having trouble filling races?"

"No, Ben," Spears said. "Because I'd be up doing what I do, and letting them worry for themselves about what goes on down here."

Ben looked at him and smiled. "Point taken. Still, I think there needs to be more communication. I think everybody needs to at least know what everyone else is up against."

A trainer and his assistant entered the secretary's office. When they both stopped at the counter, Tom watched. Hopefully they were entering horses. No. They appeared to be just asking questions, and then both walked over to the table. Ben, Tom, and Dusty knew them, but only in passing. This was their first year here at Nottingham Downs.

"Afternoon."

Everyone at the table returned the greeting. "Good afternoon."

176

It was obvious they had something on their mind. "What are the chances of us being able to move into Billy Martin's old barn?" one of them asked. "We have horses spread all over the backside."

Ben glanced at Joe Feigler; he lowered his eyes.

"How many head do you have?" Ben asked.

"Ten. Eleven with our pony."

Ben looked at Joe again. "Is there a problem with this?"

Joe hesitated and then shook his head.

"All right." Ben glanced at Dusty.

Dusty nodded. "All his stuff's stored elsewhere. It's all emptied out."

Ben looked at the two men again. "You do know that he died there?"

The men nodded, one voicing both their opinions. "Actually, since we shipped in, he was the only one that would give us the time of day. Thank you. Thank you kindly."

"Now that's uncalled for," Ben said, when they walked away. "They've been here all year and that's how we treat them. That's not right."

"I'm on it," Dusty said.

Tom shook his head. "We're a sorry lot."

"Oh, don't start that again," Ben said.

"Well, it's true. Here we are worrying about offices and crappers, and...."

Spears leaned forward; about to say something, but there was an announcement over the p.a. system. "Ladies and gentlemen, welcome to Nottingham Downs. Post time for the first race of the daily double is in thirty minutes. Don't get shut out."

Ben smiled. "Now that's what I'm talking about." He looked around the table. "Is everybody happy?"

Dawn laughed. "I will be, because I'm going home. I get to turn the ponies out today."

"Not too long, remember," Tom said.

Dawn smacked him, not once, but three times, and then again for extra measure. "Yes, Dad."

"Do you have an opinion about the offices?" Ben asked, when she stood up to leave.

"Yes," she said. "As nice as it would be to have everyone down on this floor, those offices are too dreary. I like the open window upstairs. I think it would be awesome if it can be set up inexpensively. Can you all share that room? I don't know. I think it's worth looking into. If not, then I say the big room right there. All things considered, if it were me, I'd want to see the racetrack every day. But also, I'd want to be a part of things here." She looked at Spears. "That's my opinion." She hesitated and turned to Wendy. "Is the video going to play at the same times?"

Wendy nodded. "I'll watch for the response."

"Thank you. I'll see you all later."

Ben looked around the room. This was the heart and soul of the daily business at the track; where the entries were taken in one of two entry booths, which provided privacy for the trainer who didn't want his entries common knowledge before the overnights came out. Where jockey agents vied for the best mounts for their riders and where the perpetual gin-rummy card game was played. If you wanted to know the latest about what was going on at Nottingham Downs all you had to do was hang out in the secretary's office. If you needed a license for an owner or groom or hotwalkers or your horse's papers, you were in the right place. Everything happened here, every day, as long as there was racing. He couldn't understand why Spears wouldn't want to be close to this, to be a part of it all.

He observed Spears out of the corner of his eye. The man was checking his suit-coat sleeve, dusting it off. Yes, the table wasn't all that clean, but it wasn't all that dirty either. And why was he wearing a suit anyway?

He looked at Dusty, sitting there looking at his notes. Dusty glanced up and smiled when another trainer entered the room.

"Hey!"

"Hey, Dusty."

"Hey, Ben, Tom."

They nodded and waved to the man.

Ben looked at Wendy; she too was scanning her notes. Tom pointed to the second item on her list. "Forget Me Nots?"

She smiled. "In Evangeline, Longfellow wrote, "Silently, one by one, in the infinite meadows of Heaven, blossom the lovely stars, the Forget-Me-Nots of the angels.""

"Okay...." Tom said. "That's pretty, but...." He motioned to the next two items on the list. Windows cleaned. Find new storage area for boxes. He looked at her, really looked at her, perhaps looked at her too long, not enough, just enough, because he found himself literally almost forgetting what he was about to say. "How do Forget-Me-Nots figure in?"

"Well, when I was looking out at the racetrack from the window up above, I thought how pretty it would be to have Forget-Me-Nots planted all around in front of the tote board. They're perennials and take little watering. Actually they're rather prolific, but that would be the point. They would keep growing. And they're blue, like blue grass, Kentucky, racetrack, Thoroughbreds, stars, heavenly stars...."

Tom smiled, Ben smiled, Dusty smiled, even Spears smiled.

"Now would be a good time to plant them," Wendy said.

Ben liked that idea. It had a positive feel to it, a promising feel, a feeling of hope for the future. It was a good feeling. He nodded. "Then get it done."

"Thank you, I will."

Ben looked around the table. "Getting back to the offices, I think I agree with Dawn. Those offices down the hall are too small."

Spears heaved a sigh of relief.

"They would not be welcoming and I want an open-door policy." He looked at Spears.

The man hesitated. "If I had my choice, I'd stay where I'm at." He could see right off Ben didn't like that answer. "But, I can see how my being more accessible could be a good thing, a positive move. I don't think I need to be involved in the day-to-day goings on down here, but...."

Tom and Dusty both shifted their weight. It was like a standoff.

"All right, let's look at it this way," Ben said. "Saying we close the third floor, totally. Of the two locations, that big room back there or the windowed one upstairs, which would you choose?"

When Spears hesitated again, Ben looked at Wendy. "Which one would you pick?"

Wendy paused, lowering her eyes to her notes. "Okay," she said. "This may be far-fetched, but since both the first and second floors are completely open and going to stay open, why can't we set up in both." She drew a breath, gaining momentum as she went along. "Why can't we set up what would be a very accessible office down here in the big room, one that the horsemen would feel comfortable visiting if they have concerns, and...." She glanced around the table. "Then one upstairs that would give Mr. Spears the privacy and quiet he needs, plus the professional setting conducive to receiving clients, meeting with the advertisers, the heavy-hitters, the people who could care less about the horses and only see dollars. And even better up there, if the windows clean up and they can see out, maybe, just maybe, they'll start thinking differently, and Mr. Spears, you would start thinking differently, and...."

When she fell quiet, fearing she may have overstepped her bounds, Tom looked at her with a most serious expression on his face. "Wendy, will you marry me?"

She smiled, blushed and then chuckled, all seemingly at the same time. "Can we at least date first?"

"Sure," Tom said, "Dinner, tonight at Ben's, seven o'clock."

Wendy laughed. "I'm already there."

It seemed a good time to end the meeting.

Chapter Twenty-Three

Dawn took a long hot shower, washed and dried her hair, and took a nap with the children. She fell into such a deep sleep, she dreamed one dream after another, unusual for her during a nap. When she opened her eyes, she gazed at her little ones, miracles; considering the doctors had predicted she'd never have children. She touched D.R's soft hand, marveled over Maeve's long eyelashes, and both with such red hair. She planted a kisses on their little button noses and slid her arm out from underneath the pillow.

The children's nanny, Carol, had offered to go to the grocery store and picked up everything for dinner, steaks, baking potatoes, hard crusty rolls. Randy was expected to be home to do the grilling. Dawn was going to make a salad. Glenda was bringing dessert.

"Oh, and Wendy called," Carol said. "She's bringing a fruit salad."

"Awesome."

"What do you think of her?" Carol asked.

"I like her," Dawn said.

Carol nodded. "Tom seems to like her."

"I know. It's scary." Dawn grabbed a jacket hanging at the back door and stepped into a pair of dry boots. "I'll be back in a little bit." She followed a well-worn path to the main barn, checked on All Together and the horses there, then walked to the stallion barn to say hello to Beau and Hurry Sandy. Both had been napping. "Sorry," she said, tiptoeing out. "Go back to sleep."

When Beau slept, for the most part, he lay flat out, and snored. Hurry Sandy slept all curled up like a deer and breathed so soft. Dawn approached the foaling barn quietly, thinking the ponies might be taking advantage of the lazy afternoon and napping as well. But they were both awake, standing at the back of their stalls.

She checked the pasture, probably too wet, she thought, and figured she'd turn them out in the sand paddock. At least they could roll and run if they felt like it, get a little sun on their bony backs. She put on their halters and debated which one to turn out first. She didn't want to show favoritism. When the foals on the farm are about a month old, they are taught to walk on a lead next to their mothers and were led out of the barn together that way. It transferred over into the same learned behavior pattern when they became weanlings and were led out of the barn two at a time, each with another weanling they'd grown up with.

She put lead shanks on both ponies, led Poncho out into the aisle, stopped in front of Biscuit's stall, led him out and walked them outside in tandem. They both stood looking at the pastures, looking at the horses grazing, looking at each other. When Poncho nipped at Biscuit, she laughed. It had never occurred to Dawn that they might not like one another.

"Well, there's only one way to find out." She led them into the sand paddock, turned them both to face her, which they did in a very well-behaved manner. She unsnapped the lead shanks, turning them loose, and they both just stood there. "Go!" she said. "Go play!"

They stood there still. It wasn't until she waved their lead shanks and clicked to them that they walked away, and even then they kept looking back at her unsure of what to do. Just about the time Dawn started worrying that there might be something wrong with them, Poncho dropped to his knees and rolled. He rolled and he rolled and he rolled and moaned and rolled, and rolled some more. Biscuit walked around the paddock, looking wary and then started snorting, head raised high and mane blowing in the wind.

If it weren't for his ribs sticking out and his tailbone prominent, he would almost be considered beautiful. Dawn walked out of the paddock and latched the gate none too soon. When Poncho rose to his feet, shook off the sand, and whinnied, the yearlings in the pasture below whinnied back and Biscuit took off running.

"Oh no!" For a split second, Dawn feared he was going to try to jump the five-foot fence. He put on the brakes at the last possible moment, bucked and kicked out, and he and Poncho started cantering round and round in the paddock.

Glenda was in the hayshed loading up the flatbed and came to see what all the commotion was about. "Well, look at them!"

Dawn smiled. They had every horse in all the pastures running and whinnying. "It's like they're happy just to be alive," Dawn said.

"And loved," Glenda added.

When the ponies finally stopped running in circles and all the other horses settled down and went back to grazing, it was Biscuit's turn to roll, and roll and roll. He had an odd way of rolling. "I've never seen a horse do that," Dawn said.

"Me neither," Glenda said.

He would roll on one side, then raise his hind end up, crawl on his knees a step or two, then back down he'd go on the other side, and roll some more. When he finally stood on all fours, Dawn heaved a sigh of relief.

The yearlings were wide-eyed and watching their every move, waiting for another reason to start running again no doubt. Running around was fine for them down in pastures where there was better drainage. In the pasture up here, there was standing water everywhere.

"I was planning to turn them out on grass today," Dawn said, smiling as she motioned to the stallion barn, where Beau had his head out his window, sniffing the air. "They're geldings, Beau, geldings."

The two women stood looking at all the horses, stood gazing at the farm, stood taking it all in and enjoying the sunny, warm afternoon breeze.

"Well, back to work," Glenda said, wiping her brow. When she walked back to the hayshed, Dawn went back into the foaling barn and picked out the ponies' stalls and checked their water. She decided to sweep the aisle way then and recalled the moments when each of the foals were born here.

"Randy..." she remembered saying when All Together seemed to be struggling with giving birth to Born All Together. "Help her."

"She's fine," he'd said, waiting patiently outside the stall. "She's fine."

Moments later, Batgirl entered the world. "Oh, Randy...."

When Dawn heard a nicker sounding close by, she walked out to check on the ponies. They were both standing at the gate. "Do you want in already?" It was sad to think of them being so appreciative of the little bit of time they'd had outside. But then she looked again, paying closer attention. They were both staring at the grass on both sides of the path leading back to the barn.

She opened the gate, secured their lead shanks, and led them out of the paddock. They practically pulled her to the grass and started grazing as if their very lives depended on it. "Slow down, slow down," she said, glancing at her watch. "I don't want you getting belly aches. Ten minutes and you're going in. You'll get more tomorrow."

Chapter Twenty-Four

Wendy walked through the grandstand, judging reactions to the "Beau Born" video. It was all positive. People stopped, they looked - they listened. Comments such as "Pretty horse, I remember that horse, I think that's the new owner's horse, that's nice, look how big he is..." peppered throughout. Wendy had to admit, she didn't realize how big a racehorse could be either. She was amazed too.

Tom had positioned himself by the monitor near the claiming booth just outside the paddock so he could gauge the horsemen's opinion of the video. It was somewhat mixed, but leaning more toward positive. He heard, "What the hell, Beau looks good, what else would you expect, are you a movie star now, Tom?"

Jack Burke, the complainer, walked over next to him. Tom smiled. "That's not exactly my best performance."

Jack laughed. "You looking to claim something?"

"No."

The horses were just entering the paddock. Both men turned. "I'll fight you for that one," Jack said.

"Do you want to step outside?"

"We are outside."

The two men laughed.

"Seriously," Jack said. "Are you guys allowed to claim anymore?"

"We haven't claimed any for years. We're not interested."

When Tom walked back to the barn and relayed the conversation Ben just shook his head. Tom sat down next to him. "What's the matter, old man? You look worried about something."

"Well." Ben looked at him. "I was just sitting here thinking of how nice it was when all I had to think about was this barn right here."

"Oh, not this again," Tom said, the two constantly reminding one another of their shortcomings.

"Maybe I'm trying to do too much. Maybe I *should* just let Spears do his job. What does it matter where he does it, upstairs, downstairs?"

"It matters, and you know it. Why are you second guessing yourself?"

"Because I'm an old man."

"A wise old man," Tom said. "And come this time next year, if the doors are closed and you didn't do it your way, you're still going to be an old man and then who are you going to blame?"

Ben laughed. "You."

Tom shrugged. "I can take it, but only if we've done our best and the Lord willing."

Ben sighed.

"All these years you've been saying how they should be doing this and doing that and here you are doing it. Come on, you're doing the best you can do."

Ben looked at him.

"And I for one would like to see this all put to a rest. No more doubts, no more second guessing. Forge ahead." Tom stood up. "And now, since that's all settled, I'm going to the crapper. There's one just up the way with my name on it."

Ben laughed. A few minutes later, one of the stable guards stopped by "Just to say hello." After that, the blacksmith came by to check B-Bo. Grain was delivered. The muck bin was emptied. The timer on the coffee pot didn't go off. It was a perfect racetrack afternoon.

From all directions they came, first Glenda and George, then Dawn and Randy, along with the children and Carol. Tom was already home, as was Ben. Dusty arrived next, then Wendy, and then Cracker Jack. Randy grilled the steaks outside on the back porch, Tom made a pot of decaf coffee, Dusty filled the water glasses, Glenda and Wendy set the table, Dawn and Carol fed the children.

Dawn stuck her head out the door to ask Randy, "Did you bring their headsets?"

"Yes," he said. "They're on top of the fridge."

They had a sizable library of children's movies stacked on the end table. "Which one do you want to see?" Carol asked.

"Dinosaur! Dinosaur!" D.R. said.

"Yes! Yes! Dine-thor!" Maeve said. They both ran to the couch, Maeve hugging her favorite "Dolly," and D.R. sporting his stuffed animal dinosaur hat, perched way low down on his eyes the way Tom wore his cowboy hat.

Carol "plugged them in" as she called it. "D.R., get your finger out of your nose."

"It's dinosaur nose. It itches!"

"Then rub the outside."

"Steaks are ready!" If anyone wanted them well done, they were out of luck. Randy brought the platter in and set it down in the middle of the table with great pomp and circumstance. "A masterpiece!" Everyone sat down and started helping themselves, steak, baked potato, tossed salad, fruit salad, rolls.

"Looks delicious," Cracker Jack said. In his day, as a local celebrity, he'd hosted a sports talk radio program, loved the "ponies," and was a crackerjack of a handicapper, hence his nickname. He stood over six-foot-six and was skinny as a rail. He had an abundance of wiry shoulder-length white hair. Quite a character; was the term most commonly used to describe him. He and Ben went way back.

"Fifty some years," Ben said.

Cracker Jack retired to Florida but still visited his son Jeff who was a trainer at Nottingham Downs with nine horses. Cracker Jack knew just about everything going on at the track, thanks to his son, and jumped right into the discussion at the dinner table.

"I hear tell Billy Martin's funeral was quite the spectacle."

"It was grand," Tom said. "A real proper sendoff."

"And who's this lovely lady?" Cracker Jack asked, smiling at Wendy.

"Don't you be flirting with her," Tom said.

Cracker Jack laughed. He was Ben's age. "I'm considered quite harmless unless you talk to the widows at the retirement complex."

Everyone laughed.

"This is Wendy." Tom said, "Nottingham Downs Assistant General Manager."

Wendy blushed. "Actually, I'm the administrative assistant to the General Manager."

Ben looked at Tom, then Dawn, and then Wendy and smiled. "No, I think Tom had it right."

Dawn waved her fork. "I agree."

"All right, then so it is," Ben said.

"Just like that?" Wendy asked.

Ben nodded. "Just like that."

Wendy smiled. "Can I be the one to tell Mr. Spears?"

They all laughed. "You bet," Ben said.

"I remembered when they hired Spears," Cracker Jack said. "If I recall correctly...."

A phone rang in Wendy's purse sitting on the kitchen counter. "Do you want me to get it for you?" Tom asked, being the closest.

Wendy glanced around the table. "Well, we're all here and that's Ben's new phone. No one else has the number yet."

"Then let it ring," Ben said. "Wait a minute. How is it that it sounds like a phone?"

"It's a retro ring," Wendy said.

They all sat listening; fourth ring and whoever it was hung up. Ben motioned for the sour cream. Randy passed it to him and glanced over his shoulder at the children. "D.R., quit," he said, laughing. He was picking Maeve's dolly's nose now. "I have serious concerns about that child."

Dawn shook her head. "You have to stop laughing when he does things like that. It only encourages him."

Carol sighed. "When they grow up, I fear my resume`."

Everyone laughed.

"I'm glad they got their looks from their mom," Cracker Jack said, glancing at Randy and smiling at Dawn. Flirt, flirt.

"Yeah, well I dropped your steak on the ground and wasn't going to tell you," Randy said. "But don't worry, I wiped it off."

Cracker Jack laughed and for a moment or so, they all busied themselves with eating. "So how do you plan to turn the track around, Ben?"

"Well." Ben looked across the table. "We've been trying to come up with various ideas. We raised the purses. We're trying to do a little more promoting. Dawn's been writing articles and doing videos...."

"I'm not sure what I'm going to do tomorrow," Dawn said. "It'll have to be in the morning early."

"And I fired some people."

"I heard," Cracker Jack said.

"We hired Dusty here to try and police the backside. Regardless of being independent contractors, the trainers need to operate on a certain level of professionalism. We don't want any mistreated horses. And we're going to make some improvements in the barn area, starting with the Ginny stand."

"That'll be nice," Cracker Jack said.

"We just have to take it slow, in the event...which reminds me," Ben said, looking at Tom and Dusty. "Did you find a bigger place for Rupert?"

"As a matter of fact," Dusty said, "I think we did. We have several possibilities. One is the old firehouse."

"Firehouse?" Dawn said.

"It's where they used to store the water trucks. The problem is it's up at the far end of the backside. Rupert thinks he has to be "in the middle" of things, like where he's at now."

"Another possibility," Tom said, watching the very dainty way Wendy cut her steak and chewed...chewed and chewed and chewed.

She looked at him. "What?"

He smiled. "You're just so darn cute."

She rolled her eyes.

"There's also the old maintenance shed, which is clear the other side of the backside, but...." Tom looked at Dusty.

"Rupert could have the option of staying open year-round, because there's a drive off Sycamore Street which would be another way to get in, for anyone, not just racetrackers."

"We think he might go for that," Tom said, "because that way he can compete on the same level as the other tack stores and be open to more customers. He could still shut down in the winter, but he could also stay open if he wanted to. Besides, you can see the racetrack from there. People might come just to see it."

"Well, at the moment, we don't want them seeing the backside."

Everyone agreed, particularly Cracker Jack. "It looks pretty bad compared to most."

"How did that happen?" Wendy asked.

"Well," Tom said. "Fifteen or twenty years ago, the owner before Swingline, was talking about building a new racetrack about a half hour south of here. Needless to say, it never happened, and in the meantime the barn area fell into a shambles."

"Some of the barns are still nice," Wendy said.

"Very few," Tom said. "We're going to have to change that."

"Are we talking structural or facelift?" Wendy asked.

"Both," Dusty said. "I've drawn up a list of which ones need the most attention."

Randy took a drink of water. "I fear for the racing industry."

"Oh great, now you tell me," Ben said.

They all chuckled, Randy included. "I'm serious though. It takes a hit every day. I read a report this morning that had me wanting to throw my hands up. I won't say who said it, but we all know. The article went on and on. The bottom line, they claim there are 20,000 discarded Thoroughbreds each year. Define discarded? In their terms, it's any Thoroughbred that is no longer racing. Now that pisses me off. Some of them never even raced to begin with. Come on….discarded?"

Tom looked at him. "What are you gonna do? People believe what they want to believe. I wish we could get them to come to the racetrack and see how these horses are taken care of."

Dusty nodded. "As long as we're sure every barn operates the way it should."

"Which reminds me," Tom said. "Jackson Scrimshaw called me a socialist today. He said I had my head in the clouds."

"Yeah, well," Ben said. "Jackson Scrimshaw is the kind of trainer we could do without."

Cracker Jack shook his head. "I've gotta say, I admire you all. I'm proud to call you all my friends, even you, Darlin, whom I just met." He paused, choosing his words. "But I don't see how the business can heal itself, not without drastic change across the board at every racetrack in the country."

"Right here at Nottingham would be a start," Ben said.

"And it also could be the end." He and Ben looked at one another, the two of them friends for life, horsemen, true horsemen. "I'm in," Cracker Jack said. "What can I do to help?"

A momentary silence fell upon the room. No one ate, no one spoke, no one moved. A collective consciousness passed from one to the next. "For starters," Dawn said. "You can let Dusty interview you for a thirty-second video about why you love horseracing?"

"Will I have to comb my hair?" Cracker Jack asked.

"No, I like it just the way it is. It's you."

"In that case, Darlin', gladly."

The discussion continued in earnest through dessert - delicious ice cold dirt cake and hot coffee. "You know about the proposed alliance the Jockey Club is working on, right?" Dusty asked Cracker Jack. "They plan to accredit retirement, rehoming, and retraining facilities, and they want to help raise funds for the care and retraining of the horses."

Cracker Jack nodded.

"We might want to get on board with that," Ben said. "I don't think it's a fix-all, but it's a hell of a start."

Wendy got out her note pad. "Done." It was her first executive decision.

"How do we go about making sure horses leaving here aren't going to the killers," Tom asked.

Dusty motioned for Wendy to hand him a piece of paper. "I'll take care of that. I hear Brigadier's having trainers sign a no-slaughter affidavit whenever a horse ships out. We can come up with something similar."

"Does it have to say no-slaughter?" Dawn asked.

"Unfortunately, yes," Tom said. "Otherwise...."

"I don't know if this would work, in regards to time and cost," Randy said, "but maybe a vet needs to sign off on every horse shipping out."

"That means an exam, right," Tom asked.

"Well, that would be the sticky part, time and cost-wise. Is it just a glance? Yep, he's on all fours, good to go. Or should it be more thorough?" He paused. "Actually, the more I think about it, this should probably be done by one of the track

191

vets, a salaried employee, that way the trainers and owners won't balk, and...."

"How will it work?" Glenda asked. "When you're going to ship out, you go put your name on a list, what? What about if they're just shipping out to race somewhere else? Would the same rules apply?"

Randy looked at her. "It would be a can of worms."

"But worth pursuing," Cracker Jack said. "For years, no one thought anything of sending a horse to the killers. It was considered part of the business. And so cruel."

"All right," Ben said. "We're all in agreement, we're going to do everything we can to make sure every retirement horse leaving here is going to a prospective good home."

"Did you hear about that woman in Maryland?" George asked.

"She should be shot," Glenda said. "And all she got was a slap on the wrist."

Wendy looked at her.

"She was taking in horses under the guise of finding them homes and was shipping them out of the country."

"Can't they police the boarders?" Wendy asked.

Cracker Jack looked at her. "If they have papers and are up to date on their shots, there's no stopping them. Look what's happening with people crossing the borders, let alone horses. Or even dogs for that matter." He held up his hand. "How do people live with themselves?"

They all shook their heads.

"And look at that horse that was retired and sold without papers and ended up getting raced again," George said. "How do things like this happen? He was like ten years old. Come on....he was eased for Christ sake."

"People need to take responsibility for their horses when they retire," Tom said.

"The former owner tried," George said. "They thought if they didn't pass on the papers, the horse would never be allowed to race again. I've got to be honest with you though, I never kept track of the horses we sold when Glenda and I trained. Who had time for that? And actually, most of the owners didn't care. I'm glad they care now; I'm glad they're being held accountable. But back then, it was nothing. You sold them or you gave them away, and they were gone. That was the end of it. I remember seeing where Giant Power was being raced a year after I gave him away as a riding horse. I remember thinking; someone must be taking good care of him to get run of him." George paused. "Looking back on it, I don't know if I did the right thing. He wouldn't have made a good riding horse, I can tell you that."

The majority of them nodded, remembering that horse. Tom especially. He used to have to pony him. "He was a mean son of a bitch."

"Is there a limit to how old a horse can be and race?" Wendy asked.

"Not that I know of," Cracker Jack said. "The average horse races at ages three, four, five, and six. After that, they are usually done."

"But some race as two-year olds, right?"

"Not as many as you would think," Randy said. "Though there are some that don't think two-year olds should race at all." This was a subject Randy, Ben, Tom, and George discussed often.

"I don't like racing two-year olds," Ben said.

"Why not?" Wendy asked.

"Well, in addition to their growing like weeds when they're two, there's the issue of them shin-bucking, and their knees still open. It just seems like so much of a risk to me. In my opinion, if they have issues as a two-year old, they never forget it, particularly the fillies." He looked at Randy. "Okay, and then there's Randy's opinion."

They all chuckled.

"I'm sorry, I think racing them as two-year olds is fine, as long as you know what's going on in their knees and race them lightly. I actually think it's good for them. Athletes across the board compete well as teenagers, which is essentially what we're talking about with two-year-olds. In fact, they just did a study in New Zealand and found that horses racing at two-year olds had more career starts than horses starting at three-year-old, and that's with removing the amount of starts as a two-year-old. The tally was taken from three years and up."

"I still don't like it," Ben said. "You have horses out there racing and some of them aren't even chronologically two yet."

Wendy looked at him. "How does that happen?"

"Every Thoroughbred turns a year older every January 1st," Tom said. "Regardless of which month they were born in, January 1st, they are another year older."

"That doesn't make sense," Wendy said. "So…?"

"So essentially," Glenda said, "if you have a late foal, one not born in January or February, they're running against horses far more mature than they are. It'd be like a thirteen year old trying to outrun a fifteen or sixteen year old."

"Wow, that doesn't seem fair."

"Meg wrote to the racing commission once and proposed not starting two-year olds until September of their two-year old year."

"And?"

"And…they said they'd take the suggestion under consideration."

"How long ago was that?" Wendy asked.

"Oh, about twenty years ago," Ben said. "I guess they're still considering it."

Glenda shook her head. "It makes perfect sense to me. That way they'd at least be about two and a half by then. Why not wait?"

Dusty leaned forward. "Because that's the way it's always been done."

The irony of that comment weighed on all of their shoulders. Change. It was so hard to change things.

"Just like the whip." Cracker Jack said.

Tom looked at him. "And what are your thoughts on that?" He already knew how everyone else at the table felt, including Wendy.

"The jocks are fighting it tooth and nail over in Britain at the moment, I don't see it changing there or here anytime soon, if ever," Cracker Jack said, sadly. "I think everyone's going about it all wrong, talking about how many hits allowed, where hits are allowed, the age of the horse. That's ridiculous. I think it has to be all or nothing across the board. I actually proposed once we cease using the whip totally in Thoroughbred and Standardbred racing in this country and practically got rode out of town on a rail."

Ben smiled. He'd forgotten about that.

"There was so much uproar, the sponsors wanted to pull their ads. We had more call-ins that day than any other day in the show's history. The sponsors hung in with us, but I was advised to start agreeing with the callers, mostly horsemen mind you, that maybe I had misspoken or that I was reconsidering the ramifications."

"And?"

"I had a family to take care of, so...I ate crow."

Everyone lowered their eyes, even Carol, who while enjoying the conversation, knew very little about horses aside from the fact that she was afraid of them, and was basically only listening out of politeness. "I think we've all eaten crow at one time or another in our lives, Cracker Jack."

He raised his eyes and smiled. They all agreed.

"All right, there's only a little bit of this left," Glenda said, scooping out the last of the dirt cake. "Who wants it?"

"Me," Dawn said. And they all laughed. That came as no surprise. Several of them opted for more coffee or got up to go to the restroom.

Wendy checked Ben's new phone. The call was from the phone company, welcoming him to the new plan. She sat back down at the table next to him. "This is a test," she said, and no sooner said than Tom's cell phone rang. "Don't answer it. It's just us. Just push this button right here," she told Ben.

He did, and up came a list of names. Dawn, Tom, Randy, Dusty, Wendy, Spears. "Use the arrow and then just click on the name you want." He clicked on Dawn's name. Her phone rang.

She waved to him from across the table. "Hello."

Ben chuckled.

"Glenda, I'm going to need your phone number," Wendy said.

Glenda gave it to her and she programmed it in. "George." She programmed his too, and then Cracker Jack's. "Do you want anyone else's?"

Ben shook his head. The phone was big, not as big as a regular phone, but nothing nearly as small as his other one, the one he hated. "I like this."

"It comes with a holster," Wendy said.

"It does?" When Ben's eyes lit up, they all laughed.

"It's in my car, I'll go get it. I didn't know if you'd want to use it or not."

"I do," Ben said, resting the phone on his hip, right where he would want it.

Wendy returned a moment later. Ben tried the holster on, slipped the phone inside, and sat back. "Someone phone me."

They all dialed their phones. Randy got through first.

Ben pulled the phone out of the holster. "Hello."

"Is this Ben Miller, owner of the infamous Nottingham Downs?"

Ben smiled and looked around the table at his friends, his family. Most everyone had their phones to their ears. "Yes, this is Ben Miller...a lucky man."

Tom and Wendy walked out into the night. Dusty and Cracker Jack weren't far behind them. Both men walked to their trucks, waved good-bye. Tom walked Wendy to her car. Off in the distance, Dawn and Randy, each carrying a sleepy child, walked along next to Carol. A horse nickered in one of the barns.

"Good night, Beau," Dawn could be heard saying softly.

A soft breeze rustled the leaves on the trees, a wind chime tinkled. "This is an amazing place," Wendy said.

Tom nodded. "You look good here," he said. "'Course if we could get you into a pair of jeans you'd look even more at home."

196

Wendy smiled, but it was a rather sad smile. "Is there anything about me that you like just the way I am?"

Tom smiled. "You're about as perfect as I can imagine." He kissed her gently, the first of many kisses, he hoped. "Are you telling me you don't own any jeans?"

Wendy shook her head. The kiss...the kiss. "I have jeans. I even have worn-out jeans."

Tom laughed. "I'll see you tomorrow."

Wendy nodded. She waved to Glenda and George; coming out onto the porch. "Good night."

Tom watched her drive away, and glanced at Glenda and George, now standing at his side. "Do you think she's the real deal?"

Glenda looked at him. "Oh, is that romantic or what?"

Tom chuckled. "What's happening to me?"

"Well, offhand," George said. "I'd say you're falling in love."

Tom looked at him. "I don't even know what the word means. Does it mean I'm looking forward to seeing her tomorrow?"

George put his arm around Glenda. "Yes, and it means not being able to imagine a day without her."

They looked in the window at Ben, doing dishes in Meg's kitchen.

"Love hurts," Tom said. "It hurts already."

George smiled and patted him on the back. "Take the good with the bad. It's worth it. We'll see you tomorrow."

Tom strolled through the barns as he usually did every night, except this wasn't a typical evening barn check. This had been a special night, their first kiss. When he walked into the kitchen, Ben was still drying dishes."Let me see that new phone of yours."

Ben unholstered it and handed it to Tom. "Urgent phone call?"

"You might say that. I think it's more of an overdue one." Tom scrolled down to Wendy's name and pressed dial.

Two rings and her voice came on the line, "Hello, Ben."

"It's me," Tom said, pausing. "I want to meet your boys."

"Okay."

"Good night."

Chapter Twenty-Five

It was the day of B-Bo's race, a crisp morning, and lots to do. By eight-thirty, three of their horses had tracked and Dawn was headed up to the Henderson barn to video Cracker Jack's interview on why he loved horseracing. She smiled when she saw him standing under the eaves of the shedrow. It looked as if he'd made an attempt to comb his hair and it actually looked worse than normal.

His son Jeff agreed. "Mess it up."

Cracker Jack shook it hard, roughed it with his fingers, shook it some more side to side and back and forth, and posed again. "Better?"

"Much," Dawn said.

"Good. But you'd better hurry because I think I'm going to faint. I'm all dizzy now."

His son laughed.

"Here comes Dusty," Cracker Jack said.

Jeff Henderson led his "big horse" out of the stall, his father's favorite, and walked him up the shedrow. Cracker Jack stood next to him and reached up and smoothed the horse's mane. "There's no sense both of us looking crazed."

Dawn smiled. He didn't look crazed. He looked like a Harvard Professor she once knew, down to the Henley sweater, Khaki pants, and scuffed penny loafers. Dusty had a script and nodded for Dawn to start taping. "We're here today on the backside of Nottingham Downs with Cracker Jack Henderson. Some of you may remember Cracker Jack as a handicapper and talk-show host."

Cracker Jack smiled and looked at the camera.

"And this here is Kentucky Bandit, owned and trained by Jeff Henderson." Dawn zoomed in on the horse for a second, a handsome horse with big knowing eyes and a wide blaze.

"How do you feel about the future of horseracing, Cracker Jack?"

"Well, I have my concerns." He hesitated, looking at Kentucky Bandit. "I remember when this horse was born. I remember the anticipation. The hope."

Dawn zoomed in on the two of them. "I remember seeing him run for the first time. I remember when he broke his maiden. I remember the night he got sick and we all sat up with him right here at this track. I remember tears of joy..." his voice cracked, "in the morning when he finally stood back up, wobbly on his feet, but standing."

Dawn struggled to keep her hands steady.

"I think if I had to sum up Thoroughbred racing today, I believe I'd have to say we're somewhere between fear and hope, just like that night. We don't know where the industry is going, which direction it needs to take. We just know we want to get there. We want to get back to the joy, back on our feet. It's all about the horses. And say what you want, but a Thoroughbred wants to run."

Dawn stepped back, slowed the video down....and faded away.

"That is a wrap!" she said, hugging him and hugging the horse, hugging Dusty.

Cracker Jack wiped his eyes. "I'm glad I only did radio all these years. This would have killed me a long time ago."

His son patted him on the back, tears in his eyes as well. "Way to go, Dad. Us Hendersons will all be known as wusses now."

Wendy was not at her desk, so Dawn left the video and a note, and headed back to the barn. With B-Bo in the eighth race, once they were done with the horses this morning, she'd have time to go home, be with the children, turn the ponies out and be back at the track in plenty of time. Whenever they had a horse in, Ben stayed at the track all day, and one of them had to be at the barn at all times.

"Why don't you go get something to eat," she suggested.

"All right." Ben walked up to the track kitchen.

Red was untacked and in his stall eating hay and Tom was gone, so Dawn started doing up the horses. She had them all done by the time Tom and Ben returned.

"I'll be back around three-thirty," she said, and left.

B-Bo nickered for hay. "Sorry, buddy." He was being "drawn" for the race. No hay. No full belly for the athlete about to perform.

"Don't you want to hear the news?" Tom asked.

"No. Tell me when I get back."

He'd already shared the news with Ben. Rupert had decided to move his tack shop to the old maintenance shed with the Sycamore Street entrance and having given it more thought, he seemed rather excited about the prospect.

"Did you talk to him about ordering in the soft whips?"

"Yes. He said he'd order in ten of them. Any more than that and he wants us to cover the cost upfront. He said he won't be able to return them. His cost is over $45 each."

Ben shook his head. "How many jocks do we have here?"

"At least seventy or so."

"That's a lot of money."

"That's what Rupert said." Tom smiled. "I think it would be almost worth the investment and just hand them out. That way, how can they complain?"

Ben looked up from his desk. "Where are you going?"

Tom was looking in the mirror and combing his hair. He put on his cowboy hat. "I thought I'd go over and see how Wendy's doing with the offices." He stopped in front of B-Bo's stall, but only for a second. They had a firm "don't mess with a horse the day of a race" policy. He was just checking to see if he was emptying out. He nodded to Ben. There were manure piles everywhere. When B-Bo raised his head and snorted, Tom walked on, chewing on a toothpick.

"You're just like your old man," he said, referring to Beau Born. "Make him proud."

Tom checked Wendy's office, then walked down to the second floor "mirror room" and found her there. "Wow!" he said.

"I know." She nodded. The windows were perfectly clear and sparkling clean. "It was some kind of finish and all on the inside. The maintenance men said it came right off."

Tom looked down at the racetrack. "What a view. Maybe we can rent this out as a penthouse and make big bucks."

"Actually," she said, hands on her hips as she looked around. "Mr. Spears' desk will go right there, the rest of his furniture over here, and my desk will go right here."

Tom smiled. "And he's okay with that?"

"He seems to be. Ben says he doesn't want a desk, so I thought the big table in Mr. Swingline's old conference room could go right there." She pointed to an area on the far side of the room.

"Here, look," she said, tugging Tom by the arm and taking him to the exact spot. "You can see the entire racetrack from here, even some of the backside."

Tom smiled. "He'll like that, that's for sure. What about the big room downstairs?"

"Well, I haven't gotten that far, but having both areas as offices seems to please Mr. Spears. This way, if he needs quiet, or a reason to get away...."

Tom shook his head and sighed.

"I know you don't want to hear this, but there are times, lots of times actually, where the everyday routine of the racetrack has no bearing on what he does."

Tom shook his head. "You're right; I don't want to hear that."

Wendy smiled. "Think of it like this: When Lee Iacocca came in and turned Chrysler around, do you think he was out on the factory assembly floor every day?"

Point taken. Tom studied her eyes. "Who are you?"

Wendy laughed. "I am Nottingham Downs' new Assistant General Manager."

"Does Spears know about that?"

Wendy shook her head. "It's not important. I know." She looked around the room. "Unfortunately, all of this can't be done until Monday." When her phone rang, she looked at the Caller ID. "It's Ben. Hello."

"Hello. I was just sitting here looking at this phone and I like it. Thank you."

"That's it?"

"Yep, that's it." Click.

Wendy hung up and looked at Tom. "Ben likes his phone."

Tom laughed. "I know. He called me earlier too, told me to meet him up at the kitchen. We may regret his having that phone."

Wendy smiled.

When they heard a noise behind them they both turned. "Well, look at you," Tom said. It was the bugler, all decked out in a red Hunt Coat with tails, riding breeches, black patent leather boots, and black velvet riding hat. Joe Feigler stood at his side.

"I've been practicing all week," the young man said. "Listen to this." He raised his bugle and played the race announcer's tune.

"Now that's just plain beautiful," Tom said.

Joe had to agree. He held out his hands. "Something special, just for today."

"Forever," Tom said. "The Lord willing."

Joe nodded. "Well, I didn't know. He came into the secretary's office, and...."

The young man was busy tuning his bugle, paying them no attention.

"I'm sorry," Tom said. "I should have told you."

"I thought it was a joke, you know, like one of those singing telegrams."

"It's no joke," Tom said.

"Well, I figured I'd better bring him up, just to be sure." Joe turned. "Oh by the way, the jocks are having a fit."

"Why?"

"The new whips."

"That damned Rupert." Tom shook his head. "All right, I'll go talk to them."

Tom entered the jocks' room and traded fake punches with Johnny. "Hey, Tom."

"Johnny."

Juan Garcia glanced up from across the room and nodded. There was definitely some tension in the room. Tom sat down. "Well, who wants to go first?"

Everyone looked at Juan, the leading jockey, the leading "Miller barn" jockey. "Ben should have talked to us about this," Juan said.

"About what?" Tom asked. "Ordering in some soft whips so you all could give them a try and see how you like them? I don't understand what the fuck the problem is?"

Questions followed a collective wind taken out of their sails.

"Is that it?"

"Is that all?"

"For the time being, yes."

"But...?"

"Come on," Tom said. "This isn't rocket science. Racetracks all over this country are facing this issue. I don't know about you, but I wouldn't want to take anybody else's word for it. I would want to know firsthand if it makes a difference."

Silence....

Tom looked around the room. "Has Pastor Mitchell been in yet?"

Juan nodded. "Yes."

Pastor Mitchell came into the jocks' room every day of racing to say a prayer for the jocks' safety.

"Good," Tom said. "Amen."

Tom phoned Ben on the way back to the barn. "I'm going to go talk to Rupert. I think maybe I'm going to go kick his ass."

Ben sighed. "Let it go."

"Come on, Ben. We're bending over backwards to get along with this man, and look what he does."

"Never mind Rupert, I think you need to go talk to the Stewards. Tell them what we're doing. They need to hear it from one of us."

"But who knows what all Rupert is saying," Tom said.

"It's not about being right; it's about doing the right thing. Isn't that what you just said to me the other day?"

"Something like that," Tom said. He glanced back at the grandstand. "All right. But if God's not looking and I catch Rupert alone one of these days, I'm still going to kick his ass."

All three Stewards looked up when they heard a tap on the door. "Gentlemen," Tom said.

They waved him in. "Have a seat, Tom."

Tom took off his hat and sat down. The last time he came before the Stewards was years ago as Ben's assistant trainer. That day left a bad taste in his mouth. He looked each one of the men square in the eye. "Ben and I would like your opinion on the soft whip."

All three men sat back and crossed their arms. They'd heard.

"I asked Rupert about ordering some in, so we could see what they're like, and maybe have some of the jocks try them out."

All three men nodded.

"Good." Tom sat there for a moment.

"Anything else?" the state-appointed Steward asked, the man in the middle.

"Nope, I think that just about does it." It's not about being right, it's about doing the right thing, Tom said in his mind. It's not about being right. "Thank you for your time."

Chapter Twenty-Six

When Dawn walked into the foaling barn and both ponies came to the front of their stalls, nickering to her, she felt like a kid at Christmas. The sun was shining; there was no standing water in the pasture. This was their day and it was as if they knew. Dawn put on their halters and lead shanks, led them out of their stalls and out of the barn, one on each side, and walked them to the pasture. They both turned to face her, both stood like gentlemen to be released, and both took off trotting. They rolled, they bucked and played, and then they grazed.

They looked so happy. Occasionally one or both of them would raise their head and look at the other horses, look at the barn, look at Dawn. Then they would graze some more. The horses in the other pastures seemed perfectly bored with the newcomers' presence today. They were old news, just two more horses that belonged here.

Carol walked the children down to visit and they all stood watching the ponies. D.R. leaned down so he could see through the fence rails. "Pretty horsey, Mommy."

Dawn smiled. It was going to be nice having horses the children could be relatively safe around. When Poncho walked over to the fence to investigate this little person, Biscuit followed. They both sniffed his hair and he giggled. Maeve touched Poncho's leg and he leaned his head down and licked her hand.

"Okay, that's enough," Dawn said. "Let's take this a little at a time." She glanced at her watch. "Oh my gosh, speaking of time." The ponies had been out close to a half hour; time for them to come in. Dawn climbed the fence, lead shanks in hand, and both ponies trotted off.

D.R. and Maeve giggled and clapped their hands. "Run, horsey! Run!"

"No, don't," Dawn said, motioning for them to stop clapping. "Don't."

Carol laughed. All this time living on the farm and this was the closest and most she'd ever done with the horses. "What if they won't let you catch them?"

"Oh, they will," Dawn said, walking around as she tried to coax them to come to her. 'I'll give you carrots."

The two ponies kept trotting and playing, pushing at one another.

"Enough." Dawn gave up and walked to the gate, thinking she'd go get some grain to entice them. The ponies stopped and looked at her. Was she leaving them? Poncho lowered his head, appearing totally puzzled. Biscuit stood at his side.

"Look," Carol said.

Dawn turned, and as soon as she turned, the ponies started trotting and playing again. She quickly put her back to them and opened the gate, hesitated, and here they came, at an obedient walk and stood to have their lead shanks snapped.

"Lesson number one," she said to Carol and the children. "Lead the way and they will follow."

Carol laughed.

"That's good boys."

It had been a long time since there was this much excitement during the races at Nottingham Downs. At times, it rivaled a circus. The track announcer Bud Gipson, the photographer Denny Sergeant, and Cracker Jack Henderson were all old friends and hammed it up over the loud speaker. Add this to the video playing Cracker Jack's morning performance and the new bugler, who was a huge hit. Most everyone seemed to be having a fun time. Some of the spectators had actually ventured outside, a spillover of sorts, capturing the mood of the day.

"Yes, but will it reflect in the handle?" Spears said.

Wendy shrugged, standing at his side, both staring out at the racetrack in what were to be their new offices. "Probably not today, but hopefully it's a step in the right direction."

Spears glanced at her and waved his hand. "This is all superficial."

"Yes," Wendy said. "But sometimes you have to look good to feel good."

Spears smiled. "I wish some of your optimism would rub off on me."

Wendy nodded. "Me too."

Spears chuckled. "I don't know what to do. I mean, I know what to do, I just don't know how to go about getting the end results we need in the short time that we need them."

Wendy looked at him. She liked Spears, she always has. She felt he was a good man and a hard worker, and he had always treated her well, but admittedly....

"Ladies and gentlemen," the track announcer said. "You have only two minutes to wager on the seventh race. Do not get shut out!"

Wendy couldn't help but notice how Spears cringed at that announcement. "I have to ask you, do you want to be here at Nottingham?"

"I don't know," he answered honestly. "I really don't know."

She looked out the window and motioned to Ben, making his way slowly to the paddock from the barn area. "He wants you to want to be here, he wants you to care. And the only way he thinks that will happen is for you to get caught up in the passion."

Spears watched as two men approached Ben. Ben shook their hands, patted them on the back, and walked on. "I can't imagine getting that much respect."

"Imagining it is the first step," Wendy said. "That's what my father used to say."

Spears glanced at her. "You've done well. I'm sure he's proud of you. What does he do for a living?"

Wendy smiled. All these years as his administrative assistant and he'd never asked her anything about her family, about her life. "He's a Presbyterian minister."

"Here?"

"In Florida."

Ben stood leaning on the rail nearby the paddock to watch the seventh race.

"And they're off!"

It was a mile race, a ten-horse field.

Wendy wished she had Dawn's video camera. Not to video the race, that was being done. She'd video Ben, she'd zoom in close, and she'd capture his expression. Even at this

207

distance, she could see the intensity in his eyes, the love of the sport, the passion…the passion he hoped would take hold of Spears.

"That morning you spent with him at the barn," Wendy said. "How did that make you feel?"

Spears smiled. "Like I was playing hooky."

"Because…?"

He glanced at her and then watched the horses in the stretch run. He watched and he watched and he watched. "Because it was fun."

"And it is Bold Bigilo, neck and neck with Flim Man. Bold Bigilo, Flim Man….head to head, nose to nose. Bold Bigilooooooo. Ladies and gentlemen, there is a photo for the win. Hold on to your tickets. What a horse race, ladies and gentlemen! What a horse race!"

Spears smiled. "What, is he on speed?"

Wendy shook her head. "I think he's just 'having fun.'"

Spears laughed. "Is that a gotcha?"

"Yes. Something like that."

Spears nodded.

"Do you want to go down to the paddock? B-Bo is in the next race." Wendy looked down the racetrack to the gap. No Tom, no Red, no Dawn, no B-Bo yet.

"B-Bo?"

"That's Native Beau Born's nickname. Oh, look." She pointed. "There he is." Tom, astride Red and leading B-Bo, had just appeared from the barn area. Dawn walked alongside them.

Spears drew a breath and sighed. "I wonder if that would be considered a faux pas, us going down for the racetrack owner's horse and none of the others."

"Good point." Wendy watched as Tom led B-Bo onto the racetrack. The horse was "dancing". She smiled. "He looks so much like his sire."

Spears shook his head. "You are light years ahead of me."

Wendy watched Tom, watched how "at home" he was in the saddle, how in command he was of B-Bo. She watched Ben as he waited for them, watched as Ben turned and walked with Dawn, following the horse, watched as Dawn put her arm around his.

She smiled. "It's been a long time since I've been this happy," she said, as much to herself as to Spears. "I've got as much at stake as everyone else in the barns. I'm one of them now. Which reminds me…" she said. "Do you have a problem with my dressing down?"

Spears looked at her. "Now that you're my partner, you mean?"

Wendy smiled. "You heard?"

"Ben phoned me. He says he has me on speed dial. It sounded like a warning."

Wendy laughed. "We can do this, Richard," she said, purposely calling him Richard for the first time. "We can. We just need to remember one thing. It's like Ben said, it's all about the horses. If we do right by them, good things will happen."

Spears hesitated. "Not to be negative, but hasn't it always been about the horses here?"

"I don't know." Wendy watched as Tom dismounted Red and led B-Bo into the paddock. "Ben says the head office lost sight of that a long time ago." She looked at him. "I for one, really think we need to put that all behind us and move forward. I think we're off to a good start." She smiled. "Look how Red just stands there. That's called ground-tying. He knows he's supposed to wait and he just waits. He knows his job."

Spears nodded.

"Ladies and gentlemen, I want to draw your attention to the monitors. For those of you who don't know Cracker Jack Henderson, talk show celebrity host and handicapper, let me introduce you."

Spears looked at Wendy, both turning at the same time. The nearest monitor was in the clubhouse. They hurried. "Damned heels" Wendy said, trying to keep up with Spears.

Cracker Jack was being taped bowing and waving to the crowd. Wendy laughed. Everyone was cheering. "Oh, if only we could bottle that enthusiasm."

Spears agreed, albeit in a more negative way. "This would hard to maintain." The two of them looked around the clubhouse. Saturdays always drew the highest attendance.

"I would have liked to have been a part of this in its heyday. No pun intended," he added.

When they heard the bugle sound, they watched as the post parade of horses walked out onto the racetrack. Wendy smiled at the casual way Tom mounted Red and took hold of B-Bo's rein when Dawn handed him over. She glanced at the tote board. B-Bo was the number five in a six-horse field. He was the favorite with odds of 3-1. The race was 6 furlongs.

B-Bo was usually never a problem in the post parade. Today he decided he was going to buck a little and act up. "Here, here," Tom said. "Save it."

Juan Garcia stood in his irons, the breeze billowing the Miller barn's red and black jockey silks. Wendy motioned to two empty seats in the club house by the window and she and Spears walked down to watch the race from there.

A man sitting at the table next to them asked who they were betting on. Wendy smiled. "I like number five."

The man nodded and looked at Spears.

"Me too," Spears said.

Wendy watched the horses turn in front of the grandstand and then break into a warm-up canter. She jumped when B-Bo bucked again.

The man at the next table chuckled. "He's just feeling his oats."

Wendy smiled.

"He's got some early speed," the man said, studying his racing form. "I'm not sure if he'll like the off track."

Wendy knew from the conversations at the farm that B-Bo liked an off racetrack. "What does the form say?"

The man looked again. "Well, he ran on an off track earlier this spring and finished second. He was making a move and then just hung."

Wendy stared. Hung? "Maybe he just got tired."

The man looked at her again. That was pretty much what he'd said.

"Plus, he hasn't raced in two weeks and he's fresh," Wendy said, repeating what Ben had said, but obviously not divulging her source.

Spears turned to conceal his smile. She was definitely getting caught up in this.

"Do you come here a lot?" she asked.

"Whenever I can. I usually go to Mountaineer."

"Well, we're glad you're here," Wendy said.

"Oh?" the man said, as if she was flirting with him. "That's nice of you to say."

Wendy smiled. "He's saying it too," she said, pointing to Spears. "Oh look, they're going to the gate."

"Ladies and gentlemen, it's one minute to post. Do not get shut out."

The man got up and left in a hurry.

Spears shook his head.

"There's Ben," Wendy said, scooching to the edge of her seat to see him. She looked for Dawn, wondered, worried for a second. "Oh good, there she is."

The horses were loaded one by one, B-Bo walked in easily.

"Wish I had binoculars," Wendy said. The man at the next table had left his. She glanced to see if he was on his way back and then reached over and picked them up and held them to her eyes. "Oh my God...."

"What?" Spears said.

"I can see them."

Spears chuckled.

"I can see them perfectly."

"And they're off!"

The man returned to his table to see Wendy, on her feet and watching every B-Bo stride through the binoculars. He motioned to Spears that it was okay. "Leave her be," he whispered.

B-Bo was a length off the lead going into the turn. Wendy wondered if that was a good thing. She turned the binoculars on Ben and Dawn, trying to judge from their reaction. They seemed okay; no worried looks on their faces.

"At the head of the stretch it is Native Beau Born challenging the leader Becky's Babe," the announcer said. "Out in the middle of the racetrack and under a hand ride, here he comes!"

"Look at those fractions," Wendy heard someone say.

She turned the binoculars on the tote board, where, where, oh there it is; 23 1/5th for the first quarter, 45 4/5^{ths} for the half.

"With a furlong left to go, it's Native Beau Born and Becky's Babe."

"Come on, B-Bo," Wendy said, the binoculars fixed on him. "Come on."

Spectators throughout the club house were cheering the horses on.

"Come on, B-Bo," Wendy said, a little louder this time.

"Come on, B-Bo!" the man next to her shouted. "Come on, B-Bo!"

Even Spears started shouting. "Come on, B-Bo!"

Wendy zoomed in on the horse's eyes. "You can do it, come on! Do it for your dad!" She shouted. "Come on, B-Bo!"

"And it is Native Beau Born taking over the lead! Native Beau Born! Native Beau Born! Na-tiveeee Beauuuu Bornnnnnn!!!"

"He won!" Wendy shouted, still holding the binoculars on him. "He won!" She looked down at Ben and Dawn, smiling, laughing, nodding. "He won!" She zoomed in on Tom and Red, watched as they cantered out into the middle of the racetrack and helped pull B-Bo up.

"Thank you," she said, handing the man his binoculars. "I'm going to have to get a pair of these." She and Spears started up the stairs on the side of the clubhouse. "Have a nice day!"

"You too," the man said, waving, laughing, and then shaking his head.

"Was that exciting or what?" Wendy said.

"Yes," Spears agreed. "Now if we can figure out how to get that feeling of involvement to spread throughout the grandstand, we might be on to something."

212

Wendy nodded, hurrying to get to the room with the windows so she could see the winner's circle. "We're working on it....we're working on it."

Spears followed.

Tom dismounted Red and led B-Bo into the Winner's Circle. Juan Garcia waved his whip to the Stewards up in their booth, a jockey's salute. Dawn and Ben took their places. The photographer stepped back when B-Bo kicked out. The horse tossed his head, slobber and sweat streaming everywhere.

"Okay, ready."

Everyone smiled.

"Ladies and gentlemen" the announcer said, on his feet. "Native Beau Born, son of the multiple Stakes winner Beau Born, leading sire of Ohio-bred two-year olds. Congratulations Native Beau Born."

Chapter Twenty-Seven

Randy had watched the race from the gap and waited to see B-Bo come off the track. The horse danced and pranced. Randy smiled at Dawn and Tom, but kept his distance from B-Bo. Horses that win and place go from the racetrack straight to the spit barn under the watchful eye of a racetrack official. The horse is to have no contact with anyone other than the trainer, pony person, and groom, only those directly associated with the everyday care of the horse.

Any person or any veterinarian other than the track veterinarian interfering in any way at this point, enroute, would be a serious violation. In the old days, the winning horses were required to have their saliva tested for drugs, hence the term "spit barn." Urine is tested now, and if the horse doesn't oblige, a blood sample is drawn.

Dawn gave Randy a hug. "What a race!"

"He run big! He looks good! I've got a couple of farm calls. I'll see you guys at The Rib."

213

"Love you!" Dawn took the shortcut down through the barns to theirs, grabbed B-Bo's halter, shank, and sheet, and hurried to the spit barn. Tom had just dismounted Red. The test barn was basically nothing more than an eight-stall enclosed barn and shedrow, with a state veterinarian's office - lab set up where normally a tack room would be.

"Native Beau Born," Tom said, leading B-Bo inside. Dawn followed them into the first empty stall; they took off his bridle, put on his halter. The state veterinarian checked the horse's tattoo for confirmation of his identity, all routine, and hung a tag on the horse's halter. Tom led him out and around to get a drink. There were fresh buckets of water hanging on posts. B-Bo dragged him to the first one, from that point on, his and his alone to drink.

Dawn headed out to turn on the wash hose and let the water warm up. There were days it was barely lukewarm. Today, it was a desirable temperature. Suds buckets and washrags were provided at Nottingham, as were towels. Tom held B-Bo and Dawn hosed him off, ridding him of most of the mud. Then Dawn switched and held the horse while Tom gave him a suds bath. They did this without thought, without plan. It's the way they always did it. Tom scraped the excess water off. Dawn wiped B-Bo's face with a towel. Tom squeegeed his legs with his hands and towel. Dawn put a lightweight cooler on the horse.

Becky's Babe, the horse that ran second, was getting bathed as well.

"I'll see you back at the barn," Tom said, hosing off the bridle.

Taking a wide berth around Becky's Babe, Dawn led B-Bo back inside. As was customary, the horse was handwalked around the shedrow and allowed to drink a little with each pass, until he didn't want to drink anymore. By then his exerted breathing was back to normal and he was practically dry. Dawn took his cooler off and led him into the stall, where an attendant stood by with a cup on a stick to collect urine.

B-Bo obliged almost as soon as he walked into the stall. The attendant whistled, which was routine. Dawn asked once when the habit of whistling to get a horse to pee, started. No one knew. It simply had always been done, the attendant said, at racetracks everywhere.

Ben stood outside their barn as she returned with B-Bo and watched the way all four of his hooves were hitting the ground, watched the flexion in his ankles, his knees, noted his breathing. He was walking good. A little tired, but that was to be expected. He'd just run a fast race on an off track, final time: 1:11 1/5.

Tom had his stall done, bed deep with straw, his water bucket and haynet full. Dawn walked B-Bo a lap around his own shedrow, a ritual she initiated years ago. She felt it helped acclimate the horse, helped to welcome them back home. "A horse knows their own barn," she'd said. "And look how proud they are."

B-Bo had his "I'm badd" walk going, all of the other horses coming to the front of their stalls. "Uh, huh, uh huh, I'm badd."

Dawn put him away and she, Tom, and Ben watched as he circled in his stall and then lay down and rolled. "I called Wendy and Spears," Ben said. "They'll meet us there."

Tom had already fed the horses their grain while Dawn had B-Bo at the spit barn. Ben had topped off all their water buckets. There was no hurry to get to dinner. They always allowed plenty of time. Ben watched the winner of the ninth and final race of the day limp into the spit barn. It was a sobering sight; one a horseman never gets used to seeing.

Tom was just walking back from the men's room and talked to the groom in passing. He relayed the information to Ben. "He tripped pulling up after the race."

The two of them stood staring at the spit barn. Both the winner and the horse that ran second were inside now. They just stared. Dawn walked up next to them. "What's going on?"

"Peek I Am pulled up bad." They all knew the horse, the trainer, the groom.

"Oh no," Dawn said.

Tom sighed. "Maybe he'll be all right. It's times like this I wish I totally believed in the power of prayer."

215

Dawn and Ben looked at him.

"'Cause I'd make everything right," he said, and walked away.

Fortunately, there were things still needing to be done in the Miller Barn. Dawn walked down to give Red a good rubdown. "Such a good boy," she kept saying to him, always. Tom did B-Bo up and brushed him. Both looked outside the stalls when they heard the sound of Randy's diesel engine truck pass by enroute to the spit barn. Both said a prayer.

The Rib was less than a mile from the barn and served great food, wood-fired grilled steaks and Italian dishes being their specialty. It was at The Rib many years ago where Ben announced Beau Born's retirement after he'd bled in a race. It was at The Rib where Dawn and Randy fought, and it was at The Rib where they made up.

Dawn's Aunt Maeve loved The Rib. "We're going to have to come again when she's in town next week."

"Who's running then?" Ben asked, joking. For years, the only time he and his wife Meg came to this restaurant was for a "win" because that was the only times they could afford it. By today's standards, the food was quite reasonable. But back then....

"So this is a tradition?" Spears asked.

"Yes, since forever," Dawn said.

Tom glanced at the door. Wendy had yet to arrive, Randy or Dusty either.

The restaurant was a familiar haunt for a lot of racetrackers. It was loud and informal, most everyone came straight from the racetrack, and the food was always delicious. When Wendy came through the doorway, Tom stood and waved her over to a seat next to him. "Hey, pretty lady."

She smiled. "What a race!"

"You should have seen her," Spears said. "She stole some guy's binoculars in the clubhouse and...." He wrapped his fingers around his eyes like binoculars, imitating her, binoculars up, down, all around. "There he is, there he is, oh look…there he is."

Everyone laughed.

"I want a pair," she said.

Dusty came in, said hello to several people at a table by the bar, and walked over and sat down. "Congratulations! He run a hell of a race!"

"Yep, he run big," Ben said, smiling.

Tom looked at Wendy. He just looked at her, and she blushed.

"Hey!" Randy barely got though the doorway when his phone rang. He motioned he'd be right there and took the call outside. Ben ordered a family-sized antipasto appetizer for everyone to share.

"Water."

"Coffee, decaf." Ben frowned.

"Two ginger ales," Dawn said, ordering for her and Randy.

"Iced tea."

"Caffeinated?"

"Sorry, make that a diet 7up." Wendy smiled.

"Rum and coke," Spears said.

Everyone looked at him. "Caffeinated?"

He laughed. "Rum and decaf coke."

"We're working on him," Tom said to the waitress. "I'll have the fake coffee too."

The waitress smiled. She had a crush on Tom. Wendy noticed.

Randy came in, gave Dawn a kiss, and sat down next to her. "That was Mom. They want Dad to come to the Clinic for tests. They're driving in Monday morning."

"Tell me your dad's not driving."

"That's what I said."

"And."

Randy rolled his eyes.

"What time?"

"They should be here around noon."

"He'll be fine," Ben said. "I have a good feeling."

217

Randy smiled, appreciating that comment.

"How's that uh…?" Ben glanced around, not wanting to be overheard, not knowing where his boundaries as concerned friend, trainer, and racetrack owner set in. "That other horse from the last race?"

"I think he'll be okay. It seems up high." Randy moved his shoulder in a discreet way.

Ben nodded. End of subject.

Several people from across the room yelled to Ben. "Nice race!"

Ben waved. "Thank you!"

Tom was looking at Wendy again, just looking.

"Quit," she said.

"What?" Tom laughed. Everyone laughed. Everyone but Spears that is, feeling a bit like an outsider.

"How's B-Bo?" Randy asked.

"Good," Ben said. "He came back good."

"He bit me," Tom said, pointing out a rip on his shirt sleeve. "He was all wound up in the post parade."

Ben nodded. "Must have been from the crowd."

Spears smiled. "Speaking of the crowd, attendance was 5700 which has been fairly normal for good-weather Saturdays, but the great news is the handle was up by about thirteen thousand. It's the best Saturday we've had in over nine weeks."

"How do you account for that?"

"I don't know."

Tom looked at him. "Wait a minute. Are you saying you keep track of weather in relation to the crowds?"

"Well, I don't personally, but yes."

Tom leaned forward. "So what's the best weather condition, a sunny day, a rainy day? We might be on to something here?"

Spears laughed. "Actually the best day we've had this year was the day between Good Friday and Easter Sunday."

"Ooh," Tom said. "I don't know what that means, I mean, really, what does that mean? Was it a pretty day?"

"If I recall correctly, it was a rainy day," Spears said.

Tom looked at Wendy, and then everyone else at the table. "This is a complicated business."

They all laughed.

Here came their drinks, here came their antipasto, here came hot Italian bread and herb butter. It was time to dig in, to celebrate. Ben proposed a toast. "To racetrackers everywhere! May they all win their share!"

When Ben made the decision to no longer run a public stable; no more training for other owners, he went into what most sports media would refer to as a rebuilding phase. His stable now consisted of Beau Born progeny. Last year was the first two-year-old crop, lightly raced at the end of the year with three wins. The scaling-back timing was great, considering little Maeve's relatively newborn age, and D.R. being a toddler.

"Life has a way," Ben liked to say. Dawn got to spend more time at home and they all got to watch the babies grow, horses and infants. They all got to work on building Beau's stallion career, building Randy and Dawn's house, building a family.

As they all sat talking, laughing, enjoying their celebratory meal, Ben's only regret was that Meg wasn't here. He lowered his eyes for a moment, talk at the table far off in the distance, talk all around them. Life going on in spite of her absence.

Dawn touched his arm gently. "Ben, are you all right?"

He nodded. "Just feeling a little sad," he said.

Dawn gave him a hug and when she did, everyone at the table silenced; a silence that spread around the room. Ben raised his eyes and smiled. "When you get to be my age, you get a little sentimental. Don't worry, I'll forget it in a moment and be fine."

Everyone laughed, some even clapped.

"It's time to go home," he said. Finished eating, they were all tired. Randy was headed back to the racetrack to check on the horse, Peek I Am. Spears had another gathering he "needed to make an appearance at" with the Chamber of Commerce. Dawn was headed home to hopefully see the children before they fell asleep. Dusty had an AA meeting to attend. Tom was going back to the track to check on B-Bo. Wendy said she was going home and straight to bed.

"Big day tomorrow," she said.

"Oh?" Tom asked.

"My sons are coming home for the day."

Tom smiled as he walked her to her car. She'd obviously called them home because of his request to meet them. "Are you going to bring them to the track?"

"Yes. I promised them lunch in the clubhouse, if you'd care to join us. They've never been to the racetrack."

"Never?"

"Never."

"Well, we'll have to make sure they have a good time." He kissed her gently and then touched the rim of his cowboy hat. "Sweet dreams, pretty lady."

Chapter Twenty-Eight

Dusty was waiting outside the tack room when Tom arrived in the morning, sitting on an over-turned muck basket, newspaper in hand, and looked like he'd lost his best friend. "You're not going to believe this," he said.

"What?"

Dusty handed him the sports page. Tom stared. It was a photo of the dinner celebration at The Rib with the caption. "New owner of Nottingham Downs devastated by the news."

"What news?"

"Read the article. It's short."

Tom skimmed the print. "It's short because it's a lie."

Dusty nodded. "Tell me about it."

Tom stood reading the article again, one short paragraph, a caption actually.

Former leading trainer at Nottingham Downs Dave Brubaker says the racetrack is doomed. "I do not see a future here." Ben Miller, new owner of Nottingham Downs fears the worst. Not even his own horse Native Beau Born's allowance win yesterday could cheer him up.

Dawn arrived and looked over his shoulder. "What are you reading?" Her eyes zoomed in on the photo and then the caption. "What?" Ben was right behind her. Should they spare him? But how? It was just a matter of time before he'd see it elsewhere. She and Tom conveyed that in a glance.

Tom handed him the newspaper.

Ben looked at the photo, looked at the three of them, and then put on his glasses to read the article. "Well," he commented.

"What the fuck?" Tom said.

Ben looked over his glasses at him. "Did B-Bo eat up?"

B-Bo? Tom shook his head and marveled. "Old man, when I get to be your age, I hope I'm half as wise." Tom walked down to B-Bo's stall, checked his feed tub, and walked back with a thumbs-up. Business as usual.

"We'll talk about this later," Ben said, and unlocked the tack room. It was a light training morning, which was a blessing of circumstance. Ben didn't have to leave the barn. He didn't have to field any questions until, around ten-thirty when a reporter showed up at the barn.

Ben told the man he was busy, but the man persisted. "I just have a few questions. The people have a right to know. Is Nottingham Downs going to close?"

Dawn phoned Wendy from Wee Born's stall. "Get Spears over here. Now! There's a reporter here. Did you see the paper? Good." She hung up and stuck her head out the doorway. "Ben, can I see you a minute."

Still ignoring the reporter, Ben walked down to Wee Born's stall. The man followed.

"Excuse me," Dawn said, implying, first off, this would only take a moment; second, this was a private conversation. The man stepped back, ended up in front of B-Bo's stall, and practically jumped sky-high when B-Bo charged to the front in what may have appeared to be an attack, when in actuality it was just B-Bo feeling good.

"I just talked to Wendy," Dawn said to Ben, her voice low so as not to be overheard. "Spears is on his way. Let him handle this."

Ben shook his head. He wasn't used to other people "handling" his business.

"Please," Dawn said. "Don't bother yourself with this."

Ben glanced at the man, now standing outside the shedrow between the barn and the road.

Dawn looked at him. "All right?"

Ben glanced at the man again.

"What time are you going to the film room?" Dawn asked.

"Eleven. Why?"

"Just wondering. I hadn't planned on going, but I might go too."

"Why?" Ben asked, and then smiled. She was trying to divert his attention. She had succeeded. Here came Spears. When he glanced ahead and saw the reporter, he crossed over to the opposite barn, and walked down and out onto the road to greet the man.

"Hello, I'm Richard Spears, General Manager at Nottingham Downs. I don't think we've met, but I want to thank you for being part of such a fine enterprise."

"Um, I don't work here at the racetrack," the man said.

"Well, that's a shame," Spears said, and pretended to start to walk away then hesitated. "Well, if you don't mind my asking, what are you doing on the backside? Are you a Thoroughbred owner?"

"I'm with the Herald, here to do a follow-up to the story in today's paper."

"Oh," Spears said. "Are you trying to correct the misquote?"

"Misquote?"

"Brubaker. He said he never said that; he said it was taken out of context. How are you going to fix that?"

"Fix it?"

"Yes," Spears said, taking out his cell phone and glancing at it. "Does a Regis Milburn work for you?"

The man looked at him. "Actually, I work for him."

"Oh," Spears said, nodding, as if he knew something the young man didn't. "Well, you have a nice day." He shook the man's hand. "Hope to see you at the races. By the way, we're not going anywhere. You might want to *start* with that in your retraction."

The man turned on his heels and walked to his car parked at the stable gate. Spears walked down to Wee Born's stall.

"Well?" Ben said.

Spears played the conversation recorded on his cell phone.

Ben's eyes lit up. "So Brubaker didn't say that?"

"No."

"And this Regis Milburn?"

Spears smiled, dialing his phone. "I'm still trying to reach him." He held up his hand. "Hello, yes, Regis Milburn please. Richard Spears. He's expecting my call."

Ben chuckled. This was a treat seeing Spears in action.

"Yes, hello. Thank you. Yes, yes, I am very concerned. I know the stellar reputation The Herald has and frankly, I was a bit surprised not only by the misquote, but with the paparazzi-tabloid type of intrusion into the personal lives of the parties in the photo, myself included. When did this become standard journalism for The Herald?" He listened, and listened, and listened. "Thank you. I appreciate you handling the matter. Thank you."

He hung up and pocketed his phone. "Done."

Dawn smiled. She was used to things being "done." She nodded her approval.

Ben patted Spears on the back. "We're going to be watching the replay of the races at eleven. I'd like it if you'd join us."

"Us?" Dawn said. Her diversionary tactic earlier was backfiring,

Ben smiled. "It's not good to say things you don't mean."

"Yes, Dad," Dawn said, teasing.

"We'll see you over there," Ben said to Spears.

The film room at Nottingham Downs was little more than a 10x10 video screen and about twenty folding chairs in a cramped space. It rarely drew a crowd. The most common attendees would be a trainer or owner, accompanying their jockey to go over why a horse didn't finish in the money, what went wrong, or what might have gotten them beat. Or, an owner, trainer, groom, wanting to watch the "win" again.

Ben, Tom, Dawn, and Dusty were on assignment, the only ones there today. Spears came in and sat down next to Tom. "Okay, what are we looking for?"

"Whip effectiveness," Tom said.

"Isn't that the Stewards' job?"

"No, they look for whip abuse."

Spears looked at him.

"And," Tom added, "lack of whip use."

"Meaning?"

"Meaning, a jock not riding to win."

Spears nodded. The horses were being loaded into the gate for the first race. "I like gray horses," Spears said.

The others just stared at him.

"Just saying," he said.

They laughed.

"Did you watch the first race yesterday?" Dusty asked.

"No," Spears said. "I was meeting with a hotdog vendor."

"Seriously?"

"Seriously."

"Shut up," Tom said.

"And they're off."

"Turn down the volume," Ben said.

Dawn turned it down completely.

The racing secretary Joe Feigler walked by the door, backed up, and came in to join them. "Is there something wrong with the volume?"

"No," Tom said. "Sit down."

Joe sat down next to Dawn. She made him nervous.

"Look! Look right there," Dusty said.

"Can we back it up?" Ben asked. "Where's the remote?"

"At home on the coffee table," Tom said. "Can everyone just shut the fuck up."

They all laughed.

"Oh look," Spears said. "The gray horse is going to win."

Tom looked at Joe. "Repeat that and you're toast."

They all laughed again, everyone but Joe that is. He didn't get the joke, didn't know how little Spears actually knew about racing.

"All right. All right," Tom said. "Now let's get serious."

Ben looked at him. "Why? I'm supposed to be inconsolable."

Dawn mimicked hugging him, as in the newspaper photo. "It's okay. Everything will be all right."

Now they had Joe laughing.

"Let's start this over." Tom said.

Joe took the remote and set the race to start again. "Volume?"

"No!" they all said in unison.

"Okay, okay, I was just asking."

This time when the latch sprung, they were all serious. "Can you slow it down?"

"I don't know. No."

"Shit!" Tom said.

Dusty leaned forward. "Did you see that?"

The number five horse looked as if it was lugging out and when the jockey hit him with the whip, he sucked back. The number three horse wearing full blinkers ducked his head. "Was that from the sound of the whip?" Dawn asked. "Why'd he do that?"

Ben shook his head. No sound was putting them into a whole new dimension. Tom watched the horses' eyes. Dawn watched the jockeys' hands. In the stretch run, every time a jockey hit a horse, she jerked. Again, again, again….the gray horse was moving up on the outside. It reminded her of "All Together". It reminded her of the day she broke down.

"No," she said. "No."

225

At the wire, the gray horse won by a head.

They all looked at Dawn. She was trembling. She looked at Tom. She looked at Ben. She drew a breath, and then another breath, and then another, and lowered her eyes. It never occurred to her until this moment, but she now needed to know, she needed to ask. She looked at Tom again. He was there that day; he was close by, on Red. He'd gotten to the filly first.

He shook his head no. No. "She was being hand-ridden," he said.

"Who?" Joe asked.

Tom hesitated and motioned to the screen. "The uh, six horse."

"It ran second," Joe said.

"Yes," Tom nodded. "I see that."

"Which race next?" Joe asked.

"All of them."

"All of them?"

"Yes, all of them," Tom said, smiling. "You're welcome to stay."

"No, that's okay. I have work to do." He laughed. "Don't want the bosses to think I'm sleeping on the job."

The remaining group watched each subsequent race, made comments, replayed a few races, and came to a conclusion, a consensus: the whip did not play a factor in the majority of the outcomes of the races. And not only that. At times, it seemed to have a negative impact, like the horse that sucked back and the horse that shied from the sound of the whip. Tom made an additional interesting observation.

"It's almost as if when they start using their stick, they stop riding. Come on, these horses don't neck rein. They talk about needing the whip to guide a horse. What happens when you start riding with one hand? You can't steer them then, you can only over-steer them, one handed." He paused a race and pointed. "Look." When the jockey was hand-riding, the horse's head was straight. As soon as the jockey took to using the whip, the horse started to lug out. Tom hit play, pause, play, pause. "See."

226

They all sat nodding.

Admittedly, talking amongst themselves, the ineffectiveness "in the outcome" of the race was most profound. "It's like beating a dead horse," Tom said, silencing the room. "There is no point hitting a tired horse. You start hitting a tired horse and then what do you get? Injuries."

Spears sat thinking, stroking his chin. He looked for Wendy, forgetting she wasn't there. "Where *is* Wendy?"

"Her sons are in town. They're up in the clubhouse." Tom looked at his watch. "Oh, shit, I gotta go."

They all stood at the same time, all stretched. They'd been watching the replays for close to two hours. Spears yawned. "I'll bet there are statistics, studies, on where a horse is most likely to break down in a race."

Ben looked at him.

"Sorry," he said. "Let me reword that."

They all nodded.

"I'll get Wendy to research this. If fatigue plays a part, it would be in the stretch run, right?"

"Right," Ben said.

"Then we'll find out. Meanwhile…?"

Now it was Ben who was yawning. "Meanwhile, the soft whips should be here in the next day or so. We'll get the jocks to try them, and go from there."

Chapter Twenty-Nine

Tom entered the clubhouse and looked around. Wendy waved. She'd been watching for him, waiting, at times fearful he'd forgotten, got tied up, anything, everything. She smiled. Her sons both turned from the look on her face.

"So that's your cowboy," her eldest said.

"Behave," she told him. "Both of you."

Tom was stopped twice on the way to their table, a trainer congratulating him on B-Bo's race yesterday. The man wasn't a close friend of Tom's, more of an acquaintance, and obviously using the encounter to impress his owners, all sitting at the table with him. Second stop, was an old flame of sorts. Tom smiled. She still looked hot! She gave him a big kiss.

"It's nice to see you again," Tom said. For the life of him, he couldn't remember her name.

"This is my husband Charles," the woman said, of the sugar-daddy-looking-type man sitting next to her. "We have a filly in the sixth race today."

Tom nodded and shook the man's hand. "I hope she runs big. Nice to meet you."

"He looks like a country western singer," Wendy's youngest said.

The other one nodded. "That one that sings about the frog in the pond."

Wendy flashed them both a stern look.

As Tom neared the table, a trainer two tables down called to him. Tom waved and turned his attention to Wendy. "Sorry I'm late," he said.

"That's okay," Wendy said, thinking, thank God at least you showed. Her sons would have never let her live it down otherwise. Mom called us home to meet her new boyfriend, only…. "And these are my sons, Matthew and Gordon. Matthew is named after his father. Gordon is named after my father."

Both sons rolled their eyes. She was being so formal, so serious, so nervous.

"Matthew," Tom said, shaking his hand. "Gordon." He reached across the table and shook his hand too. "Nice to meet you both. Your mom has told me absolutely nothing about you."

Both boys laughed. The guy was kind of funny.

Tom sat down next to Wendy and was just about to say something when another fellow trainer called to him from across the way. "There's no riff-raff allowed in here."

Tom laughed. "Fuckin' A."

Everyone at the man's table laughed. They all knew Tom, they all loved Tom. Who didn't? When he leaned forward, he realized.... "Sorry," he said, cringing from the raised-eyebrow expression on Wendy's face. "God keeps letting me down in the language department."

Both boys laughed. Their mom looked like she wanted to crawl under the table. A waitress appeared at Tom's side. He glanced around; they all had beverages already. "I'll have a ginger ale, lots of ice. Did ya'll order lunch yet?"

Wendy shook her head. She'd never noticed him using the term ya'll before.

"Well, I'm starving so why don't we order," Tom said. He looked at Wendy and grinned. "This pretty lady will probably have a salad."

Wendy smiled. "Actually, I was thinking of having a....."

"Salad," both her sons said.

"A cobb salad," she said, laughing. "With Roquefort dressing."

Both of her sons ordered the cheeseburger platter, Tom ordered a Rueben. The first race was about to run. Tom took the racing form out of his back pocket and opened it. He glanced at the tote board. "Did you guys pick a winner?"

"Um, no," Matthew said.

Tom set the form down between them. "I like Divot Dan, he's overdo, see here...." He gave them a quick lesson. "This column is their past performances. This one here is the race conditions...."

Wendy watched her sons, at first appearing to listen politely, then all of sudden getting interested. Matthew was into numbers, Gordon was into competition. They each picked a horse and watched the race. Tom's pick won.

"My horse ran dead last," Gordon said.

"Yeah, well I only beat you by one," Matthew said.

Tom looked from one to the other, sizing them up so to speak. "If you want me to throw a race and let you win, you're going to have to let me know."

Both boys laughed. "No, that's okay," Gordon said. "I want to beat you fair and square."

They ate their lunch while pouring over the horses' past performances in the next race. "How important is their time percentage?"

"You mean their speed rating?"

"Yes."

"Very," Tom said, and looked at Wendy. She was picking at her salad. "What's wrong with it?"

She hesitated. "It's...."

Tom took his fork, speared some of it and tasted. He made a face, spit it discreetly into a napkin. "Shit, we can't even complain, can we?" he said, laughing.

"But it's sour," she said. "We don't want anyone sick."

"It's a sign," Tom said.

"Of what?" she asked.

"That you have eaten one too many salads."

They both laughed. Tom waved the waitress over. "Be very quiet about this, okay?"

The young woman nodded.

"Take the salad to the chef. Wait, do we have a chef?"

Wendy nodded. "Two of them."

"Good, tell them to taste the dressing."

"Oh no," the waitress said. "Why?"

"Shhh..." Tom insisted, with that smile of his that melted female hearts. "It's no big deal. Just have them taste it. All right."

"All right."

Matthew and Gordon glanced up and went back to studying the form, handicapping. "I want the number five horse," Gordon said. He looked at the odds. 12-1. "Maybe not."

Tom looked at the form. "Don't let the odds fool you."

"What are you saying?" Gordon asked.

Tom shrugged. "Nothing."

"I like the two horse." Matthew looked at Tom. "Which one do you want?"

Tom looked at the form again. "The two horse has a good shot and so does the five. But I personally like the four horse."

Both boys looked at him.

230

"So if I was betting, I'd bet the four to win, five to place, and two to show."

As the horses were loading into the gate, here came the waitress with another salad. "The chef said there was nothing wrong with the dressing, but he gave you a new salad anyway."

"I see. If you'll excuse me," she said to Tom and her sons. "I'll be right back."

Tom looked at the boys and shook his head. "I think the shit's going to hit the fan."

Both boys laughed.

"And they're off!"

Wendy's two sons and Tom watched every step of the race. It was 5 ½ furlongs and in the stretch run, here came the number four horse. "Oh my God," Matthew said. "He's going to win!"

Tom shook his head. Were they talking about him or the horse? "He's going to come up short."

"My horse is winning!" Gordon said. "Look! Come on Satan!"

Tom smiled. The horse's name was Sattan. He was the grandson of the famous Shim Sham.

"Look! Look!" Matthew said. "Come on number two."

The three of them laughed. All three horses vied for the lead...and at the wire, Gordon's horse won, Matthew's finished second, and Tom's came in third. It wasn't even a photo finish.

Tom smiled when they looked at him for an explanation. "You win some and you lose some," he said.

"That's it? That's all you're going to say?" Matthew said.

"What? Do you think this is the first horse race I've ever lost?"

The boys laughed. If asked, they'd have to admit they'd had reservations about meeting Tom, but liked him almost right from the beginning and liked him even more with every passing minute. Wendy returned to the table, all red in the face.

Tom looked at her as she sat down and dug into her salad.

"Talk about arrogance."

"It didn't go well, eh?"

"No," she said. "Not at all. Now see, this salad is good. And yes, I do know the difference."

Tom didn't dare laugh, though he wanted to. Her sons either. "Did you tell him who you were? I mean, are?"

She looked at him. "In the end."

"The end...? What? Did you fire him?"

"No." She jabbed her salad again. "I can't fire him. I don't have the authority."

Tom looked at her.

"Besides, he quit."

Tom nodded. "I see." He looked at her sons. "Walk softly and carry a big stick," he said.

Matthew and Gordon laughed. Then here came the chef, all dressed in white, chef hat in hand, and having a meltdown.

The boys stared.

"Oh way to go, Mom," Gordon said. "You made the man cry."

"Please," Wendy said to the chef. "Sit down." She made room for him next to her.

Tom looked around to see if there was someone with a camera. This scenario almost looked staged; another sad Nottingham Downs headline. "Chef quits over rancid...."

"I am so sorry," the man said. "You were right. I tasted it. It was spoiled. It was sour."

"Which is all I asked initially." Wendy could feel eyes on her from all over the clubhouse. Damage control, she kept thinking, damage control. "Chef Diamond Lou," she said, as if introducing him. "Can we have a round of applause?"

Most everyone in the clubhouse clapped, singing his praises.

"Thank you, thank you," he said, wiping his eyes. "Thank you."

"Now," Wendy said, when things got quiet again. "Would you perhaps just like to go back to work now?"

"Yes, please," he said. "I'm so sorry."

"Yes, and so am I," Wendy said.

The chef sniffled and looked around the table. Tom nodded, touching the rim of his hat. "Afternoon."

The boys smiled. "Great burger," Matthew said. Gordon agreed.

"Thank you. Burger," the chef said. "So young." He looked at Tom's empty plate.

"Rueben," Tom said. "Particularly good."

"I leave you now," Chef Diamond Lou said. "Have a nice day."

"You too," they all said.

He put on his hat and walked back to the kitchen, tall and proud. "Thank you, thank you," he kept saying, to everyone he passed. "Thank you." He kissed the back of one woman's hand. "Salmon, yes, yes, thank you. Tarragon."

Matthew leaned forward. "Was that for real?"

Their mom smiled. "Watch the race. I need to catch my breath and eat."

Tom looked at her. "Is there any tarragon in that salad?"

She smacked him, chuckling. "Quit. Enough."

He turned to Matthew and Gordon. "Okay, I'm going to redeem myself here. Big Lucky...." He motioned. The horses were loading in the gate. "He's going to win drawing away."

"Drawing away?" Gordon said.

Tom nodded. "All on his own."

Big Lucky won by five lengths, drawing away.

When Tom excused himself to go to the men's room, Wendy looked at her sons. "Well?"

"He's nothing like Dad," Matthew said.

Wendy smiled. "There's no one like your dad. I'm not trying to replace him."

Matthew nodded. "I think he's cool."

"Me too," Gordon said.

Tom had promised them a tour of the barn area, so when he returned, he paid the bill, and off they went. "Look at you in them trousers," he said to Wendy.

She laughed. "Actually they are trousers."

"And you didn't think I'd know that?" Tom smiled.

The boys were walking ahead of them. "Don't get too close to the stalls," Tom said, as they started down the shedrow. "A couple of those horses get a little aggressive with their greetings this close to dinner time."

Ben was sitting in the tack room, having just walked back from the track kitchen. He looked up and smiled when Wendy introduced her sons. "Your mom does a good job," he said.

Both boys smiled shyly, thinking the same thing. This man owns the racetrack, this really nice old man; this is mom's boss. "Nice to meet you, Mr. Miller."

Ben asked the boys about school, what they were studying and what they hoped to be some day. "Computer Science," Matthew said.

"Geek," Gordon said, teasing. "Me, marketing."

They both attended Kent State University, which was about an hour away. One was a freshman, the other a sophomore. Ben smiled at the way Wendy looked at her sons. She was proud, and rightfully so, he thought. They seemed like nice kids. She'd done well.

The boys got to meet all the "Miller" horses once they'd been fed their dinner. They liked the fillies; all three were inquisitive and kind. Bo-T; Beau Together, the two-year old colt, showed off a little, kicking and turning around and around in his stall. He was the biggest of the five horses, owing his size to both Beau Born and All Together.

"So he'll be used for breeding?" Gordon asked.

"Well, that depends," Tom said. "He's unproven as a racehorse. He hasn't run yet."

"Yeah, but even so, with his breeding as good as you say, wouldn't it make sense to use him for breeding when he's done racing?" Matthew asked.

Tom nodded. "If he proves himself, otherwise, no one's going to breed to him, particularly if Beau Born is still standing at stud."

"Standing?"

Tom smiled. "Come to think of it, it is an odd expression. Stand at stud….hmmm."

The boys laughed. Their mom blushed.

"And now this here is B-Bo. He's by Beau Born but out of a What a Pleasure mare. Technically, the match has probabilities of producing a good sire."

"Because...?"

"It's a Nick system. It's all computerized. It tells you which stallion to breed to that's likely to be the best match, who passes on this, who corrects that. They have it all down to a science," Tom said.

"But if Beau Born is still 'standing at stud' why would anyone want to breed to him and not Beau Born?"

"Well, for one, B-Bo has Seattle Slew in his bloodline on his dam's side. He's got a different momma than Bo-T. They're both bred equally as well, but it goes back to that Nick system."

Gordon and Matthew nodded. They'd grown up with computers, so the explanation made sense to both of them.

"Plus," Tom added, patting B-Bo on the neck. "He's a racehorse. In the eight times he's run, he's only been beaten once."

"What happened that time?" Matthew asked.

Tom glanced down the shedrow at Ben, who sat shaking his head.

"He bucked coming out of the gate and dumped Juan. It wasn't pretty."

"Will they hold that against him?" Gordon asked. "Would that be a personality Nick?"

Tom smiled. "You two are quick."

"Yes, it could be. No one's allowed to forget something like that, though I for one would like to," Ben said.

"But what if it wasn't his fault?"

"Now you're talking. It's a gamble," Tom said. "It's a game."

Ben smiled. "The best game in town."

Wendy had to agree. For the first time in her five years at Nottingham Downs, she was starting to appreciate the other side of this racetrack business, the reason behind it all; the horses. "Well," she said. "We'd better get going."

Tom walked with them to the end of the shedrow, shook the boys' hands, and stepped back. "I'll see you in the morning," he said to Wendy.

"It's going to be a big day," she said. "There's a lot going on." When her sons walked away, she gave Tom a hug. "Thank you."

Tom smiled as they gazed into one another's eyes. "Good night, pretty lady," he said, and kissed her gently.

Matthew and Gordon turned and watched from a distance. Their mother had been lonely for a very long time. She wasn't lonely anymore.

Chapter Thirty

Mondays and Tuesdays were dark days at Nottingham Downs, no racing. But it was training as usual. In fact, since there was no racing, it was typically heavier traffic on the racetrack during training hours. Cracker Jack Henderson walked down to the Miller barn to say good-bye. The backside always reminded him of an ant hill; activity everywhere.

"God, I love this place!"

"Me too," Ben said, shaking his hand. "When will you be back this way?"

"In about two weeks. Let me know if there's anything I can do in the meantime. You have my number, right?"

Ben nodded.

Tom and Dawn returned from the wash rack with Bo-T and waved to Cracker Jack in passing. "I'll be back the end of the month," he said, that crazy hair of his blowing in all different directions in the wind.

"Have a safe trip," Dawn said.

"Don't take any wooden nickels," Tom told him.

Cracker Jack laughed. "Don't break any hearts."

"I don't plan to," Tom said. "See you when you get back."

At the barn, Dawn picked up right where she left off. "And then, when I went to bring them in...."

Tom shook his head. "Oh no, not another pony story."

Dawn chuckled. "I know, but they're just so cute. You should see them when they're out in the pasture playing."

Tom nodded. "Uh huh."

Ben walked out from under the shedrow. "Well, he got okayed."

"I knew he would," Tom said. "He broke really good."

Ben stood looking at Bo-T, only two years old and standing well over 16 hands; a big, strapping colt with an attitude - and now okay to run. After Dawn and Tom scraped him off, Tom put a cooler on him, hung him on the walking machine, and Dawn went to the ladies room to wash up and leave. Randy's parents were due to arrive at the farm any time now.

"Don't worry," Liz, her mother-in-law had said last night on the phone. "We'll probably need a nap; at least I know I will. Don't hurry home."

Dawn was hoping to be there before they arrived anyway, to welcome them. Randy had three castration surgeries scheduled, and wouldn't be able to swing by the house until at least two. "I'll see you all later. Dinner at seven. Tell Wendy, okay?"

Tom nodded.

"Tell her not to bring anything. It's all set. She has enough to do today."

Tom nodded again, what was there to say? He looked at Ben. "What would I have done if Dawn didn't like her?"

Ben smiled. "That would have been a problem."

"Speaking of problems, Dusty said, uh...." Tom spotted him two barns down and headed this way. "Never mind, I'll let him tell you."

Ben sat down on the bench outside the barn to wait. Dusty walked up and sat down next to him. "Issues," he said.

Ben sighed. It had been such a nice morning until now. "The feed store cut off Ace for not paying his bill. I talked to

237

them but they're not budging. Deek says he owes them close to a thousand dollars."

"And?"

"And, I'm thinking we need a certain amount of money in the Billy Martin fund to help out in these types of situations."

"The Billy Martin fund?"

Dusty smiled. "Yeah, I know, it's non-existent. But it would serve a purpose if there was one for times like these. Ace has two horses entered for Wednesday and both races are gonna go. He's got a shot in both of them. His horses have been running good."

Ben looked at him. "Then why hasn't he paid his feed bill?"

"He says he's been having some personal problems. I didn't ask for particulars."

The two men sat staring down the road between the barns, the proverbial infinity. "A thousand dollars, that's a lot of money," Ben said, stating the obvious. "He doesn't have that many horses, does he?"

"Six."

Ben nodded.

"He owes his hay man too."

Ben looked at him. "How would you handle this, even if we did have a fund?"

"Well, Tom and I were thinking, it's not like you could just give them the money and…."

"Wait a minute. *Them*?"

"We're thinking this is probably going to come up again, particularly if word gets around."

Tom walked up next to them and heard the last part. "Because if we pay direct out of the Billy Martin fund, we know Deek or someone's going to say something to someone about it."

"Which is why we're thinking that if a fund is set up, the person getting the funds is going to have to be held accountable for it, you know, sign a promissory note or something, since the bills would be paid directly."

Ben shook his head. "I'm afraid of the can of worms this is going to open. What happens if they don't pay it back?"

"Well," Tom said. "We've given that some thought."

"We're thinking maybe the note should tie into their horseman's account in some way."

"Aw, Jesus, now you know that's not going to fly," Ben said.

"I don't think you want to get into asking for collateral," Dusty said. "We can always refuse them stalls next year if they're not paid up. That's one option. Also, we're thinking we could probably get close to a thousand for Billy's tack and belongings we've got stored. We could put that into the fund to start."

"And that way, it really is a Billy Martin foundation in a way," Tom said. "Dusty and I are each going to put in five hundred dollars too, so that'll help."

Ben sat thinking. "Well, work out the kinks I guess and go for it. Just be prepared for how you're going to say no when the times comes if this gets out of hand." Ben looked around. Activity everywhere, people working hard, bathing horses, doing horses up, grooming horses, putting horses on and off walking machines, horses kicking and bucking and playing, horses coming and going to the racetrack, hopes and dreams following them, riding on them.... "Did Dawn leave her camera?"

"Yes," Tom said. "Why?"

"We need to film this," Ben said. "Go get it."

"What do you want me to say?" Dusty asked, used to having a script of sorts.

"Just tell is like it is," Ben said, "Because it just doesn't get any better than this."

Rupert had enlisted quite a bit of help to relocate his tack store and liked the idea of his moving more and more. He had his own "john" which wasn't much, just a toilet and a sink, but it was certainly more than they had at the other location.

"It's like moving up town," he said.

Tom chuckled. "Does that mean you have no excuse to be full of shit now?"

Rupert laughed. "Oh by the way, your whips came in." He glanced around at all the boxes, all the tack, all the grooming supplies. "It's in a white box about this size."

After a little searching, Tom found the box and opened it. The whips had good grips, had a nice feel. He hit the side of his leg with one and smiled. "I'm liking it!" From there he and Dusty headed to the grandstand. Ben had said he'd meet them there to see the progress on the offices.

Wendy had been up and down the elevator at least a dozen times, had long since given up waiting on it to go from floor to floor, and took to the stairs instead. She had her hair pulled back in a ponytail, was wearing a short-sleeve shirt, jeans, and her paddock boots, and had sweat on her brow.

Ben sat down at "his table" in the glass-front room and looked out at the racetrack. It was a good fit. Wendy smiled at him sitting there. He looked almost as much at home as when he sat at his big kitchen table. "Much better than a desk," he said.

When Tom and Dusty entered the room, they were impressed.

"Next." Ben said, waving them in as if holding court.

They laughed. Tom didn't see Wendy at first. She was over in the area where her desk had been set up and leaning down to put something into one of the files drawers. When she closed the drawer and stood up, Tom turned.

"Well, hello," he said. "Look at you."

She smiled. She figured there would come a day when he wouldn't take her breath away just by looking at her the way he was looking at her now, but until then, she couldn't help but blush.

He took off his hat and placed it over his heart. "Could I have this dance?"

She laughed.

"I'm serious," he said.

"No. I'm not dancing with you," she said. "I don't hear any music."

"I do," he said, putting his cowboy hat back on in that irresistible way of his as he walked toward her. "They're playing our song. Don't you hear it?"

Ben and Dusty laughed, which saved her from blushing again. "No, but I do like to dance though. So maybe someday."

Spears entered the office just then, with details of what he said was good and bad news. "Which do you want first?"

"The bad," Ben said.

"We are now onboard with the Jockey Club Equine Injury Database. It's still in the planning, but it's going to happen. Fatalities from all the racetracks will be recorded, taking into account track conditions, a horse's age, number of races, distance, all of that."

"And that's the bad news?" Tom asked. "How do you figure?"

"Well, near as I can discern, the statistics do not cover injuries, just fatalities. I don't think that's the figures you want, not to mention the statistics are only now being compiled."

Ben shook his head. He was right; that's not the figures he wanted, nor the time frame. "So what's the good news?"

"The good news is, since we re-surfaced the racetrack four years ago, our injuries are way down, as opposed to the fatality records from the six years prior to that."

Tom sat back. "Are we talking hauled off injuries?"

"Yes. Hate to say it, but it seems to be the only clear way to account for them. If they make it back to the barn...."

Tom nodded. "This goes back to what Randy was saying. We need to keep track of horses coming and going."

"What do you mean?" Spears said.

"Well, I don't know if any other track is doing something like this. I've never heard of it if they do, but when we were talking about the slaughter issue and how to try and prevent that, he suggested that maybe a horse should have an exit exam. If that horse isn't hitting the ground on all fours and not headed for rehab, it shouldn't be allowed to leave."

Spears saw dollar signs, and not in a good way. "Are we talking about a veterinarian doing the exams?"

"Perhaps," Tom said. "Or a vet tech."

"So it would just be a quick physical exam?"

"Yes, and they'd probably have to draw blood. Drugs can mask a lot of pain."

Spears nodded. "Are there certain times for shipping horses in and out?"

"Yes," Dusty said. He, Tom, and Ben shook their heads at the reality of that. "They can ship in and out anytime but during training hours in the morning."

"But doesn't the guard check them in and out?"

"They check their papers, Coggins test certificate, health certificate - that type of thing."

"And Randy thinks...?"

"A sound-to-go exam certificate is in order," Tom said.

"What are the liabilities of a veterinarian saying the horse is good to go and having it turn out not to be?"

Ben scratched the back of his neck as he looked around the table. So many things to think about. "It would be a start, a trial, to see if would work. Even if we end up saving just one horse."

Tom and Dusty nodded. Wendy nodded. And fairly soon, as he sat there thinking about it, Spears nodded. "Oh, by the way," he said, changing the subject when several men from maintenance entered the room hauling additional furniture. "Starting Wednesday, it's buy one hotdog, get the second one free."

Tom smiled. "Same price as now."

"Only technically," Spears said. "It's two for one, but you only pay for the one. No, now don't laugh. This is very serious business. No one will be mad if you give one away, but if you try and charge less than the average price, for the same hotdog...."

They all laughed.

"For how long?" Dusty asked. Racetracks everywhere offered free hotdogs routinely as promotions. "You said starting Wednesday."

"We're committed to three million hotdogs in the next five years. And," he said, holding up his hand when their mouths dropped. "They're all natural."

"Well then," Tom said. "I think we're making progress. We've made a commitment."

Everyone laughed again.

"And on that note," Wendy said. "Look. The 'Forget Me Nots' have arrived." The landscape crew were carrying flat after flat across the track to the tote board on the infield. "I'll see you guys later. Go check out downstairs. It's all done."

Tom, Ben, and Dusty took the elevator down and marveled. Another table with ten comfortable chairs had been set up in the middle of the downstairs office. They all sat down. Spears' desk was at the far end, Wendy's to the side of his, and the most important feature of all, an open door.

Joe Feigler walked in behind them. "Did you guys hear about those steeplechase horses. Day one and already two broke down."

"Where?"

"I don't know, I didn't read the whole article. It's under investigation." Joe sat down and sighed. "We have a problem of our own." All three men looked at him. Just what they needed, more problems. "Rickety entered that Beckon horse of his again. It's run dead last his last four times out. It's done."

"Lose the entry," Tom said.

Joe looked at him. "We can't do that. Besides, he said the horse has nowhere to go and that by Nottingham Downs' rules, if he doesn't run him he loses his stall."

True. They all knew the rules. Though the time frame was not etched in stone, the idea was to not have horses stabled on the track that weren't running. Worse, was horses stabled at Nottingham Downs and running elsewhere, a more common offense. Horsemen don't pay for stalls; they stable horses at a racetrack free, with the agreement to race the horses.

"Ah, Jesus," Tom said. Ben and Dusty's sentiments exactly.

"I'll take care of it," Dusty said.

"How?" Joe asked.

"Well, I'm not sure. I'll go talk to him."

Ben nodded and looked at Joe. "Meanwhile, you go talk to the Stewards. We need them to back us up if Rickety won't pull the entry."

Tom looked out the window and smiled. Wendy had a can of spray paint in her hand and was mapping out a pattern for where to plant the "Forget Me Nots."

Mim Freemont limped into the room and stood supporting her weight on her cane. "I don't like where the Ginny stand's going."

"Why not?" Ben asked.

"It's going to scare the horses," she said.

Ben stood up. Mim wasn't one to be dismissed easily, nor would he care to. "Let's go take a look." She had her golf cart parked right outside the secretary's office. Ben stared at it. "Come on," she said. "I ain't got all day."

Tom and Dusty piled in the back, Ben climbed in next to her.

"I told the men to wait and they'd better have waited." She took them by way of the path leading from the Winner's Circle to the track kitchen and stopped mid-way. "Look," she said, pointing. "See. It's going to cast shadows."

"Fuck," Tom said, agreeing.

Ben sighed, all four of them just sitting there for a moment. "Drive onto the track."

Mim pulled down to the gap, Tom hopped off the golf cart, opened the gate, and hopped back on. Steve Simmons yelled to them from his barn. "What's going on?"

"Nosey old coot," Mim said. "Nothing!" she yelled. "Mind your own business."

Steve laughed.

Mim stopped midway on the track and there they sat, assessing the situation. Steve walked out to join them, and then here came Sally Jensen and several others from inside the track kitchen.

"What's going on?" Sally asked.

Tom looked at Ben. Did he want to talk about this with everyone? Apparently. Why not? "Mim thinks the horses might get spooked from the shadows." Here came some more people, and then the work crew. All climbed over the fence to join them.

The foreman didn't quite comprehend the problem. "Well, it'll cast some shadows, but...."

Mim looked at him; she and this man weren't on the best of terms already. "There's an old saying, 'Horses are only afraid of two things; things that move and things that don't.'"

All the horsemen and horsewomen nodded.

"All right then," the man said. "You'll need to go talk to whoever it is you need to talk to, so they can figure out what they want us to do."

"Well," Ben said, somewhat reluctantly. "That would be us."

"So what do you want to do?"

Time is money; Ben could hear Spears saying in his mind. "Give us a minute. We need to think this through."

Everyone had an opinion: move it here, how about over there, this won't work, yes it will.... Ben posed the consensus to the foreman. "How much trouble would it be to move the stand right up against the back of the track kitchen, make it narrower but longer, and also put in an access door from the kitchen?"

The man stood looking the area over with a keen eye.

"See, the thing is," Tom said, "The horses are used to the kitchen building being there. And set back far enough, it shouldn't cast a shadow."

The man glanced up at the sun and had to agree. The shadow would be on the outside of the fence. "It's still going to be a different structure."

"That's okay," Tom said. "They'll get used to that; shadows that change with the movement of the sun, no. They don't race the same time each day. It would be a whole new ball game each time they saw it in a different way."

"That's a concrete block wall," the man said, motioning to the kitchen. "It won't be easy knocking it out."

Tom smiled. "Do you want Mim to do it?"

"Mim...?" When he realized Tom was referring to the old woman giving him the evil eye, he smiled. "No, that's okay, we'll get it done."

Chapter Thirty-One

Dawn greeted her mother-in-law Liz and father-in-law Randy Senior with genuine love and concern, and disbelief. To look at the man, one would never suspect a potential time bomb ticking inside his chest. He looked happy, he looked strong, he looked healthy.

"I'm fine," he insisted. "Wish everyone would stop worrying."

D.R. squealed and ran into his arms. "Grandpa!"

Randy Senior picked him up and twirled him around.

"Stop that," Liz said. "Stop."

Randy Senior handed him off and picked up little Maeve. "How's my girl?"

"Gampa, Gampa!" She made funny faces when he kissed her on the nose.

"So where's Randy?" he asked.

"He'll be home soon," Dawn said. "He had some surgeries to do. He won't be long. Maybe you'd both like a snack and a little rest after the long drive?"

"I could go for a cup of coffee," Randy Senior said.

"I have some made, come sit." Dawn pulled chairs out around the kitchen table. Randy Senior sat with Maeve in his lap, arms around his neck. Liz sat hugging and loving D.R. "to deffis."

Dawn laughed. First time she heard one of them use that expression, Randy had to explain. Deffis? "Mom doesn't like saying 'love you to death.' It gives her the creeps. Love you to deffis is more to her liking."

Dawn's too. "We're having Chinese for dinner."

Randy Senior's eyes lit up. Whenever they came to town, he asked for Chinese. The nearest Chinese restaurant back home near their farm was over an hour away.

Dawn poured them both a cup of coffee. Randy Senior took a sip. It was nice and hot but awfully weak, in his opinion. "It's decaf," Dawn said. "We are all on decaf in support of Ben. It's the only way he'd give up caffeine. He said he wasn't going it alone."

Randy Senior took another sip and then stared into the cup. "Can you at least make it a little stronger next time?"

Dawn chuckled. She had no complaints about her in-laws. They were both such nice people, so easygoing. After they had a light snack, Randy Senior sat down in front of the television and promptly fell asleep. Liz took a nap with D.R. and Maeve. When Randy came home, Dawn met him out on the porch and motioned for him to be quiet.

"They're all asleep."

He walked with her to the foaling barn. It was time to turn the ponies out. All six dogs came running from the back of the house where they'd been napping on the deck and followed along. Poncho could care less about the dogs, but Biscuit didn't want anything to do with them. He stepped back and snorted.

"They're putting on weight," Randy said.

"Not fast enough. Yes, I know, I know," she added, when he started to say something about slow being better. "Still…."

Randy smiled. "If everyone's asleep, do you want to go up in the hayloft?"

"No," she said, laughing when he pulled her close.

He kissed her. "But I love you," he said.

"I love you better," Dawn said, imitating D.R.

Randy sighed, holding her. "How's Dad look?"

"Actually I think he looks really good." They both turned when the dogs started barking. A strange car. Poncho and Biscuit ran to the gate. "You're kidding me," Dawn said.

Randy stared. It was Linda Dillon. "What's she doing here?"

"I don't know." Dawn waved. "Be nice," she said.

247

Randy just looked at her.

When Linda parked her car and got out, both ponies nickered.

"Hello," Dawn said.

"Hi, Dawn," Linda said. "Randy."

He nodded.

"What's going on?" Dawn asked. "What can I do for you?"

"Well, I'm just passing through. I got a job up in Canada. I'm going to be a clocker at Archbine." She smiled, looking at the ponies. "Do you mind...?" she asked, wanting to go over and pet them. Poncho had taken to pawing.

"No, go ahead," Dawn said.

Both ponies seemed happy to see her. "I didn't realize you were going to keep them. I thought you'd sell them."

Dawn walked over, shaking her head. "No, this is their forever home."

Linda smiled, rubbing both horses on their foreheads. "They're good boys. They'd have to be, to put up with me."

Dawn studied her expression. "Are you okay?"

Linda nodded. "I haven't had a cigarette in two weeks and I'm off Oxyfil. I found I didn't need it. I'm not in pain now that I'm not riding. The nightmares are gone too."

Dawn smiled. "How's Maria?"

Linda turned. "She's fine." She was asleep in her car seat.

"Daddy!" D.R. screamed, running toward them. Grandma and Grandpa Iredell were right behind him with Maeve. "Daddy!"

Randy picked him up and gave him a kiss. "How's my little man?"

"Grandma Grandpa is here!"

"I see," Randy said. He gave his mom a kiss on the cheek and shook his dad's hand. "How was the trip?" he asked, leaning down and picking Maeve up with his free arm. "Give Daddy kiss."

Maeve kissed him on the nose, and Randy laughed. They all laughed, and then all looked at Linda. "Oh," Dawn said.

"Sorry. This is Randy's mom and dad, Randy Senior and Liz, and this is our son D.R."

"Short for doctor," Randy Senior said.

"This is our daughter Maeve."

"Hellwo," Maeve said.

Linda smiled.

"And this is our friend, Linda Dillon."

Everyone smiled. Even Randy smiled, out of politeness. Our friend?

Maria woke to the sound of their voices and started crying. "That's my little girl, Maria," Linda said, walking toward the car. By now, Poncho and Biscuit had gone back to grazing. As far as Randy was concerned, the visit was over. He glanced down the drive. Ben's truck had just turned in off the road. Tom was right behind him.

"Baby, baby!" Maeve said, clapping her hands and squirming out of Randy's arms.

Wendy pulled in right behind Tom.

When Linda took Maria out of her car seat and put her down, they all laughed when Maeve hugged her tight. "My baby! My baby!"

Ben walked over to greet everyone. Tom waited for Wendy and followed. More introductions. Tom smiled. "This is my friend, Wendy. Nottingham Downs' Assistant General Manager and the love of my life."

Wendy blushed. Then here came Dusty, and right behind him, Glenda and George with all the food. "Would you like to join us for dinner?" Dawn asked Linda. "There's plenty. I ordered enough Chinese food for an army."

"Uh, thank you," Linda said, glanced at everyone self-consciously. "But I uh...."

Little Maeve had hold of Maria's hand and was already leading her toward the house.

"You've been outvoted," Randy Senior said.

The two little girls looked so cute walking together.

"Horsey," one would say.

"Horsey," the other would add.

"Doggies!"

"Doggies!"

"Doggies, no!"

"Doggies, no!"

Dog kisses all over their faces, little arms flailing, giggling.

"No, no, doggies! No! No!"

Everyone carted several bags of Chinese food, Linda included. Tom carried the carrot cake. Wendy looked inside the cellophane lid. "I love carrot cake."

Tom smiled. "I love you."

Wendy nodded, say it. Say it, she told herself. Say it. "I love you too."

Tom leaded down and kissed her. 'Thank you," he said.

"For what?" she asked, walking alongside him.

"For loving me, for coming into my life, for having such fine sons."

"Did you like them, really? They really liked you."

Tom nodded. "They're good boys."

Wendy smiled, thinking; I'm dreaming. I'm dreaming, I'm dreaming, and any moment now, I'm going to wake up. The two of them had lagged back and were relatively alone. Tears welled up in her eyes as she recalled something her husband had said as he lay dying in her arms.

"I can't love you any more than I already do and you can't love me any less. I wouldn't take you with me even if I could. Live...."

She looked up at Tom, with happy tears trickling down her face.

"What are you doing crying?" he asked.

"I'm living," she said, smiling. "I'm living."

The food was set up on the kitchen island. Dawn had the plates and silverware all set out, glasses, ice, juice, water. She made a fresh pot of coffee, stronger this time. Everyone helped themselves.

"Did you get me and D.R. our worms?" Tom asked.

Dawn chuckled. "They're rice noodles."

"That's what you think," Tom said, holding one up and swallowing it little by little.

D.R. did the same. "Worms."

There were enough chairs combined between the kitchen table and dining room table to seat everyone. Liz fed Maeve. Linda fed her daughter Maria.

It was a homey scene the likes of which Linda hadn't seen in a long, long time. "Thank you, Dawn," she said. "This is very nice of you." She and Liz talked about the children's ages, food likes and dislikes, habits. They talked about the weather in Florida. "Too hot for me," Linda said.

They talked about the weather in Illinois. "It's the best time of year," Liz said. Everyone was relaxed, everyone was happy. "D.R., what are you doing?"

He had his ear to his plate. "Listening to the worms," he said.

Randy shook his head and cast a glance at Tom. "Those are not worms, son. Don't listen to Uncle Tom." He paused. "They're eels!"

Everyone laughed when D.R. squealed in delight!

Linda sighed. There wasn't a person at the table with a care in the world. They all had nice big houses: they all had secure lives.

"So what time are your tests tomorrow?" Ben asked Randy Senior

"Nine."

"Do you have to fast?" Dawn asked.

Linda looked from one to the other. Liz explained. "He's having tests on his heart tomorrow at The Clinic. Back home they said he needed surgery, otherwise...."

"Otherwise, hell," Randy Senior said. "Who'll run the farm?"

"Me, and we'll hire help?"

"What do you farm?" Wendy asked.

"Pigs, Whiteshires," Randy Senior said. "I've farmed pigs all my life."

Randy smiled. "That's why the two of us, me and my sister Linda, grew up to be vets."

"You sister's named Linda?"

Liz nodded. "I love that name."

"My mother's name was Linda," Dusty said.

Dawn went back for another serving of cashew chicken. "My cousin's name is Linda."

"I had an Aunt Linda," Tom said.

"I *have* an Aunt Linda," Glenda said.

Linda smiled. Something as simple as having the same name as some of their loved ones, made her feel at home in a way. When it came time to cut the carrot cake, she felt welcome enough to take on the task. Wendy passed each slice down the table.

By the time they'd finished dessert, Randy Senior was yawning.

"I'd better go bring the ponies in," Dawn said, glancing at the clock.

"I'll go with you," Linda said, picking up Maria to carry her along.

"I'll watch her," Liz said.

Linda hesitated. She was hoping just to make a discreet exit. "Okay. Thank you."

She and Dawn walked to the foaling barn, with all six dogs weaving in and out around them. "I've never seen a Standard Poodle as a farm dog," Linda said.

"He's a rescue," Dawn said.

The ponies picked their heads up from grazing. When Dawn opened the gate and turned her back, they both walked over to her. "It's a game we play," Dawn said.

Linda smiled. Dawn handed her a lead shank. Linda took Poncho, Dawn took Biscuit. Their hay and grain was already set up in their stalls. Dawn motioned which stall was Poncho's. They led the horses in, took off their halters, and stood outside their stalls watching them eat for a moment.

"I fed them a box of Quaker oatmeal once," Linda said in a sad soft voice.

Dawn looked at her.

"It's all I had."

"What did you eat?"

"That night, nothing."

They both stared in at the horses. "Is everything all right? Are you looking forward to your new job?"

Linda nodded. "The pay is good, and I'm told there's affordable housing and daycares nearby."

Dawn looked at her.

"And if I can't clock a horse, then who can?"

Dawn chuckled.

"I'll be fine. We'll be fine." Linda said, and paused. "Maria's the best thing that ever happened to me. I'm not going to let her down."

The two of them walked back up to the house. "It's getting dark earlier and earlier," Dawn said.

"I wonder if they have daylight savings time in Canada?"

"I think so," Dawn said.

Randy Senior and Ben were sitting on the porch. Apparently Ben was bringing him up to date about the racetrack. Dusty and Tom came out to join them, and then Randy. "Mom's insisting on doing the dishes. I told her to use the dishwasher, but she said that it takes longer."

"Let her do it," his dad said. "She's a nervous wreck. I'll be glad when tomorrow's over, for her sake more than anything."

Randy nodded.

"And by the way, son." His dad lowered his voice. "I know there's nothing wrong with me, but if something happens, have your mom sell the farm and move her here. All right?"

Randy looked at him. "All right."

Linda slipped past them, as sad as if it were her father saying that, and went to check on Maria. She and Maeve were watching cartoons, wearing headsets. Dawn walked in behind her. "Oh those," she said, from the look on Linda's face. "Our nanny Carol insists on them."

They laughed.

Liz had most of the dishes washed. Wendy was drying silverware. She handed another towel to Linda, Dawn wiped the tables off, and they were done in no time.

253

When the dogs all ran up onto the porch, barking, Maeve and Maria threw off their headsets and took off running. More kisses, more squealing, more, "No, doggies, no!"

The women all walked outside. "Well, we'd better get going," Linda said, picking up Maria. "Thank you for dinner. Thank you for everything."

"You'll keep in touch, right?" Dawn said.

Linda nodded.

"How far are you going tonight?" Wendy asked.

"Till I get sleepy," she said, yawning.

Ben looked at her. "There's a room at the house, if you want to stay the night. We're up early. You can get an early start in the morning."

"Thanks, but I...." She looked at them, all of them. What she wouldn't give to have a family like this, even if it was for just one night. The way they were all awaiting her answer, the caring looks in their eyes. It was as if she *was* family. "If you don't think we'd be a bother."

"No, no bother," Ben said.

"Thank you."

Linda gathered hers and Maria's overnight bags from her car. Wendy stood by, holding Maria, practically asleep and with her head resting on Wendy's shoulder. Tom, Dusty, Glenda and George did night check in the barns. Ben walked on ahead to the house.

"I feel bad Ben thinking he has to put me up for the night," Linda said.

"I don't think Ben thinks he *has* to do anything. He wants to."

After being inside Dawn and Randy's huge Colonial house for the evening, Ben's farmhouse wasn't quite what Linda had expected. It was as if she'd stepped back in time. Low ceilings, wide open-arch rooms, large eat-in kitchen, sink and cabinets all on one wall, an ancient refrigerator, old fashioned hardwood plank floors. It reminded her of her Nana's house, her Nana's kitchen.

"The spare room's just down the hall," Ben said.

It was a small room, a double bed against the wall, a dresser and chest of drawers. The bed had a yellow chenille spread and two pillows with shams matching the sheets. "Like I said, it's not much," Ben said, looking around.

"It's heaven," Linda said.

Wendy put Maria down gently on the bed. She was sound asleep, so precious the way she curled herself into a little ball, making soft nestling noises, little sighs. Ben smiled, shook his head, and walked on down the hall. "Good night."

"Good night," Wendy and Linda said.

Ben's house was a quiet house, even with the hardwood floors. Wendy and Linda tiptoed back down the hall when they heard Tom come in the back door. "All is well," he said, in a normal tone of voice.

"Shhhh…" Wendy said. "Maria's sleeping and Ben went to bed too.

Tom smiled and lowered his voice. "Ben can't hear a thing when he goes to sleep. You could have a party out here." He reached into the fridge for a bottled water - held it up to see if they wanted one. Both shook their heads no, both said, "I'm stuffed," at the same time and both chuckled.

A slightly awkward moment descended upon them. What to do? It was obvious Tom didn't want Wendy to leave. It was also obvious Linda didn't want Wendy to leave. Tom walked into the living room and reached for the remote. "Let's see if there's a Larry Levinson movie on. I love that guy's movies, I always cry at the end."

Linda laughed. "You…cry?"

"Yeah, sit down. You'll see. I don't cry a little either> I cry a lot."

When the three of them laughed, Wendy glanced down the hall towards Maria's temporary room. "That's all right. She's used to noise," Linda said. "We lived over a bar in Florida," she added. "The rent was cheap."

The three of them got comfortable on the couch, Tom and Wendy at one recliner end, Linda the other. One commercial, then another, and another, and Tom's cell phone rang. It was Randy. "Yeah. What's up?"

"One of the horses at Shifting Gears is down. I think I'm going to need your help."

"All right, pick me up," Tom said. He glanced at his watch. "I'll be back in a little bit. Don't go," he told Wendy.

"Why? What's wrong?"

"A horse is down at a rescue farm. I'm going with Randy. It's not far. It's just up the road."

"Down...?" Wendy asked.

Tom nodded. "Not good when they won't get up." He saw Randy's truck coming up the drive, kissed Wendy good-bye, nodded to Linda, and left.

Wendy stared at the television for a moment. "I don't want to cry at a movie."

"I don't either," Linda said.

Wendy tossed her the remote. "Find something happy."

Linda flipped through the channels. There weren't that many. Apparently Ben didn't have cable. There was an old rerun of an "I Love Lucy" episode playing. "Do you want to watch it?"

Wendy nodded. "Why not?" She glanced at the door.

"I think you've cast a spell on him," Linda said. "Tom."

Wendy smiled. "Actually I think he's cast a spell on me."

"You two seem good for one another."

Wendy paused. "I never thought I'd love another man."

Linda smiled. "I never thought Tom would love one woman."

Wendy chuckled. "I keep thinking I'm going to wake up one day soon and he's going to be the Tom everyone told me he used to be and not even remember my name."

Linda shook her head. "I'd lay odds against that."

Wendy looked at her. "That means the odds are in my favor, right?"

Linda smiled. "Right."

Lucy was hiding in the closet, covered in flour. "Lucy! Lucy, where are you?" Ricky searched their apartment. There was flour everywhere. He traced the footprints and opened the closet door.

"If you don't mind me asking, where is Maria's father?"

256

"Ah," Linda shook her head. "There were *no* odds there, none whatsoever. I was just a speed bump in the night." She reached for an afghan off the back of the couch and covered up in it. "Life sure has its twists and turns."

Wendy nodded. "You can say that again."

"Lucy! You have some splainin' to do. Look at you!"

"Oh, Ricky!"

Wendy and Linda laughed. There was always a happy ending with "I Love Lucy," no matter what. "It's a shame it didn't cross over into real life, huh?" Linda said, yawning.

Wendy reached for the other afghan. This must be Tom's, she thought. It had the scent of his cologne. What was it? She sighed. "You know, there's a part of me that wishes I could see a little of the old Tom, the Tom that...."

When she hesitated, blushing, Linda laughed. "I hear it was one hell of a ride."

Wendy looked at her and shook her head. "Go to sleep."

"I'm just sayin'!"

Wendy turned off the lamp next to her and snuggled into the afghan.

Lucy was crying happy tears in Ricky's arms.

"Oh, Ricky."

"Oh, Lucy...."

Wendy opened her eyes and turned. There was someone in the kitchen. Tom? No, it was Ben. She glanced at Linda, waking now also, and little Maria waking up next to her. "She came out in the middle of the night." Linda said.

Wendy smiled, rubbing her eyes. "I can't believe I slept that soundly."

"There's coffee made," Ben said. "And some oatmeal."

"Thank you," Wendy and Linda said in unison.

Wendy wondered where Tom was. "What time is it?"

"Ten to five," Ben said. "Tom phoned. They're still at Shifting Gears."

Wendy stared. "Where?"

"The rescue farm."

"Is this horse okay?"

Maria climbed into her mother's arms.

"They're hopeful." Ben hesitated at the door. "I'll see you later. We don't lock the door. Just pull it shut."

"Ben," Linda said. "Thank you."

He nodded. "You take care of that little one."

"I will."

"Let Dawn or Wendy know how you're doing. All right?"

"All right."

Chapter Thirty-Two

Ben walked through the stable gate and greeted the guard. "Good Morning."

"Mornin', Ben."

"Is everything okay? Anything I need to know? Anything you need me to do?"

The man smiled. "Everything's good."

"That's what I like to hear," Ben said, walking on.

"But there is one thing."

Ben dropped his head and turned around.

"Just kidding."

Ben shook his head and laughed. Dawn had fed the horses their breakfast, made coffee, and was taking leg wraps off Bo-T. She looked up. "Tom's on his way. He just called."

"Everybody clean up?"

"Yep." All the horses had eaten their oats.

Ben walked into the tack room and stood looking at the training chart on the wall. B-Bo was scheduled to walk, Whinny and Wee Born were marked to gallop, Batgirl was going to be breezed and Bo-T was scheduled to pony.

Randy's father's medical assessment was scheduled for nine this morning. They were told it would take up to four hours. Dawn had offered to go stay with Liz at the hospital, but Randy Senior insisted Dawn go to work.

"Work, work, work," Liz had said in response, rolling her eyes.

Randy hoped to get there for the evaluation and recommendations. "You can if you want," his dad said. "But I'm not having surgery. There's no two ways about it."

Tom showed up a few minutes later, sporting a fair amount of dried manure on his jeans and looking "rode hard and put away wet."

"I ain't had that much fun since I stayed up all night with the Inkster twins."

Dawn shook her head. "Do you want to pony Bo-T first?"

"Might as well."

"How's the horse doing?"

Tom hesitated. "I need to tell you something about that bad-ass husband of yours."

Dawn smiled. This was going to be good. She'd just talked to Randy. He was fine. Tired, but fine.

"I'm serious," Tom said.

Dawn paused.

"He doesn't know the word "quit." And if that horse makes it, he owes his life to Randy and them two crazy women."

Dawn smiled.

Tom grabbed Red's saddle and bridle, walked down to tack him up, and here came Dusty. "Wait till you see."

"What?" Ben asked, fearing the worst of whatever it was.

Joe Feigler made an announcement just then. "Attention, horsemen. Be aware of the Ginny stand. Make sure your horses get a good look at it. We don't want anyone dumped on their heads. Have a good day."

Ben smiled.

"Like I said, wait till you see it," Dusty said. In addition to having Joe Feigler make the announcement several times this morning, Dusty had visited every barn to warn them personally. "So far only a few of the horses have spooked from it."

"How's it look?" Ben asked.

"Unbelievable," Dusty said.

259

"Well, no time like the present," Ben said. "I'll see you up there, Tom. Dawn, do you want to come look?"

"I'll be up in a few minutes."

The Ginny stand was a big hit. Ben heard comments along the way. An occasional "It's about time," didn't dampen his spirits one iota. It was a fine Ginny stand, a positive statement, a testament to the importance of the employees on the backside. As he and Dusty stood admiring the structure; a min-version of a grandstand for spectators, Dawn walked up next to them.

"Wow! Now that's nice. I like it."

Tom, astride Red, led Bo-T onto the racetrack and the big colt snorted and balked, then stomped. Ben laughed. "Ah, you gotta love him. If he isn't a chip off the old block, I don't know who is." Of all the horses Beau Born had sired thus far, this is the one that most resembled Beau in Ben's eyes.

The sun was just coming up over the trees and shone on the infield. "Diamonds on green velvet," Dawn said, of the dew. She didn't get up to the track this early in the morning very often. She usually had her hands full at the barn. The first time she ever came to the racetrack was a morning just like this.

"Oh look," she said. "The Forget Me Nots."

Ben and Dusty gazed at them and smiled. "They look like they've been there forever," Ben said. Dawn and Dusty agreed.

"What *was* there before?"

"I don't know. Grass?"

Dawn walked back to the barn and was happy to see Randy's truck parked next to it. He was sitting in the tack room, having just poured himself a cup of coffee. She gave him a hug. "I'm so proud of you."

"For what?"

"For everything," she said. "Did you stop by the house and see your dad?"

He nodded and took a sip of his coffee. "I've never seen my dad scared, ever. Not even when our bull penned him in the barn and it looked like he was about to kill him."

"What did he do?"

"Then?" Randy smiled. "He told me to go tell my mother that if all went well, we were having sweetbreads for dinner."

Dawn smiled. "Do you think he's scared now?"

Randy nodded and for a second, a split second, tears welled up in his eyes. "I'm exhausted," he said. "He'll be fine." And just like that, he was smiling again.

"You two are too much alike," Dawn said, smoothing the side of his hair back.

Randy kissed her, finished his coffee, and was off again.

"Go see the Ginny stand," Dawn called to him.

He nodded.

Wendy arrived at work a little earlier than usual for a Tuesday. Oddly enough, her days off were Saturday and Sunday, both the biggest race days. Since she'd worked Saturday morning and all day Sunday, she certainly could have stayed home today. But she had too many things she wanted to get done.

First on her list, was making sure the finish work on the offices was underway. She made several trips up and down the stairs, and at one point walked into the secretary's office for a drink of water. Two men at the entry booth motioned discreetly in her direction. "Who's that?"

"That would be your Assistant General Manager," Joe said.

"You're kidding?" Not only was she dressed in jeans, boots, and a casual shirt and looked like she belonged here. She was sweating.

"Hey, Joe," she said in passing as she wiped her brow. "How's it going?"

"Good," he said. "We're going to have a full card."

She gave him a thumbs up, not exactly sure what "full card" meant, but the way he'd said it, she figured it had to be good. And back up the stairs she went. Ever since she'd worked on finding advertising space for the jazz band that played at Billy Martin's funeral, she'd been kicking around

261

the idea of coming up with a new front-cover design-layout for the racetrack program. As it was now, it had only the name Nottingham Downs across the top, a photo of three horses in a race in the middle and a blank space across the bottom for the date. There was so much wasted space, not to mention suggesting nothing about the uniqueness of this racetrack, no signature statement; no slogan.

She sat down at her desk, stared out at the infield and smiled. What was it about those little tiny flowers, the Forget Me Nots that changed everything? "It's like a promise," she said, and took out a note pad and started sketching.

"Nah!" She crumbled that piece of paper and started another drawing.

Her cell phone rang. "Hello."

"So, you spend the night at my house, first time, and I'm not even there," Tom said. "What's that all about?"

Wendy chuckled. "How's that horse doing?"

"I think he might make it. It was touch and go for a while. Hey, I was thinking. What about you and me go on a real date tonight? Dinner, dancing if you want? "

"Okay. Where are you?"

"I'm sitting outside the barn waiting for Juan. He's going to come gallop Whinny and try out the soft whip. She hates a whip."

"I'll watch for you."

"Are you up in your office? Isn't this your day off?"

"Yeah, but I'm working on something."

"Is Spears there?"

"No, not today. I'll be by the barn a little later. I have something I want to show you and Ben and Dawn." She sat watching out the window, watched and watched, and then finally spotted Tom on Red, leading Whinny. When they came in front of the grandstand and he and Juan looked up, Wendy waved.

Winning Beau, "Whinny" was a bay filly. Wendy was learning the different colors of the horses. Whinny had a black mane and tail and black legs, characteristics of a bay. The horse was sired by Beau Born but was not an offspring of All

Together. She smiled, feeling rather proud of herself for remembering all this information, even if she couldn't recall Whinny's dam's name.

She watched as Tom turned Whinny and her jockey around, watched as he glanced over his shoulder to see if any other horses were approaching, watched as he and Red galloped along next to Whinny, watched, watched, watched….and caught her breath when Tom let Whinny go and she took off so fast, running so hard. She watched as the filly galloped all the way around the track…never took her eyes off of her.

Juan asked Whinny for more run down the stretch, trying out the soft whip again and then again, and then once more as they approached the wire.

Wendy watched it all. The jockey stood up in his stirrups after he passed the finish line. She looked for Tom. He was on Red out in the middle of the racetrack on the far turn. When the filly galloped up next to him, he reached over and took hold of her rein.

"Wow."

She stared at her sketch, an only slightly better version of the previous one; crumpled it also and feverishly started sketching another. The program should show everything, all aspects of the Thoroughbred's life, not just the racing, but the babies, the barns, the training, the caring, and yes, she gazed at the Forget Me Nots, it should show the day when they no longer raced. It had to show it all. This wasn't just about racing. This was about the life of a Thoroughbred. She couldn't draw fast enough.

Ben was anxious to hear Juan's opinion of the soft whip. He stood smiling at the playful way Whinny nipped at Red and chuckled when Red pinned his ears at her and she lowered her head as if to say, "I'm sorry." Was it his imagination or was she coming off the track calmer than usual?

Juan seemed reluctant to talk about it at first. "I don't know, I…."

Tom smiled. "Have you ever known a jock to be speechless?"

"You suck," Juan said, laughing. He hopped off Whinny and walked along with Ben as Tom led the filly back to the barn.

"Well?"

Juan looked at him. "If you say I should try it in a race, I say that is your choice."

Ben nodded and patted him on the back. "Thank you." There was a lot said and unsaid in that exchange. Juan walked off, tapping the side of his leg with the whip. Ben walked away, smiling. Dawn and Tom gave Whinny a good suds bath and they too noticed a difference in her behavior: calmer, happier, playful. Ben stood at the barn, thinking. When a horse wins a race easy, they also cool out easier as a rule. They're not wired as tight, so to speak. A common bragging rights expression about their "not even breathing hard" under those circumstances came to mind. He'd always, always associated it with their not running as hard. But there were many occasions when they'd run their fastest race, and yet, since they'd win easy - no one challenging them at the end - no one whipping them to run harder, just hand riding....

Ben sighed. Another expression came to mind, "You can't teach old dogs new tricks." Oh yes you can, he said to himself. If someone could prove to me that whipping a horse stresses that horse, I'd damned sure make a change. He'd read a study once that supported the theory that shipping horses, whether by van or trailer, regardless of vehicle size, stressed a horse.

The study was disputed by many horsemen, particularly the ones that raced off the farm, but Ben stopped racing off the farm shortly thereafter that. Upon observing his own horses before and after shipping, he found that even if they ran well, they were different horses shipping in and out and running the same day. Yes, they liked being back home, but they seemed to dread going back to the racetrack next time around. Stress? Anticipation? They all shipped well. It wasn't that. He'd never had a bad shipper. The day of a race, horses aren't given hay; there was nothing to distract them on the ride there. On the way home, they had a full haynet hanging in the van. The study said horses just having to work at keeping their balance in a moving vehicle, particularly on the starts and stops, plus loud traffic noises seemingly coming out of nowhere, added stress. Even a horse that walked off the van, looking cool and calm, had been stressed.

"What's the matter?" Dawn asked, from the expression on his face when they returned to the barn.

Ben shook his head. "The older I get, I think too much."

Probably the most convincing comment for him was, "Do they ship Derby horses in the day of a race?" No one would even think of doing that. They arrive at the track days before the race. They get settled in, they....

"Old man," Tom said. "You worry me when you think too much."

Ben laughed. "I worry myself. Stand in line."

The rest of the morning went fairly fast. By eleven, the horses were all done up and Dusty had made several trips to the barn. "I'm getting so I dread seeing you coming," Ben said.

Dusty smiled. "Rickety's still not budging. I'll tell you, I almost wish I still had my stalls. I'd offer him a killer price and take the horse off his hands. But then even if I did, I don't know what I'd do with it. I asked Randy and he said Shifting Gears is full."

"What we need," Tom said, "is a transition barn; somewhere to put these horses in the meantime."

"Do you mean there's more than one," Dawn asked.

"I'll bet there's one in every barn," Tom said, "Particularly this time of year."

Dawn sighed.

"What about Brubaker's old stalls?" Tom asked.

Ben looked at him. "What are you saying?"

"I'm saying," Tom said. "Thoroughbreds need transition time anyway. Why not have a barn, half a barn, whatever, where these types of horses can go?"

"And who takes care of them, who feeds them?"

"You're starting to sound like Spears," Tom said.

Ben held his hands out. "You know he's going to ask."

"Yeah, I know."

The four of them turned when they saw Wendy coming down the shedrow, looking every bit the horseperson, except for when she would duck and shy if a horse rushed its stall webbing. She had a notepad in her hand.

Tom smiled, a smile that took Dawn somewhat by surprise. "Oh my God, Tom, you really are in love, aren't you?"

"Big time," he said.

"Okay," Wendy said, approaching them. "I'm no artist, but...I've been thinking and thinking. We need a slogan." She dodged B-Bo, who lunged at her playfully, mouth open. "We need a more positive image."

All four of them looked at her, no argument there from any of them.

"Now, again, I'm not an artist. But I think you'll get the gist of it. This is a sketch for our new program."

"New program?" Ben said, motioning for her to hand it to him.

She gave it to him and held her breath.

Across the top of the page read, "Nottingham Downs" and underneath it, "Where Thoroughbreds Reign and are Never Forgotten"

She'd drawn the tote board with the Forget Me Nots dotted underneath it. Behind the tote board on one side, was a foal standing next to its mother in a pasture, on the other side, was a horse and rider going over a jump, three other horses stood grazing in green pastures, a cowboy on a trail. In the middle of the page, was a horse race, the whole field of horses and not just the winners. Underneath the horse race, was a drawing of the grandstand and backside barns.

"It's busy, I know. It's just a rough idea, and I have to work on the slogan a little more. But...."

"Well, it certainly says a lot more than the old one," Dusty said. "Well, not says, but...."

"Is it too busy?"

They all shook their heads.

"What's usually on the back?" Dawn asked. "I can't remember."

266

"Precious advertising," Wendy said.

They all nodded. Enough said.

"I like it," Ben said.

"Me too," Tom said. "That cowboy on the trail horse, is that me?"

Wendy chuckled. "No, not really, well... maybe."

He smiled.

She looked at all of them. "I basically just wanted to get some idea of what you thought about changing the program."

Dawn nodded. "I like it. I'm not so sure about the cowboy," she said, teasing.

They all laughed.

"I think it's great," Dusty said.

"Okay," Wendy said, "If we're all in agreement that it's a good idea to change the program, what do we think about the slogan."

"Well, it goes along with what we were just saying," Dusty said. "When a racehorse leaves here, their lives are not over. At least they shouldn't be. They're just moving on."

"Did you just make that up?" Tom asked.

Dusty stared and shrugged. "I guess so."

"Write that down," Tom said to Wendy. "That's really good."

Dawn's cell phone rang. She excused herself, stood outside the tack room door to take it, and lowered her eyes. "Are they sure? It hasn't even been three hours yet."

"They're sure," her mother-in-law said. "It's what he's been saying all along. He's fine."

"Is Randy there?"

"Yes."

"Did he ask them questions?"

"A million."

Dawn heaved a sigh of relief, covered the phone long enough to say, "Randy's dad is fine, no surgery needed," and got back on the line. "Do we want to go out to dinner and celebrate?"

"No, he says he just wants to stay at the farm and visit now that this load is off everyone's mind."

Dawn smiled. She could almost hear him saying that. "Okay, well, figure out what you guys want to eat, and we'll go from there." She hung up, knowing he'd say pizza. The nearest pizza place was even further from their farm back home than the Chinese restaurant.

"How cold's it supposed to get tonight?" she asked.

"It's going to be warm," Tom said. "Why?"

"They're going to go home in the morning, so I'm thinking we'll eat out on the deck if it's going to be warm."

Tom glanced at Wendy. Their date plans, a *real* date.

"What?" Dawn said, picking up on something between the two.

"Nothing," Wendy said. "That's sound great. What can I bring?"

"Now wait a minute. Come on, what's going on?"

Tom shrugged. "We were gonna go dancing."

"Oh," Dawn said, as she thought, you Tom? Dancing? "Okay, stop by, say hi and good-bye, and if you feel like eating, fine, and if not, go. They're leaving for home early in the morning, so…."

Wendy smiled. "That sounds good. Can I bring anything?"

"No."

Tom walked with Wendy down the shedrow and around the corner. "Are you sure about this? Listen, you come first, okay?"

"Okay, but no. Besides, it's not like we've had this planned for a long, long time. We'll do it tomorrow. I like being part of a big family gathering. I miss that."

"All right." Tom gave her a kiss. "I'm going to pick you up though. Text me your address and directions."

"What time?"

"Seven or so. I'm going to try and take a nap first."

"Oh, that's right. I forgot. You were up all night."

Tom kissed her again, and then again.

Dunnigan, a trainer in the barn across from theirs, cat whistled at them. Tom flipped him off, they both laughed, and Wendy departed. "I'll see you later."

Chapter Thirty-Three

Dusty walked back down to Rickety's barn, half-hoping the man wouldn't be there, but he was. Not only that, he seemed to be waiting for Dusty's return, gunning for him. "I can't have you and Ben telling me what to do with my business. A man has a right to make a living."

Dusty looked at him. "Well, that's just the point. You aren't making any money with that horse. He's done. You need to do right by him."

"If he hits the board even fourth, I'll get at least $750."

"Yeah, and he can also break down and you get nothing. Come on, Rickety, this is me you're talking to. You think I was just born yesterday. He's not going to hit the board unless the rest of the pack falls down in front of him. Come on."

Rickety shook his head.

"Is $750 all you want?"

"Well, that's just this week. I can run him back next week too."

Dusty stared at the man. Was he senile? "Give me the horse now. I'll take him right now. $1200."

Rickety appeared to be giving the offer thought, but then shook his head again.

"And..." Dusty said. "You'll be the first trainer to enter a horse into our "Forget Me Not Remember the Horse Program." Think about how that'll make you feel."

"The what?"

"The Remember the Horse Program. You've heard about it before, right. I think I recall you saying you thought it was a good idea."

Rickety stood looking at him, as if trying to register all this.

"I'll come get him in the morning. All right? This is him right here, right?" The horse was a large chestnut with four white socks. "You want the money in cash?"

Rickety nodded in a half-hearted way.

Dusty sighed. He needed to seal the deal. "Uh, the newspaper will probably want to interview you too. And we'll do a video and play it all day in the grandstand. This is a good thing you're doing, Rickety. I'm glad you agreed," he said, talking fast. He shook Rickety's hand. "I'll see you in the morning."

Ben smiled when Dusty told the story. "What did you call it?"

"Well, I can't remember the exact term. I suppose we're going to have to come up with one if we're going to do this."

Tom agreed, half asleep and stretched out on the cot in the tack room. He covered his face with his cowboy hat.

"Did you see all the scratches up at Aqueduct?" Dusty asked.

Ben nodded. "The racetrack business is at a crossroads."

"It's about greed, old man," Tom mumbled. "And not just horseracing. All sports."

"Yes, but we're dealing with living creatures."

"I hear ya."

"What?"

"I said I hear ya."

Dusty poured himself a cup of coffee and sat down. "With purses that high, people make careless decisions, or should I say callous decisions."

Ben looked at him. "I'd be interested to know how long the horses that broke down were in training."

"And the condition of the track; it'll be interesting to see the findings of the investigation."

"Aqueduct yet, and the caliber of horses they get up there." Ben shook his head.

Dawn had left to spend time with her in-laws back at her home. The blacksmith was due any minute, Randy was due any minute. It was going to be a busy afternoon in the Miller barn.

"I'm going to head over and see Wendy," Dusty said.

Tom raised his head. "What for?"

Dusty laughed. "Business."

"Oh. Okay," Tom said, getting comfortable again.

Ben called after him. "Let Joe know we're taking over Brubaker's old stalls."

"I will."

Tom got all of a fifteen-minute nap and woke up cranky. Randy wasn't in the best of moods either, even with the good news about his father. He was just plain too tired. When he left the racetrack he decided to go by the Club for a quick swim, hoping to revive himself before going home, and ran into Spears there.

The man was sitting poolside, sipping a rum and coke, and reading. Randy dove into the water, surfaced half a lap later and lay on his back, staring up at the ceiling while he floated.

"What are you drinking?" Spears asked.

"Beer sounds good," Randy replied.

Spears motioned to the bartender, and then Randy. The bartender nodded. Randy got out of the pool, grabbed a towel and sat down at Spears' table. He glanced at Spears reading material - charts, not a novel.

"What can I say? I'm a workaholic."

"What are you trying to figure out?" Randy asked. "Thank you," he said, to the bartender and downed a big swallow of ice-cold Bud. "Ah, that hit the spot."

"Well, between you and me, until I present it to Ben, I'm thinking we should shorten the amount of racing days in next year's meet."

"How many?" Randy asked, taking another swig of beer.

"Well, that's what I'm trying to figure out. A shorter meet, theoretically would mean more horses in a race, which would equal more revenue."

Randy looked at him.

"Believe it or not," Spears said. "Bettors are discerning. Just because a race only has five or six horses in it, doesn't mean they're going to wager a bet on one. Fans bet more when there are full fields."

Randy gave that some thought. "Wait a minute. The beer must have gone to my head."

Spears laughed. "Yes, more horses, one would think would automatically mean more wagering in a race, but if you dig deeper and study why...." He held up the charts. "It seems to all come down to choice. The fans want more choice, more to choose from. It's about winning, but it's also about playing the game. Do you want another?" Spears motioned to Randy's empty beer bottle.

"No, thanks," Randy said. "I'm done. I'll see you later. Thanks again." As he was leaving, he ran into Harland, Dawn's cousin Linda's husband. "I'll guess we'll be getting together for dinner in a few days."

"Yes, Aunt Maeve's coming to town."

"Who's having it? Us? You?"

Harland laughed. "I don't know."

"We're so informed," Randy said, chuckling. "Well, wherever it is, I'll see you." Uncle Matt was playing cards in the Captain's room. Randy walked in and shook his hand. He liked Uncle Matt, and Uncle Matt liked him; always referred to him as, "One hell of a man."

"Oh, look, you have three aces," Randy said, teasing. "Is that a good thing?"

The men at the table laughed, Uncle Matt included.

Randy checked on the horse at Shifting Gears on his way home. The horse didn't look great, but at least he was standing and responsive. Karen and Veronica were their usual, optimistic and worrier selves. This was a big horse. It was going to take a lot to get him back in good flesh. But he was in good hands. Both women were experienced at taking their time trying to rehabilitate a horse in this condition.

Randy drove on home and smiled at the scene laid out before him as he started up the driveway. His dad was pulling D.R. and Maeve round and round in circles in their wagon in stops and starts and the two children were teetering back and forth, laughing and giggling.

Dawn and his mother were sitting on the porch, drinking lemonade. Admittedly, several years back, when Dawn suggested they build a house on Ben's farm, he'd had mixed feelings. He'd always hoped to go into business with his sister; a veterinarian also. He could run the large animal practice. His sister specialized in small and exotic animals. It would make a nice mix. He'd soon realized though there was no way Dawn would ever leave Ben. He was like a father to her.

He thought about what Spears said about shortening the meet and how it would affect him directly. Less racing days would mean less Thoroughbred racehorse business, not that he couldn't use a lighter work load for that time difference each year. Beau's breeding schedule kept them all busy from January until March. Not racing until April might work out great.

"Why so serious?" Dawn asked, when he got out of the truck.

He smiled. "I was planning our future."

His dad waved at the children. "Your future is right here."

"Is Cindy happy?"

His mother looked at him. "Yes. Why?"

"Just wondering."

They all turned when Ben's truck pulled in off the road. He drove slow. He always drove slow. There were the children and the dogs to watch out for. Plus he liked looking at the horses in the pasture. The ponies were grazing. He smiled. Dawn was getting such pleasure out of those two ponies. He parked by his house and walked up to Dawn and Randy's. It was a beautiful day.

"Would you like some lemonade?" Liz asked.

"Don't mind if I do," Ben said, sitting down on the top step.

She poured a glass and handed it to him. "Thank you. I heard the good news," he said.

"I'm never going to doubt him again," Liz said.

Ben smiled. Randy Senior was making slower and slower circles. He was dizzy, the children were dizzy. He laughed. Tom pulled in off the road in his truck, parked next to Ben's, and got out and motioned he was going to go in and get some sleep. He walked into the house and straight upstairs and into his room, not noticing anything out of the ordinary. But Ben did. After he'd had his lemonade and visited for a little while, he walked home and was no sooner in the back door when his gaze fell upon the kitchen counter.

It wasn't the note that caught his eye; it was the dishes being done and put away, the counter clear. He staggered for a moment, in a state of shock. The note was from Linda Dillon.

"Ben, I cleaned up a bit. I didn't know how else to thank you. You have no idea what your kindness has meant to me. Linda."

Ben glanced around. It looked like she'd even mopped the floor. He sat down at the kitchen table and took off his hat. In his mind's eye, he could almost see Meg standing by the sink. She'd be looking out the window, looking for someone, but who...?

"Company," she said. She always loved company. She loved this kitchen. She turned and looked at him. "I love *you*, Mr. Miller."

He nodded and wiped his eyes. The last dish she made in this kitchen when she still had the strength had been lasagna, his favorite meal. A pan of it was in the freezer still, after all these years.

He laid his hat on the table. What was that she used to say when she'd get the spring cleaning bug? "Letting go of something doesn't mean you can't hold on to the memory."

He walked over to the freezer, dug out that pan of lasagna and looked at I, and smiled. It was all shriveled up and didn't even resemble anything edible, let alone lasagna. "I think I should have taken it out sooner." He dumped it down the disposal and ran water. "I shouldn't have waited."

He glanced in the sink when it was all said and done and smiled. Linda had scrubbed the sink too, and even the faucet. "Come to think of it," he said. "It needed done." When he heard the sound of a car, he gazed out the window. It was Charlie and Gloria. Perfect timing.

He walked out to greet them, shook Charlie's hand, and hugged Gloria. She was getting tinier and tinier.

"You look so good, Ben!" she said.

"So do you two!" Gloria smelled like lilacs. She always smelled like lilacs. Ben sneezed. When he'd had the stroke years ago and Gloria literally saved his life, that's all he remembered of that day, the smell of lilacs. "Come on inside, I'll put on some coffee."

"Oh, we can't have coffee," Gloria said, "not unless it's decaf."

"Then you're in luck," Ben said, chuckling. "That's all I have."

They had a lot of catching up to do. It had been months since their last visit.

"You *own* the racetrack?"

Ben laughed. "Yep, hard to believe, huh? Wait," he said, and took out his cell phone. "Watch this." He pushed a button and a second later was talking to Dawn, on speaker phone yet. "Gloria and Charlie are in town. Did you place the pizza order yet?"

"Yes, but I can add to it. What would they like?"

"The works," Charlie said. "I've given up enough."

Gloria laughed. "Works for me. I don't eat that much anyway."

Charlie and Ben smiled. That was one of her favorite sayings. Ben made a second pot of coffee. "What can it hurt?" he said. More catching up.

"Charlie, tell him," Gloria said.

Charlie hesitated.

"It's all right." She covered his hand with hers.

"You tell him," Charlie said.

Ben glanced from one to the other. He didn't have to be a mind-reader to suspect bad news.

"Charlie was diagnosed with prostate cancer."

Ben looked at him.

"No surgery, just radiation. And they're watching his PSA's."

"It could come back, and it could not," Charlie said.

275

"We're thinking positive," Gloria added. "It's not coming back."

Ben nodded.

"If it comes back, I'm done," Charlie said. "The radiation near killed me, and it was hard on Gloria."

Gloria looked at him. "I'm sorry."

"I know. You kept it to yourself, but I could tell."

"Being a nurse has its disadvantages," Gloria said, squeezing his hand. "I've seen the worst."

Ben looked from one to the other and couldn't help but think of Meg. He was holding her hand that same way as she took her last breath. He shook his head. "Well, I'm all for thinking positive. Come on. Let's us go bring your things in while we still have our senses."

Charlie and Gloria laughed and wiped their eyes. Whenever they came to town, they usually stayed with Dawn and Randy. "You're staying here this time," Ben said. "Randy's mother and father are in town. There's plenty of room here. By the way," he added, as they walked outside. "Tom's in love."

"What?" Charlie said.

"You're kidding," Gloria said. "Who? What's she like?"

"You'll meet her at dinner. She's Nottingham's Assistant General Manager."

"Do you like her? Does Dawn like her?" Gloria asked.

Ben nodded. "You'll both like her too."

Chapter Thirty-Four

D.R. and Maeve's nanny Carol was officially given the night off so Liz could "dote" on the children. Carol was like family and lived in her own suite at Dawn and Randy's. Occasionally she went to stay and visit with her daughter and grandchildren, but this was her home. She joined in with helping get ready for dinner. She always enjoyed Liz and Randy Senior's visits, and always enjoyed seeing Gloria and

Charlie. When they all gathered, it was always a party. For the most part, everyone was always happy.

For some reason, as she looked out the kitchen window she recalled the morning Shadow Pine died. He wasn't old, he wasn't sick. He just lay down in the pasture and died. She could still see Randy kneeling down next to him. She could see Dawn standing there, crying. Ben, sad. Tom, holding his hat in his hands. George and Glenda beside themselves.

"What happened?"

Randy shook his head. Shadow Pine was a favorite of all of theirs. He was coal black, stocky, happy. "That only happened after he was gelded," Randy told her. "It changed his attitude in an instant." He was a good racehorse. He was loved. He was buried right here on the farm. They rarely talked about him and when they did, it was always about the good times.

"Where's Tom," she asked.

"He went to get Wendy," Dawn said.

It was a beautiful evening, warm, with a gentle breeze. Tom followed Wendy's directions across town and turned down the road to her cul-de-sac, modern houses, nice size, nice landscaping. Wendy's house was the first house in the turnaround; a red brick and white vinyl-sided split level. He parked in her driveway and just sat there for a moment. It didn't look to him like the type of house she'd live in, and if it weren't for her car parked there....

I know so little about her, he thought.

There was a basketball net hung over the garage door, a spotlight. He could imagine the boys shooting hoops well into the night. He started his truck up and was just about to back out of the driveway when Wendy walked around the side of the house.

He felt like a deer caught in the headlights. Did he really just want to leave, to run? Why was he still sitting here?

Wendy smiled a tentative smile. It was if she could read his mind.

"I wasn't sure this was your house." he said.

"Actually, it's not. It's my mom and dad's. We took it over when they moved to Florida a few years ago."

"You look pretty," he said, but said it sadly.

"Dawn called. She wants us to pick up a bag of ice."

He nodded.

"I'll get my purse," she said. "Do you want to come in a minute?" Maybe she sensed he was going to leave, maybe she sensed his fear, maybe she had no inclination, maybe....

He got out of his truck and followed into the house, stood just inside the door. The living room was rather formal. He never quite understood "formal living rooms." What was the point? There was a family room, down three steps, a large television, comfy-looking furniture, tidy but with a lived-in look.

She walked out of the kitchen and their eyes met. "What?" she said.

Tom shook his head, thoughts swirling and swirling. "I'm thinking," he said, glancing up the stairs. "That there's a really nice bed up there, and that...." He reached for her hand. "Why don't you show me the way."

Chapter Thirty-Five

It was a party indeed! Tom and Wendy arrived a little late but the pizza hadn't been delivered yet. Everyone sat around laughing and talking, snacking on cheese and crackers, chips and dip, listening to music, and being entertained by the children. What a celebration! Randy Senior had gotten a clean bill of health. Charlie had gotten a new lease on life. Bo-T was okayed out of the starting gate, and Ben had survived another woman in Meg's kitchen.

It was definitely a banner day!

Here came the pizza and salads, the tables were already set, and everyone sat down.

"A moment of silence," Gloria said, and they all held hands. "Amen."

Wendy smiled, but was a little puzzled. She'd noticed before that no one here said grace at meals, something her father had always insisted on. She asked.

"Well," Dawn said, glancing at Tom. "By consensus, we decided after much discussion, and I mean much...." They all chuckled. Heated discussions would best describe those conversations around the table. She looked at Tom.

"I don't think with children starving all over the world, that it's appropriate to thank God for the food we eat. I don't think he has anything to do with it."

Gloria sighed. "And while I don't agree totally, I came to realize that maybe Tom was right."

"Well, halleluiah," Tom said, smiling.

"It's just that he made some good points," Gloria said. "We all still pray, we are all still grateful for our many blessings. But...."

"How could I thank God for feeding me, sinner that I was," Tom said, "and think for one minute that he wouldn't feed innocent children if he could. Yes, I know it says in the bible that Jesus fed the multitudes with five loaves of bread and two fish, but I think that was meant metaphorically."

Dusty looked at him. This religious side of Tom never ceased to amaze him.

"I think it actually meant spreading the word. There were so many people; the ones far, far away couldn't hear him. So they would all turn and share the message heard from the person in front of them, and were all fed."

Glenda, George, Randy Senior, and Carol nodded. "He convinced me," Liz said.

Wendy smiled. "Amen."

Charlie and Ben looked at Tom and then at one another. "Who would've thought?" Charlie said.

Ben nodded. "I know."

D.R. squealed. Here came the dogs.

"Down! Down! Down!" they all said, even Gloria. "Down!"

One by one, the dogs lay down, panting. They'd obviously all been in the pond.

Maeve giggled and waved her hand like a magic wand. "Down! Down! Down!"

Liz gave her a hug. "Oh, I'm going to miss you two." She hugged both grandchildren.

Randy Senior rolled his eyes. "Oh, Liz, don't do this to yourself."

She wiped her eyes. "I'm okay. I'm okay."

D.R. looked at her. "Grandma, don't cry. It be better."

Wendy glanced around the table at all of them looking on sympathetically, all caring, all happy, and yet all sad for a moment. She couldn't help but smile.

"Welcome to the family," Tom said, noticing.

"Thank you."

Dessert was Twinkies and ice cream. Oh good, Wendy thought. I'm not even tempted for once. "Fried Twinkies," Glenda added, "Crisp on the outside, warm and gooey on the inside, cold ice cream all around. You have no idea if you've never had one. How many do you want?"

Wendy sighed. "Oh dear. Two I guess."

"Just one for me," Gloria said. "Well, maybe two. But I usually don't eat much."

Little Maeve made a mess of hers and had it all over her face. D.R. ate three. "He'll never go to sleep," Dawn said. "He'll be bouncing off the walls."

Randy laughed. "That's the point. He's going to stay awake with Grandma all night." He turned the music up and Maeve started dancing. It was dusk, which signaled the timer for the tiny white lights threaded through the landscaping to come on. They looked like fireflies, hundreds of them.

"Oh, how pretty," Gloria said.

This was a "sing-along" family. The songs on the piped music were their favorites.

"Dance, Daddy, dance," Maeve said, reaching up her arms.

Randy picked her up and swirled her around. "My girl, my girl, my girl," he sang. "Talking about my girl, my girl."

Tom and George chimed in, "Do, do do..do do do doo... do do do dooo do do..."

"I got sunshine on a cloudy day! When it's cold outside, I've got the month of May."

Everyone sang along, laughing, pointing, swaying.... making words up along the way.

"I don't need anybody."

"Cause I've got my girl."

"Do, do do do do do doooo."

"Me, Daddy, me, Daddy," D.R. said.

Randy picked him up, a child in both arms, and they all sang the last verse, Wendy included. "That's all I can talk about, talk about, talk about is my girl!"

D.R. wiggled out of his dad's arms when the song was over, ran to his grandpa, and Randy handed Maeve to his mother.

"Oh no," Dawn said, laughing. Randy's, Tom's, and George's favorite song was coming up next.

"My turn, my turn," Tom said.

"Duke, Duke, Duke, Duke of Earl, Duke, Duke."

Everyone laughed. The trio stood together: Tom in the middle, Randy and George on each side of him. "Duke of Earl, Duke, Duke, Duke of Earl, Duke, Duke...."

Tom took the lead, singing to Wendy. "As I, I walk through this world, nothing can stop the Duke of Earl, and you, you are my girl, and no one can hurt you, oh no."

Wendy laughed.

"Yes, well I...." They all twirled. " I...I'm gonna love you, oh oh...let me hold you darlin'. Oh yea, yea, yea, yea...."

They all three turned around in a synchronized circle and leaning forward, moved three steps one way and three steps back. By now everyone was laughing so hard they had tears in their eyes.

"Boom ba ba boom ba ba boom ba ba boom." The rolled their arms, looking every bit a DooWap trio. "Ooh, ooh, ooh ooh, ooh...Duke of Earl. Ah ah ah ah.... Oooh ooh ooh, ooh ooh, ah ah ah ah."

Their audience roared, the children clapping their hands and squealing!

"I'm going to love you," Tom sang, all three pointing, twirling again, arms criss-crossed on their chests. "Cause I...I...." The grand finale. "I'm the Duke of Earl. Yeah, yeah, yeah...."

Everyone clapped, squealed, and whistled. The performers took a bow. Another bow.

"What's all this commotion?" they heard someone say.

"Hey, T-Bone," Randy said. It was the old farmer from next door. They hadn't heard his truck pull in with all the noise they were making.

"A little birdie told me someone was making fried Twinkies over here tonight."

Glenda smiled. She'd dropped him off a casserole earlier today. The man was getting as skinny as a toothpick. "Have a seat. You want some coffee with it?"

"Sounds good, don't mind if I do."

He shook hands with all the men, smiled and nodded to all the women. "I don't think I know you," he said to Wendy.

"And you won't," Tom said. "She's mine."

Wendy chuckled. "Possession is nine-tenths of the law."

The old man liked that. "I've been possessed all my life."

They all laughed.

"Can I have this dance?" Tom said to Wendy, leading her away. She melted into his arms. It was an Anne Murray song, one of her favorites. He sang along softly. She loved the sound of his voice, his embrace, the smell of his skin. "When we're together, it feels so right. Can I have this dance, for the rest of our lives?"

"Yes," Wendy said.

Tom twirled her around and pulled her back into his arms. They weren't far from everyone else, but in a world all of their own.

"If you break my heart, I'll never speak to you again," Wendy said.

"That'll never happen," Tom said. "Ever. It's not possession; it's a commitment, as God is my witness."

Wendy looked into his eyes, as they both listened to the words of the song. "Would you be my partner every night?"

"Yes."

"Yes."

When Wendy kissed him, everyone clapped, and they both laughed.

"I got the point," T-Bone said. "You don't have to show me!"

As near as anyone could figure, T-Bone had to be at least eighty years old, but was as spry as ever. The only thing slowing down was his appetite. He and Ben and Randy Senior and Charlie talked about their current health limitations. He was sorry to hear about Charlie's "run-in with cancer." He shook his head. "Don't let it get you down. We're all going to die someday from something."

Charlie laughed. "Thank you for that bit of encouragement."

T-Bone nodded, spooning the last of the Fried Twinkie into his mouth.

Randy Senior looked at the three of them; they were only slightly older than him. He looked at Randy and his grandchildren. He looked at his wife Liz.

"So how are things back at the farm?" T-Bone asked him.

"Well, it's a lot work. I don't mind work though. What I do mind, is not seeing my kids and my grandkids as often as we would like. I never thought they'd move away."

Randy heard that, Dawn heard that, Liz heard that.

"Dad," Randy said.

"It's okay," Randy Senior said. "It's okay."

"I'm a racehorse vet, Dad. I have to be where the racetrack is."

"And your sister?"

Randy hesitated. "When her internship is up…."

His dad nodded. "I just never thought you would both move away."

What could Randy say? What could anyone say?

Cat Stevens was singing all about the first cut being the deepest.

"So, Liz," Randy Senior said. "I say we sell the farm and move near one of them and hope the other one will follow."

Tears welled up in his wife's eyes. "Don't say that if you don't mean it."

"I mean it."

Randy walked over and shook his dad's hand and gave him a hug. He hugged his mother. He hugged Dawn.

"Now wait a minute. I ain't selling you my farm," T-Bone said.

They all laughed.

When the Cat Stevens song ended and the theme from Sesame Street came on, the dogs started howling. Everyone knew the words to this one. "Sunny days ~ ~ !" Little Maeve clapped her hands. "Keeping the clouds away ~ ~ !"

Chapter Thirty-Six

Tom and George did night check in the barns; Wendy and Glenda walked along behind Ben, Dusty, Charlie and Gloria as they walked to Ben's house. The dogs followed. "I'll see you all tomorrow," Dusty said. T-Bone had left a few minutes earlier. It was a full moon. Glenda settled into their truck. Wendy stood by Tom's truck to wait. Rotty, the standard poodle, sat down next to her.

All was well with the horses. George climbed in behind the wheel, they waved, and Tom turned to Wendy. "We have a choice," he said, wrapping his arms around her. When Rotty barked at him, he laughed. "I can take you home now, or I can take you home early in the morning."

Wendy hesitated. "The house is full. I don't think I'd feel right."

"The first floor's full. I'm up there," he said, pointing to the second floor.

Wendy stared. "I didn't even realize there was an upstairs."

"It's just a bedroom and a bath." He smiled and kissed her. "We'll be all alone. I promise to be good."

She chuckled. After all, she did admit she wanted to see this side of Tom. She drew a breath and sighed. "I married my childhood sweetheart, Tom. My father's a minister."

"And...?"

"And." She shrugged. Back at her house earlier, that was pure passion. What she was feeling now was passion. "What's our future?"

"Our future? You and me are destined to be together. When your sons are okay with it, were going to get married. I asked and you said yes, remember? And we're going to live happily ever after."

"Where though? Here, my house, where?"

Tom looked at her. "Wow, you are serious, aren't you?"

Wendy glanced around the farm, the barns, the pastures, the sky, the sounds of the horses, the dog at her side. "I can't ask you to leave all this."

Tom smiled. "Good, so since that's all settled, come on." When he tugged her toward the house, she laughed. "Shhh..." he said, "We don't want to wake the grownups." Rotty walked along next to them and lay down on the porch outside the screen door. Wendy patted his head and rubbed his belly and then followed Tom inside. When they came back outside at four-thirty in the morning, the dog was still guarding the door.

It was the coolest morning they'd had in months, a hint of the inevitable change to come in the weather. The horses were all "wound up." Dawn attempted to hand-walk Bo-T around the shedrow and promptly handed him over to Tom.

He chuckled. "I have one to pony for Gibson. You gonna go do it for me?"

"It would probably be safer than walking *him*." She watched Tom muscle Bo-T down the shedrow. Ben glanced out at them from his desk in the tack room. Bo-T was higher than a kite, as racetrack expressions go.

This colt just might be the one to rival Beau Born, he thought, and went back to studying the condition book. The race for Bo-T on Saturday was 6 furlongs. He would prefer to start him at 5 or 5 ½ furlongs, but they stopped writing those races this time of year. That's another thing he'd change. "Next year," he said to himself. "Ah, Jesus, now I sound like Spears."

Bo-T swung around the corner of the shedrow, kicking, bucking, kicking, and bucking some more. "Hey, now, hey, now," Tom sang. "Don't treat me wrong, now…."

There was a race on Sunday, going 6 ½ for two-year old maidens, even further than he wanted to go, but the pace would be different, slower, probably a better choice for a first-time starter.

Bang!

Bo-T kicked one of the shedrow railings. It sounded like a gunshot and caused an avalanche of horses bucking and kicking in their stalls. Ben shook his head. It doesn't take much to spread racing plates. His shoes were just reset yesterday.

Training a horse to run at its best, its peak, giving it the best possible opportunity to run well and finish strong is an art in itself, he'd explained to Dawn when she first came to the track. Today was Wednesday. Ideally, he'd run him on Friday. But there was no two-year old race for Friday.

Ben sat scratching the back of his neck. Bo-T was not one to be rated, even when working in company, let alone a race. He always wanted to charge to the lead and stay on the lead. Here came Bo-T again, still bucking and kicking. "Enough of this." Ben stuck his head out of the tack room. "Tack him up. Let's gallop him before he hurts someone or himself."

Since this wasn't scheduled as a training day for Bo-T, Tom put him away and headed up to the kitchen to grab Johnny. Back at the barn, Ben glanced at Dawn down at Bo-T's stall, bridle and exercise saddle in hand, and…. "What? You need a butterfly net to catch him?"

Dawn shook her head. Bo-T was still showing off. Every attempt to get a hold of his halter set him off all over again. He was having fun! Discretion being the better part of valor, Dawn walked back to the tack room. "I think we'll wait for Tom," she said rather matter-of-factly. Ben nodded in agreement. His days of wrangling two-year olds were long past.

"Everyone's loving the Ginny stand," Tom said, upon his return. "It's a full house!"

"Did you see Johnny?" Ben asked.

"Yep, he'll be down in a few minutes. Is he tacked?"

"Nope." Dawn handed him Bo-T's bridle and exercise saddle. "He's all yours." The horse was standing at the front of his stall, bobbing his head up and down as if was about to take flight, and kicked and kicked and kicked.

Ben walked up to the racetrack, climbed the steps to the Ginny stand and took a seat on the bottom bleacher. He was one of at least twenty owners and trainers sitting there, and if asked, that's all he considered himself sitting there, an owner, trainer.

"This is nice, Ben." Lucy Davis said.

He nodded, and then debated whether or not he should say, 'Thank you.'

"It's about time," he said, instead, as one of them.

They all agreed.

Mim drove up in her golf cart and got out and climbed the steps, using the railing and her cane for support. She sat down next to Ben.

"Mim," he said.

"Ben."

Ben leaned forward and looked past her to see Tom on Red, leading Bo-T and Johnny. He sat back and crossed his arms, watched as they walked out onto the racetrack, watched as they jogged down past the grandstand.

"Is that Beau Together?" Mim asked.

Ben nodded.

When Tom turned them around, Red and Bo-T broke into a nice canter, but by the time they got down in front of Ben, Bo-T was fighting to run off. Johnny had a strangle hold on him, as did Tom, and still....

"Hold him, hold him," Ben mumbled under his breath. "Hold him...." The last thing he wanted was for him to run off, and there's only so much a pony can do to keep a horse in

287

check if it's hell bent on running off. As they started down the backside, Bo-T settled down a little, no longer climbing, and started galloping in a strong, even stride. "All right, all right," Ben said, in his mind. "All right, you can let him go."

As if he could hear him, with the very next stride, Tom let Bo-T and Johnny go and the colt galloped on strong. No playing, no looking around, no fighting, just a good racehorse gallop. Ben nodded. He galloped strong around the turn. Oh no, Ben thought, looking down the stretch. There were two horses working on the rail.

Bo-T came up on them with ears pinned and tenacious. When they crossed the wire he was better than two lengths in front of them. Ben took off his hat and stared down at the floor.

"I take it that wasn't the plan," Mim said softly.

Ben shook his head and raised his eyes just as Johnny and the large colt galloped into the turn. Tom was waiting for them out in the middle of the track. When Ben drew a breath and sighed, Mim patted him on the back. "He's grand looking, Ben. I'll give you that."

Ben nodded. Small consolation at the moment.

As they paraded in front of the Ginny stand, Johnny looked in at Ben and drew a breath and sighed. It was as if time stood still for Ben then, as if everything and everyone was moving in slow motion. Bo-T walked off the track next to Tom and Red, Johnny turned and smiled. Bo-T looked so much like Beau Born, for a second....

Mim touched his arm. "I had a dream the other night," she said, "where you turned this all around. And it was almost as good as it used to be, and in some ways even better."

Ben smiled.

"I don't believe in dreams as a rule, but I'm sure hoping this one comes true."

Dusty, Dawn, and Wendy walked down Rickety's shedrow, halter, lead shank, pen, pad, and video camera in hand. Rickety looked up as they approached. Dusty saw the horse's stall empty. His heart dropped.

"He's on the walking machine," Rickety said. "I've done already cleaned that stall once today."

When they all three turned, Renegade Man looked at them and nickered imploringly.

"How long have you been walking him?" Dusty asked.

Dawn shook her head. "I don't want to know," she said, motioning. "Let's just get on with this."

Dusty produced the money. He had Rickety sign a Bill of Sale. Wendy had the horse's Registration Papers. Dawn filmed Rickey signing them over. She filmed Dusty congratulating him for being the first owner-trainer at Nottingham Down to provide a horse to the Thoroughbred Rehoming Project. She filmed Dusty shaking the man's hand.

The horse was so tired of walking around in circles on the walking machine; they unhooked him and were able to switch halters right then and there. Rickety smiled a big grin for the video camera.

"He used to be a good horse," he said.

Used to be? As they started down the road between the barns Dawn took the horse from Dusty and walked on ahead. "That man won't be getting any stalls here next year," she said.

Dusty and Wendy nodded, following along. From the look in Dawn's eyes as they'd left Rickety's barn, that didn't come as a surprise to either of them.

Dawn patted the horse gently on his shoulder. "Nottingham Downs is going to be the standard that horsemen will have to live up to and other racetracks aspire to. Put that on the video."

Dusty nodded, camera rolling. "I already have it."

Chapter Thirty-Seven

The jockeys sat waiting. Ben had called for a short meeting, scheduled for just before the first race, and they all had a feeling it was about the soft whips. They were right. When Ben, Tom, Dusty, and Spears entered the room, Ben got right to the point. "You all know me," he said. "You know where I've been, which is right here at Nottingham Downs my entire racing life, and you know what we're up against. We're trying to save Nottingham Downs and maybe even more importantly, we're trying to save Thoroughbred racing."

He glanced at Spears. His turn. "I just read a startling statistic today. A racetrack an hour up the road had only seven hundred and fifty spectators yesterday. Seven hundred and fifty. Can you imagine a rock star singing for seven hundred and fifty people?" He paused, glancing around the room. "The first thing I thought was, does it matter to a jockey if no one sees him ride in a race? If no one sees him win? If no one sees how he puts his life on the line every time he gets on the back of a Thoroughbred?"

Silence....

"Well, I hate to say it but that seems to be where it's headed, for the majority of the tracks at least, for the majority of you, and me." He paused, just long enough. "But the good news is, this past month at Nottingham Downs has people sitting up and taking notice. We're making a change. We're a racetrack that cares and people like that. My phone's ringing off the wall. People are happy with what's going on here, and not just in the industry."

He looked at Dusty. His turn. "The horses matter here, you all matter here. There is no way any of us on this end would be here today, without you jocks."

They all hooped and hollered. It wasn't often they heard such a statement.

"We're concerned about your well-being; we're concerned about the horses' well-being."

Tom spoke next. "We're wanting more input from all of you. We want to try and make things happen. One, and I'm sure you know where this is headed, we want to be the first race track where a soft whip is the norm. No more fucking beating a horse up. It's over. The public doesn't like it, we don't like it. I'll bet even you all don't like it."

Another wave of silence flooded the room.

"We want to do it. We want to make it happen. We want to do it for your safety, and we want to do it for the horses' safety."

Silence still....

Tom smiled. "But we don't know how to make it happen. We're clueless."

The jocks all laughed.

"That, and..." Tom said. "We don't want to make decisions that you all have to live with, if you're not onboard." He shrugged. "So, how do we go about making this happen?"

"You're asking us?" Juan said.

"Who else? You're the ones out there every day. It's going to affect you the most."

The jocks looked around the room at one another.

"We have an open-door policy here at Nottingham Downs," Spears said. "What concerns you, concerns us."

"Thank you for your time," Ben said. "Be careful, be safe." With that, the four of them turned and walked out of the room.

They met with the Stewards next. "We just want to keep you informed," Ben said. "We want us all to work together." Spears passed out a copy of an article published in a national magazine about "The Downside of Thoroughbred Racing."

"It ain't pretty," Tom said.

Ben had already read it, Tom had read it, Spears had read it, Dusty had read it. They all read it again along with the Stewards who were seeing it for the first time. "So again," Ben said, "in wanting to keep you informed and all of us working together, we want you to know we're going to be addressing these issues. It doesn't appear to be getting better, it's getting worse."

"All this has been said before," one of the Stewards commented, shrugging. "It'll pass."

"Not at this racetrack," Tom said. "You're not listening. We're going to change racing as we know it. This era here," he said, as he waved the article, "this is over."

The man sat back, slightly miffed, and found himself being scrutinized by Ben. "Since I'm new to this someone will have to tell me. Do you have a contract? When is it up?"

Spears wished Wendy was here. She'd know.

"The end of the year," the Steward said.

"I see."

Spears scanned the article for the umpteenth time, read parts of it out loud. "Mandatory necropsies of all euthanized horses. Stiffer penalties for drug violations for horses tested. More random testing of the field after a race."

Ben nodded. "We're not waiting until next year on this. So you," he said to the Steward in question. "You need to either get on board or there's the door."

"I am on board, Ben. You know that. I was just saying...."

"I know, I know," Ben said. "Racing has been under fire before. But nothing like this. This is not going away. And you know what, racing *needs* to be held accountable. Every horse that leaves Nottingham Downs, we're going to know where he's going. No more killers. No more performance-enhancing drugs. No more. One violation and they lose their stalls. One! If that's tougher than what's mandated by the state, then so be it."

When Ben turned and walked out, Dusty and Spears followed. Tom looked at the three Stewards and the one in particular. "It's not good to piss him off," Tom said. "God bless you all."

"We're all on the same team, Tom," the man called after him.

"Precisely," Tom said, giving them a thumbs-up over his shoulder.

The three men looked at one another and sighed collectively. "Mark this date," the Steward sitting in the middle said. "History is being made."

Chapter Thirty-Eight

Wendy looked up from her desk when they entered the office and smiled. "How'd it go?" When Tom filled her in, she looked at Ben. "Oh my."

He sighed. "I rarely lose my temper."

"It sounds like it was warranted."

Ben nodded. "Even so…."

The four men sat down at Ben's desk table and all glanced out the window when they heard the sound of the bugle announcing the post parade for the first race. Something as simple as that seemed to lighten the mood. There were about fifty people outside watching the horses walk onto the racetrack.

The bugler was fast becoming a hit. Not only did he blow the bugle announcing the race, he usually followed that up with another tune. The fans were loving it. He was like a racetrack pied piper. On Sunday when he played "Run for the Roses" people had tears in their eyes.

Ben, Spears, Tom, and Dusty went over their list of concerns. Ben was impressed with how many were brought up and how many had solutions already underway. Dusty was proving to be the voice of the horsemen and women. He shared some of their questions, their hopes and their fears. "The biggest worry is that we won't be here next year, and that many of them will have nowhere to go."

"Well, they're not alone in that," Ben said. "How are you doing with the HBPA?"

"Good," Dusty said. "We're working on making them a formidable voice. They feel, particularly the last three or four years, that their presence had been diminished."

Ben nodded. "I'm glad you're on top of that."

Tom smiled. "Damn, old man, listen to you. You're getting good at this."

Ben laughed. "I guess I did kinda sound like an exec-u-tive."

"Speaking of which," Spears said, smiling as he exaggerated straightening his tie. "I have a meeting with the Andrew Lang Beiber Cultural Society. The founder was big into racing years ago and with his passing, they want to do a tribute in the form of a stake race next year."

Wendy held up her hand without looking their way. "I've got the stats. They're on your desk upstairs."

"What about the possibility of offering horsemen's insurance?" Tom asked. It was a topic brought up when Billy Martin passed away.

"I'm getting quotes and close to narrowing the choice of underwriters," Spears said. "When I get it all together, I'll present it." Another item checked off the list."Which brings me to one of my main concerns. I don't have all the figures complete, but on the subject of racing days, shortening the meet...."

"I'm all for it," Ben said. They all were.

"There won't be an issue with less days," Spears said. "I have the ball rolling on that, but night racing one night a week, that's going to be a different thing." He surveyed the disappointment on their faces. "I'm hopeful though, and I'm working on it."

"What about doing away with the cost of parking and admission?" Tom asked.

"Well." Spears sat back. "From all indications, eliminating a parking fee and the cost of admission works in some aspects and others it does not."

"Meaning?"

"Meaning...." He walked to his desk and came back with a list of figures. "At the end of the day, the take is just about even."

"You mean if they don't pay admission and parking, that money goes to betting?" Tom asked.

"Yes. That's the plus side. The downside is how it plays out at the end of the day."

"You mean, the handle as opposed to generated revenue?" Tom said.

Spears looked at him.

"I'm getting it," Tom said, laughing. "And anytime you want to ride a horse it's okay with me."

They all laughed, Wendy included.

"Next?" Ben said.

"A chapel," Dusty said, glancing at his list. "Pastor Mitchell's thinking maybe he could set up one where Rupert used to be."

"What's wrong with where they're at?" Ben asked.

"Come on, Ben, it's a shared space. They meet in the HBPA office," Tom said. "He would like a sacred space."

"A sacred space?" Ben sat back. Spears sat back. "Do you really think that's necessary on a racetrack?" Ben asked. "There are churches everywhere. There's two right across the street."

Dusty and Tom just looked at him.

"All right," Ben said. "Nothing fancy though, right?"

Both men shook their heads. They had no idea what Pastor Mitchell had in mind. They'd just promised to help.

Wendy looked up when someone entered the office. It was a jockey, one that had obviously just ridden in a race judging from the dirt on his silks and boots. "Hello," she said.

Juan nodded and glanced over her shoulder. "Ben...?"

"Yes." He waved him in.

"The jocks would like to meet with you all after racing today. All right?"

"All right," Ben said. "Good." When Juan turned around and walked out, Ben shook his head. "I can't believe I didn't watch the race. We're sitting right here, and...." He pointed outside. "We're right here."

"Welcome to my world," Spears said.

Ben nodded and lowered his eyes to the table.

"I know you don't like monitors, Ben," Wendy said. "But I can have the announcer piped in."

"That would probably be a good idea," he said, dumfounded as he looked out at the racetrack. The horses from the first race were already back in the barn area. The horses for the second race were already in the paddock. Here came the bugler again.

"Last on the agenda," Spears said, "The juggling of the pari-mutual employees. If we declare full time as thirty hours a week, six hours a day with full-time benefits secured, starting next year, we can cut our workforce back a third by four o'clock each weekday."

"You mean when the crowd dies down?" Dusty asked.

"The problem with that is, years ago people didn't mind standing in line. No one likes waiting now."

"How much does cutting back save us?" Ben asked.

"Frankly, not enough."

"What's the alternative?"

"Not messing with their hours and keeping a crowd here until the last race."

Chapter Thirty-Nine

Tom had a horse to pony in the fifth, saddled Red, and walked him down toward the tack room. Ben looked up and then glanced at his watch. "Why so early?"

"Well, dear," Tom said. "I thought I'd ride on down and check out Rupert's place, that's if you won't mind my being away for awhile."

Ben laughed. "You're such an ass."

Tom led Red outside and mounted. "I'll be back."

"I'll be here."

Tom rode down between the barns thinking, how many years have we been partners? Eighteen? Twenty? "Hey, Joe," he said, to one of the grooms. The man waved. Twenty one? Yes, twenty one. Damn, that's a long time.

Rupert was standing outside his new store. "I think you need a hitching post," Tom said. He dismounted Red and dropped his reins, ground tying him. "Well, look at this," he said, walking inside the store. "This looks great. Was all this stuff in the other place?"

"Yep, stacked on top of each other."

Tom stepped back. "It looks good. Has the secret shopper been by yet?"

Rupert laughed. "You ass."

"Wait a second," Tom said, laughing himself. "That's the second time someone's called me that in less than five minutes."

"If the foo shits, wear it," Rupert said.

"All right, just for that I'm leaving." Tom walked out and get back on Red.

"Thanks, Tom."

He nodded.

"I think this'll work out good."

"I think so too."

"Hey, Tom," another pony boy said in passing.

"Who do you have?"

"Gleason's. How about you?"

"Wilson's."

Tom rode Red down to the Wilson barn and sat outside waiting and thinking and yawning.

"And they're off."

He turned in the saddle. From this barn, he could see the horses going down the backside, but lost them as they went into the turn. He could hear the call of the race, but it too came in waves. From the sound of the crowd cheering as the horses ran down the stretch, a favorite must have been winning. The roar built to a fevered pitch, louder, louder, and louder, and then nothing.

He yawned some more. It's all Wendy's fault, he said to himself. She kept me up too late. Wilson's groom led their horse out and handed him over to Tom. He'd ponied this horse before. It had a nervous little twitch, wore full blinkers, and once literally tried to climb in Tom's lap.

"Let's see if we can keep your feet on the ground this time."

The horse sighed.

"Yeah, I know, that was last year. I'm just reminding you," Tom said.

His groom laughed. She was about nineteen and thought Tom was absolutely the most gorgeous cowboy she'd ever laid eyes on.

"Here, here," Tom said, when the horse started acting silly. He smoothed the horse's mane, patted him gently on the neck. By the time they got up to the racetrack, the horses from the previous race were coming off and back into the barn area.

"Who win?" Tom asked.

"Jasper Run."

"Was it close?"

"Photo."

At Nottingham Downs, horses were ponied to the grandstand and handed over to their grooms at the paddock entrance. Years ago, ponies were allowed inside the paddock, which served to help calm the Thoroughbreds. Having the same horse standing in front of the stall that just led them there added a feeling of safety; a small herd amongst a larger herd. Too many horses in the paddock added chaos at times though and about ten years ago the new rule came into effect. Ponies were to wait out on the track. Once the horses were saddled and riders up, the grooms or trainers or an occasional owner led the horse out to pony boy or girl for the post parade.

The bugle sounded!

"God, I love that," Tom said. He nodded to the musician.

The bugler waved and as he walked back inside, played a rendition of "Here Comes the Sun." Definitely fitting for this gorgeous day; the sun had just peeked out from behind the clouds.

For races going 5, 5 ½, or 6 furlongs, once the horses are loaded in the gate the pony boys and girls gather in the chute on the backside and out of the way. For mile races or longer, they gather to the back of the quarter pole chute.

Tom's horse warmed up nicely and was relatively calm. The jockey was a "bug boy;" an apprentice. Tom told jokes as they cantered toward the starting gate and the jock laughed.

He'd started out a little nervous, this being only his fourth mount. The race was a flat mile. When his horse loaded easy, Tom turned and cantered Red toward the quarter-pole chute.

The number nine horse being loaded reared and unseated his jockey. The gate crew handler lost his grip on the reins and the horse did a 180 degree turn and took off running. There are two outriders in every race, lead ponies for keeping the peace, catching loose horses, being there for an injured horse, the jockey....

"Loose horse!" Tom heard someone yell and turned in his saddle. The horse had gotten a jump on the outrider stationed at the back of the starting gate and was running in Tom's direction. The outrider stationed at the front of the starting gate was already galloping his horse into the first turn in pursuit of catching him the other way if he got around that far.

When Tom saw the racehorse charging toward him, reins over his head and almost getting hung up in the rein loop with each stride, he didn't think twice. Judging which path the horse might take to get around him - from his being on his right lead, Tom took to the outside. Red danced and cantered in place, all pumped up in anticipation. When the loose horse was about a furlong away, Tom nudged Red and Red took off, eyes wide and determined. The horse galloped up next to him, Tom and Red closed the gap between them, and again, gauging the Thoroughbred's stride, when the horse reached out with his inside lead, his inside front leg, on the next stride, Tom leaned way over as far as he could, as low as he could, and grabbed hold of the horse's reins.

"There now, there now," he said, again and again, to calm the horse. "There now."

The horse pulled up easily, was much obliged to turn around and canter alongside them back to the starting gate, and the crowd started cheering. Tom nodded, his way of saying thank you with his hands full, and the crowd clapped and cheered some more.

Wendy watched from the office window above, shaking her head, her heart still in her mouth. What if he'd gotten hurt, what if....?

Tom handed the horse over to two of the gate crew and since the other horses were all still loaded, waited behind the gate until this horse was loaded and latch sprung.

When horses break out of the gate for a mile race, the gate crew goes into quick action. They all climb onto the gate, the tractor driver turns the gate instantly, and they all barrel down the track to the chute and out of the way.

Tom chose to take Red the nearest path, the gap between the winner's circle and paddock, and stood there with Red still slightly wound up, his sides heaving. "Good boy," Tom said, patting him on the neck. "Good job."

The track photographer turned his camera on him, snapped several pictures and called to him. "Showoff!"

Tom laughed, shaking his head. "Don't try that at home."

Everyone within hearing distance clapped and yelled!

The horses were running a tight race down the backside. When Tom leaned forward, resting his arm on Red's neck as he watched, the photographer took another photo of him. The Wilson horse that Tom had ponied for the race ended up running fourth. The loose horse ran second.

Wendy posted a notice on both the inside and outside of the jockeys' room door stating that the requested meeting would be held up in the dining area of the clubhouse after the last race and that food would be served.

"Are you kidding me," Tom said. "Do you have any idea how much jocks eat?"

Wendy chuckled. "I confess. I had two ulterior motives. One, I didn't want anyone in a hurry to leave. Meetings don't go well under those circumstances, particularly if someone is hungry. Two, I wanted to let Chef Diamond Lou showcase his talents."

"Chef Diamond Lou? You're kidding. That's really his name?"

"Yes, that's really his name." She looked up at him. "By the way, did you know that horseback riding is the third most dangerous sport in the world?"

Tom looked at her. "You mean it's not number one? Damn!"

"I'm serious," Wendy said. "I read an article about it this afternoon after you practically stood on your head to catch that horse. See?" She pointed to her computer.

Tom glanced at the screen. Having someone worry about him was new. He wasn't so sure he liked it. "Yes, it's dangerous, Wendy. Horses are unpredictable and all that, but it's what I do. Are you coming upstairs?"

Wendy hesitated. "I'm sorry, it's just that...."

"It's all right, come on, let's go. We don't want to worry Chef Diamond Lou, do we?" He took her by the hand.

"This is my tenth trip upstairs today," she said. When Tom just nodded, Wendy sighed. "It's just that my husband didn't think he'd ever get hurt either."

"I'm not your husband, yet. I'm not dead, yet. And I can't live that way, Wendy. Okay?"

"Okay," she said. "I'm sorry."

Tom stopped and looked at her. "Sorry for what?"

"For loving you," she said, somewhat angrily, and pounded the stairs as she walked on up.

Tom shook his head, smiling as he followed her. "Now that I can understand."

Wendy kept walking and never looked back.

Most of the jockeys had already arrived and were helping themselves to the grand buffet Chef Diamond Lou had laid out before them. Ben, Dusty, and Spears milled about. Tom went straight for the roast beef and mashed potatoes. The jockeys that had ridden in the last race straggled in after showering, filled their plates, and everyone sat down. Conspicuously absent was the presence of alcoholic beverages. Two waitresses went from table to table, pouring water and hot coffee.

"Decaf?" Ben asked.

"Yes," the woman said.

Ben laughed. "No democracy here."

Wendy smiled. "Dawn said not to let you be tempted."

When Chef Diamond Lou came to check on their meal and Wendy introduced him, he took a bow and everyone cheered.

"We're having entirely too much fun," Tom said.

Everyone laughed again.

"Speaking of fun, weren't you supposed to call me?" Jockey Nancy Davis teased from across the room. "I've been waiting by the phone for weeks."

Tom smiled, pretended to be "busted" with Wendy standing there, and they all laughed again. "Seriously," he said, "I'd like to introduce you to my future wife. She's a little pissed at me at the moment...." He smiled when she sighed and shook her head. "See, she's giving in already."

Wendy laughed. Tom was just plain irresistible.

"She brought up a good point today though," Tom said. "It's about the danger of horseback riding. I'm sure you all know that it's the third most dangerous sport in the world. I confess I didn't know. I'd actually never given it much thought."

He'd silenced the room. He had a way of doing that. "I hope we all keep that in mind when we decide what's best for each of us here today. Our safety and our well-being."

Every jockey stood and clapped. Ben stood and clapped, Dusty stood and clapped, Spears stood and clapped. Wendy stood and clapped. Chef Diamond Lou wiped his eyes and clapped as well.

"All right, let's eat," Tom said.

Chef Diamond Lou walked from table to table answering questions about the different entrées, and was "so happy." He thanked Wendy every time he passed her and would give her a big hug and say, "Hugs, hugs, hugs," and would hug her again. "I will do your wedding, yes?"

"Sure," Wendy said, being hugged to death.

"Yes, yes, I go now." He bowed out of the room waving like royalty amidst hoots and hollers and cheers.

"This really is delicious," Spears said.

"The coffee's even good," Ben said, pouring another cup. "Are you sure it's decaf?"

Wendy nodded. "They promised."

When they'd all eaten the main course, their dishes removed, and were being served dessert; a four-berry torte drizzled with dark chocolate and topped with whipped cream, Tom tapped his water glass with a spoon.

Everyone looked up and laughed.

"Well, now that I have your attention," he said. He'd sensed a change in the mood the last couple of minutes and hoped to lighten things up again. It was time to get down to business. Ben looked across the tables at Juan, the leading jockey. From the way all of the other jockeys were looking at him, he was the apparent spokesperson.

Juan cleared his throat and took a drink of water. "We've given this thought. We have actually thought about it more than you all know. We want what's best too. We appreciate that you bought the soft sticks for us to see."

The jocks all nodded.

"I told you, I would try it. I will. But we are not sure one rider trying it out will tell us anything."

Ben listened. They all listened.

"We want to help you, Ben. We want to help you all. We want to help ourselves."

Ben nodded, thanking him.

"You say you want to change all of us to a soft whip by next year. We only have a few months left for this meet, so that's not that far away." Juan looked around the room. "We know what you are trying to do. You want to help racing. We do too. We want to win races."

Tom looked at Ben. He looked at Dusty and Spears. He looked at Wendy. "We see no reason," Juan said, "to not change to soft whips. If everybody uses them, we are all the same. There is no disadvantage. But none of us know how it will turn out."

Tom smiled. This seemed to be headed in the right direction.

"Not unless we try it now."

Ben sat back. "What are you saying?"

"I'm saying we're ready to try it. With everything you have done and all that you are all doing to try and save this racetrack, we think it's the least we can do."

"Thank you," Ben said.

Juan smiled. "There is one more thing, actually two things. Our biggest fear is being accused of not trying hard. If the horse does not respond to the soft stick, we do not want blamed."

Ben nodded. That was understandable. "There might be some kinks there to work out. What's the second thing?"

"Uh...." Juan looked around the room at the other jockeys. "We want to know who's paying for these new sticks."

Ben smiled, the others laughed. "We'll take care of that."

"Thank you, Ben."

"No," Ben said. "Thank you. All of you."

Chapter Forty

Dusty, Tom, and Wendy pulled into the driveway of the Shifting Gears Thoroughbred Rescue Farm, parked their vehicles and walked into the barn. "Oh no," Veronica said. "What's the matter?"

"Nothing." Tom smiled.

"Why do you always do that?" Karen said to her. "You give me a heart attack."

Dusty laughed. He'd known these two women for years. They never changed.

"I'd like you to meet Wendy," Tom said. "She and I are planning on getting married."

"Oh dear," Veronica said.

Karen laughed. "Don't mind her. Congratulations!"

"Thank you." Wendy shook her hand, and then shook Veronica's hand. "It's nice to meet you both. I've heard great things about you."

"Which is what we want to talk to you about," Tom said. "We want you to help us set up an "in between kind of Thoroughbred layover rescue in the meantime try and find them a home" program."

Karen smiled. "Come on. Let's go in the tack room and sit down."

Veronica tagged along behind them. "Is this for horses in the future? Do you have some already?"

"At the moment, we have one," Dusty said.

"What shape is it in?"

"He looks pretty good. He just needs some rest. We hope."

"Who does he belong to? Who's was he?"

"Well, he belonged to Rickety."

"Ah, Jesus," Veronica said, plopping down in a chair.

"The horse is at the track," Tom said. "He's getting good care."

"Who's taking care of him?" Veronica asked.

"Me," Dusty said.

"Oh thank God."

Karen agreed. "When does he have to be outta there?"

"Well, see, that's just it," Tom said, motioning for Dusty to explain.

"We're trying to come up with a way to keep horses in situations like this at the track for at least a week or so," Dusty said. "Maybe a little longer if need be."

"Horses on the track need a little time to come down off training," Tom said to Wendy. "Their grain needs to be cut back gradually, things like that. And if they've suffered an injury, they need stall rest, hand walking, that type of thing."

Wendy nodded, thankful for the explanation.

"Right now we have nine stalls," Dusty said. "What we're wanting to do is offer the horsemen the option to donate the horses to the rehab and rehoming program, and of course ultimately to find them homes."

"A major problem," Wendy said, "is we can't have people coming to the racetrack as prospects for these horses because of the liability. They can't ride them, they can't try them out. We need to work with a program like yours."

"But we don't have any room," Karen said.

"You know we'd like to help, but we're full," Veronica said, with tears welling up in her eyes.

Wendy hesitated. "Randy said you might know of other rescue organizations and I'm thinking maybe we can assist you in building a network, so that when a need arises...." She touched Veronica's arm. "I can help with that. I know very little about horses, but I know a lot about networking, and..." she added, "fundraising."

The two women looked at one another.

"I'm so tired," Veronica said.

"I know." Wendy could see that. The woman was near exhaustion. They both were.

"People start out caring, and they work hard," Karen said. "And then they just give up."

"We're not going to give up," Tom said.

They could hear the horses munching hay, hear them sigh.

"Do you remember Janie Pritchard?" Tom asked.

Both women nodded, both wiping their eyes now.

"She told me once, that a heart only beats when it has just cause. She said the sound of two hearts beating, one human, one horse, was a symphony."

Wendy looked at him, with tears welling up in her eyes.

"I hear music here. Music the world needs to hear. Listen...."

Dusty looked away, with big tears running down his face.

"We'll be back tomorrow," Tom said.

"Meanwhile," Wendy said, wiping her eyes and reaching inside her purse for her business card. She wrote her cell phone number on the bottom. "Call me if you need anything."

"Thank you," Karen said. "We will."

"Bless you both," Dusty said.

The three of them walked out into the night.

"I'll see you tomorrow," Dusty said.

Tom nodded. "Good night."

"Good night, Dusty," Wendy said.

When Dusty got into his truck, Tom looked at Wendy. "I keep promising to take you dancing," he said.

Wendy smiled. "I'm too tired."

"Perhaps just one dance," he said, taking her into his arms and swaying slowly, holding her tight. "I love you, pretty lady."

"I love you too, cowboy."

Veronica and Karen stood in the barn doorway, arms linked and smiling at the sight of them dancing under the stars.

Mid-morning, Ben walked over to the secretary's office and entered three horses.

"What?" Joe said. "You showing off now too?"

Ben chuckled.

"Did you see the newspaper?"

Ben nodded, smiling. Front page of the Sports section was a photo of Tom resting on Red after catching the loose horse. The caption read: "All in a Day's Work at Nottingham Downs."

"Everyone's talking about the jocks and the soft whips," Joe said.

On such short notice, it was impossible to get an article in the paper, but Dawn had managed to get a blurb in, promising details to follow. It was placed strategically on the Breaking News page.

Ben turned when he saw Spears. He still didn't look totally approachable, but at least he was making an effort to waltz through the secretary's office from time to time. "Have you seen Wendy?" he asked.

"She was just here," Joe said. "She said she was going to be up working on a video."

"Thanks." Spears nodded and walked away.

"What do you make of him?" Joe asked. "Seriously, just between you and me."

Ben looked at him. "I think he's doing a hell of a job."

When Joe smiled, Ben turned to leave. "Where's this video stuff done?"

"Up in filming."

"Which is where?" Ben asked.

"Up next to where Bud's at."

Ben rode the elevator to the third floor, walked down the corridor past the empty executive offices, and climbed a short flight of stairs toward the announcer's booth. Wendy was in the tiny room just this side of it. She looked up and smiled. "Hi, Ben."

"Morning." He sat down next to her and glanced at the small television screen in front of her. "What's this?

"It's the video we're going to run today." She played it for him. The two of them watched Rickety posing for the camera and bragging. It showed the horse being led down between the barns."I had to voice-over here." It showed the horse being turned loose in his new stall. It showed Dusty patting the horse on the neck. "Wishing you well on your next career, Renegade Man," Dusty said. "You'll always be a winner."

"I like it," Ben said. "What did you have to voice over?"

"Dawn," Wendy said. "She was not happy with Rickety."

Ben nodded and stood up to leave. "This looks good. Thank you. You're doing a good job."

Wendy looked up at him. "Thank you."

Ben started out the door and looked back. "Did you see the morning paper?"

Wendy smiled. "I saw it. I ordered a framed copy for my desk."

Ben looked at her. "Tom's who he is. Don't take that away from him."

Wendy nodded. "Thank you for the advice. I just wish his job wasn't so dangerous."

Ben smiled. "What's dangerous is that stairway," he said, pointing. They were like steep steps leading to the top of a lighthouse. "I'll yell I'm okay when I get to the bottom."

Wendy chuckled, and a moment later, heard. "I made it!" She laughed, and then sat reflecting on what he'd said. Had Tom talked to him about it? Or was he referring to Tom's comments at the jockeys' dinner? Either way, she felt as if she'd just gotten some fatherly advice she should heed. "He's right," she said out loud. "Tom's who he is."

After she dropped the video off in the media room, she walked to the barn, and saw Rotty sitting in the passenger seat of Randy's truck parked outside. "Hello," she said. "What are you doing here?"

Randy came out from under the shedrow, piled some items into one of the truck compartments and smiled. "He wasn't feeling so good this morning. I thought I'd take him in and get him checked out."

"Wassa matter?" she said, petting the dog and smiling when he licked her face and wagged his tail. "Wassa matter? Wassa matter?"

Randy chuckled. "What is it with women when they talk to dogs?"

Wendy shrugged. 'I'll see you later, Rotty," she said.

Randy climbed in behind the wheel and sat marveling. When Wendy walked away, the dog starting crying. Not a little cry, a loud howl. Randy rolled up the windows. Last thing he needed was for the dog to spook a horse with this mournful sound. As he backed the truck up and started to pull out, Rotty pressed his nose against the window pane.

Wendy looked at him. "Geez, that's heartbreaking. I hope he's all right."

Dawn appeared at her side. Rotty never took his eyes off Wendy. He just kept staring woefully, staring and staring and howling and crying. Dawn and Wendy heard him still crying even after Randy pulled out on the highway.

From there, Wendy walked to the barn where Renegade Man was being stabled, found Dusty there, but no Tom. "I think he's up with Pastor Mitchell where Rupert used to be," Dusty said.

Wendy was pleasantly surprised to be greeted by several people as she walked through the barn area.

"Good morning."

"Mornin'!"

"Good morning, Wendy!"

"Good morning!"

"How are you doing?"

"Good, good. How are you?"

"Mornin'!"

Tom was indeed with Pastor Mitchell. They were going over ideas about how to convert the once-upon-a-time-two stalls-turned-tack-store, into a chapel.

"Hey," Tom said, giving her a hug. "I missed you."

"Me too."

"So what's up?"

"Um...." She didn't know what to say, just a rush of thoughts. I'm sorry I made you feel bad about your job. I'm sorry it's dangerous. I'm sorry, I'm sorry, I'm sorry. "I just saw Randy. He has Rotty with him. Something's wrong with him."

"I know. He cried all night. It was weird."

"Well, I'd better get back to work."

Tom smiled. "Are we still on for lunch?"

"Oh! I'm glad you said that. No. I got a call from Karen and Veronica. I'm going to go over and meet with them again. She said they were up all night and came up with some ideas and lots of questions. Dawn's going to meet me there."

Chapter Forty-One

Gloria and Charlie met Ben for lunch at the clubhouse and the three sat talking about old times. Gloria loved the clubhouse; she always did, and loved the new menu choices. "Even though I don't eat much."

They hoped to get on the road to home by three, with plans to stop in southern Ohio overnight. "We don't want to get tired out," she said, hugging Ben and getting into their car. "We'll see you next time."

Ben shook Charlie's hand. "I'll be here. You two take care." As he stood watching them drive away, a feeling of incredible sadness washed over him. He walked to the barn and lingered in front of each horse's stall. Red wasn't in his stall. Tom was probably ponying a horse.

He wondered whether Tom would move out if and when he and Wendy got married. It made sense, since Wendy had her own house and her sons. He sat down in the tack room. The house will be awful quiet, he thought. Sure, they'd still have their dinners together often, all of them, but at night, when they all left, it would be just like after Meg died, too quiet, too lonely, sad.

"What's the matter with you, old man?" Tom said, returning with Red.

"Well, I was just sitting here thinking."

Tom grinned. "Haven't we talked about that before?"

"Yeah, I guess we have," Ben said, laughing.

Tom unsaddled Red and laid the saddle and saddle pads on the ground just outside the tack room. He rubbed Red's back vigorously with a towel. Red loved that. Tom glanced at Ben. "What?"

"Where are you going to live when you get married?"

"Is that what this is about?"

"Well, yes. I'm used to you being there."

Tom looked at him.

"I don't like good-byes," Ben said. "Charlie and Gloria leaving. I thought, what if I never see them again?"

Tom took Red's bridle off and patted him on the butt. He totted down the shedrow and into his stall, happy as could be. Tom heaved his saddle up onto the rack, hung up his bridle, and laid the saddle pad out in the sun, then walked down to Red's stall, picked his feet, and snapped his stall webbing closed.

It was time to run stalls, pick out the manure piles, wet spots. But first things first. He sat down in the tack room, leaned his head back against the wall, and sighed. "I don't want to leave the farm, Ben. I can't imagine living in a suburb on a cul-de-sac. It ain't me."

"But if it's what Wendy wants?"

"Well, see, that's just it. I'm not sure what she wants. I don't even think she knows what she wants. She has her boys

311

to think about. They're in college, but they need a place to come home to, Thanksgiving, Christmas, spring break, whenever they feel like it. That's their home."

Ben drew a breath and sighed, scratching the back of his neck. "Maybe I can rent out the upstairs."

Tom laughed. "Oh, so now you're kicking me out?"

Ben laughed as well. "You're a pain in the ass."

Tom reached for a sponge and the saddle soap. "Don't worry, old man. We'll work it out." The barn area loudspeaker crackled and they both stopped to listen.

"Congratulations, Mim Freemont, for saddling two wins back-to-back! Way to go!"

"Hot damn!" Ben said. He and Tom walked out onto the road between the barns, waited, and when they saw her coming down the road on her golf cart behind her horse on its way to the spit box, they waved. "Congratulations!"

She waved back. "Thank you!"

Randy pulled his truck in behind them. Tom looked. "Where's Rotty?"

"I dropped him off at home. They couldn't find anything wrong with him."

"Well, I'm stopping for earplugs," Ben said. "He starts that howling again tonight I'm going to be ready."

"You, needing ear plugs?" Tom said. "You're kidding me, right?"

"Oh, and Dawn told me to remind you tonight we're all eating at Glenda and George's," Randy said.

Both nodded, remembering. Tom wondered if he'd mentioned it to Wendy.

Dawn and Wendy followed Veronica and Karen from stall to stall, sad beyond belief at the condition of the some of the horses, appalled that anyone would allow a horse to go without food and proper care.

"Let me give you some advice," Veronica said. "Don't even go there. It'll just tear you up inside." She walked on.

312

"Now this one here, this is the one that Randy and Tom had to come help us with the other night."

It was a large chestnut gelding that someone had sent to a farm after an injury. "You don't want to know the details," Karen said. "Randy thinks he's through the worst of it. He and Tom took turns the other night bracing him against the wall to keep him standing. If he had gone down chances are he wouldn't have gotten back up. He wouldn't have had the strength. He's such a sweetie too."

Dawn and Wendy just shook their heads.

"The thing with me is," Karen said. "I had to stop passing judgment. It was the only way I could keep going."

"Not me," Veronica said. "I judge them all."

"Yes, and that's why you have an ulcer."

It was an old argument between them.

"And now that you've seen the worst," Karen said. "Let's go see the success stories."

Wendy and Dawn followed along. "Do you take before and after pictures?"

"Yes," Veronica said. "But I don't post them or anything. I want to allow them some dignity. I wouldn't want to be shown like that."

"But what about as far as getting funds?" Wendy asked. "Do you think it might get more donations if people could see how they come in?"

"From a certain group, yes. But let me tell you," she said, sliding the back barn door open. "Strictly speaking, financially, the people that respond to that type of photo, good hearted and all, caring people mind you, they turn out to be one-time donors. You get a check and you never hear from them again."

Two large gray horses and one bay picked their heads up from eating a round hay bale in the paddock and nickered. They were thin, but shiny and bright-eyed. They were happy and content. One of the grays walked over to the fence.

"This one loves people," Veronica said. "Even after...." She bit her bottom lip in an attempt not to break into tears. "I wasn't always like this."

Dawn pet the horse's face, straightened his forelock, and laughed when he sniffed her hair, snorted and sneezed all over her. "How long has he been here?"

"About two months now. He's just about ready to go if we can find him a home."

"How often do you place a horse?" Wendy asked.

"About one every couple of weeks. Some come back."

"Why?"

"People," Veronica said.

"We screen them. Sometimes I think we screen too much," Karen said. "Some of the homes we think will work out best, don't, and...."

Dawn looked at the bay. His ribs were still showing. "How long has he been here?"

"About four months. We almost lost him twice."

Dawn and Wendy found themselves shaking their heads again. They could only imagine how he looked when he arrived.

"Come on, let's go inside."

They followed the women into their house and sat down at the kitchen table. The two were a wealth of information. They had a long list of Rescue Farms in the state. "Transporting the horses in a weak condition is very risky. Again, if they go down, particularly in a trailer...."

"So most of the horses that come to you are in...?"

"Bad shape? Yes."

"Do you ever get a horse that maybe just can't run fast anymore?" Wendy asked.

"No. Unfortunately they're probably in good flesh, and we all know what that means."

Wendy stared.

"Killers," Dawn said, shuddering.

"Which brings up a good point." Karen sorted through a pile of articles and handed one to Dawn. "You might want to have two vets okay horses that need put down once they are in your care. All it takes is one vet like this and the rest are suspect."

314

Dawn skimmed the article and handed it to Wendy. "This is all so complicated."

"You want to hear about complicated. The biggest obstacle in the rescue business is other rescue businesses. Not to mention the animal protective rights movement."

"What do you mean?" Wendy asked.

"Well, for instance, we had this really nice mare, she was barren, neglected, a little on the small side, but just as sweet as can be once we got some groceries in her. So we find her a home, twins actually, two teenage girls, and because there were two people going to be riding this horse, somehow one of the other rescue places, I won't say who, felt that we were setting this horse up as a riding academy horse. It was ridiculous. They contacted the family and scared them to death with all their questions, and the girls weren't allowed to adopt the horse."

"That's another thing. Expenses need to be paid, so there are adoption fees, but some are ridiculously high. But! On the other hand, the fear is, if the donation is too low, say less than what a killer would pay, then you open yourself up for that type of scam."

"Seriously?"Dawn asked.

Karen fished out another article about a woman in Indiana that was passing herself off as a rescue organization and supplying. Dawn handed it back, she'd read enough. She looked at Wendy and shook her head.

"And then there's the picketers."

"Picketers?"

"Are you anti-slaughter or for the slaughter of animals?" Veronica asked.

Wendy and Dawn just looked at her. Was she kidding?

"It's a major issue in the country. You're going to be asked, trust me."

"Well, what do you say?" Wendy asked.

"We are both anti-slaughter. But…."

Dawn and Wendy stared. "But?"

Veronica's eyes filled with tears again. "Don't," Karen said. "See the thing is, we do everything we can for every

315

horse that comes to Shifting Gears. But we can't always save them. Sometimes they're too far gone. Sometimes they cross that line and there's no bringing them back."

Veronica's shoulders trembled. "I hate this part."

"So in that case, when that happens, we have to call a renderer. We are not zoned to bury animals. Even if we were, we have no equipment."

Dawn and Wendy sat back. "So, then they pay you for the body? Is that what you're saying?"

"No, we pay them. We don't know what they do with the body. When I think of hungry animals everywhere," Veronica said. "I don't know. We're a lot of help, aren't we?"

"Yes, actually you are. More than you know," Dawn said. She looked at Wendy.

Wendy glanced at the list of the rescue organizations. "The ones that have checks next to them, that means…?"

"It means they are good people."

"Two checks?"

"Good people who do good."

"The ones that….?"

"Walk the walk and talk the talk."

"The ones with X's?"

"Not so good?"

"Two X's."

"Red Herrings. They only take the ones they want."

"As opposed to? Just so I understand clearly."

"As opposed to the ones that will take the horses in the most need."

Dawn nodded. Wendy nodded. "What do you fear the most?" Wendy asked.

"I fear the day will come when we have to turn a horse way," Karen said.

Veronica lowered her eyes. "I fear that day is not far away."

Chapter Forty-Two

Ben owned Glenda and George's home, a partially remodeled farmhouse built in the late 1920's. It sat about half a mile up the road from Ben's farm. T-Bone's farm was sandwiched in the middle, a long, narrow seventy-acres used mainly for making hay. Ben offered to buy T-Bone's farm years ago but the man refused to sell. He said the only way he was leaving was going to be in a pine box, this was his home. Ben felt the same way about his place, so that was that. When T-Bone reached the age when he could no longer farm the land on his own, Ben leased it from him and T-Bone supervised the hay-making each summer.

Wendy got the grand tour. "This is so nice," she said of the house, the way Glenda had it decorated; the down-home warm cozy feel. From the back porch, you could see all of Ben's farm, the barns, the horses in the pasture. You could see Dawn and Randy's house. You could see the dogs.

"Oh no," Glenda laughed. "Here they come!"

Up and over the ridge, three of the Labs ran through the edge of the pond, two stopped for a drink and Rotty brought up the rear, barely at a trot. Randy shook his head. "He's really in a funk."

They all hurried back inside before the Labs bounded up onto the back porch. Surely the dogs were going to be dirty and wet. Yes! They lay down panting and licking themselves. It was as if they'd conquered Mount Everest. Rotty climbed the steps and heaved a sigh.

"That's so sad," Wendy said. "Look at him."

He perked up at the sound of her voice behind the screen door, walked over to look in, and started crying and wagging his tail. Everyone stared. He was looking at Wendy as if she were his long-lost friend. When she pressed her hand against the screen he wiggled all over and licked her hand.

"Walk away," Randy said.

Wendy walked into the living room, out of sight, and Rotty strained to see her and started whining.

"Come back."

Rotty wagged his tail, his eyes pleading for attention.

"It's you," Randy said.

"Me?"

"You must remind him of his owner."

"I thought you were his owner."

"We are now. He's a stray. He was abandoned."

"Oh, that's right," Wendy said. "That's so sad." When she walked back over and stuck her hand out the door, Rotty rolled onto his back to have his belly rubbed. "Oh my gosh."

"She has that affect on me too," Tom said.

They all laughed.

"Is he allowed in?" Wendy asked. He wasn't dirty at all.

Glenda nodded.

Wendy opened the door and in he came, all wiggly and happy as could be. He walked over to the water dish on the kitchen floor, lapped some up, and walked back and stood next to Wendy. "This is unbelievable," she said, down on her knee and petting him. "Look at you, you sweetie pie." A little attention and he seemed perfectly content to go back outside. He lay down next to the other dogs and rested his head on Sloopy's back.

"What do I do if he does this again when I leave?" Wendy asked.

"Simple," Tom said. "Don't leave."

Everyone chuckled.

"He'll be fine," Randy said. "The more he sees you, the more secure he'll feel."

Wendy shook her head. "Why would anyone abandon him?"

Randy shrugged. "It might not have been by choice. He could have wandered off, got lost. She could be gone."

"You mean dead?"

"Who knows."

Wendy sighed. "This has been a rather depressing day."

Dawn agreed.

"Let's eat," Glenda said. Traditionally, whenever they ate at George and Glenda's, women sat at the kitchen table and

318

the men sat in the living room. George, Randy, Tom, and Dusty filed in and found their seats. Ben chose to sit with the women today.

Dawn smiled. If Carol were here and not home putting the children to bed, she'd say he had his "I've been thinking – I'm up to something" game face on.

"Great sauce," he said.

Glenda had made meat sauce with lots of sautéed mushrooms and roasted garlic. It was one of her signature dishes and always served over angel-hair pasta. Tom of course added Tabasco to his.

"Delicious," everyone muttered, all with their mouths full.

Wendy passed the bread and then the butter.

"I've been thinking," Ben said.

Dawn smiled. He was an open book. "Oh? About what?"

Wendy leaned back to look at Rotty. He was resting contentedly.

"About forming an alliance."

"An alliance?" They were already incorporated.

"You know, like an "all for one - one for all kind of thing." A pact. A commitment."

"I ain't pricking my finger and bleeding for you, old man," Tom said.

They all laughed, Ben included.

"No, now hear me out. Say if someone wanted to build a house on the property, just like you two," he said, gesturing to Dawn and over his shoulder to Randy. "I mean, what if Dusty would want to build a house here someday," he said.

"I'd want a yurt," Dusty said.

Everyone smiled.

"What if we wanted to build a rescue barn?"

Everyone stopped eating for a second.

"Or Randy's parents? What if Tom and Wendy wanted to build a house here someday? Or her sons? Or D.R. or Maeve?"

Dawn smiled. She was on to him. This was about Tom and Wendy. He wasn't fooling anybody. Not even Wendy, the relative newcomer.

Dusty came into the kitchen for seconds. "Frankly, I'd like to live above a barn just once in my life. I'd like to hear the horses while I sleep. I'd like them to know I'm watching over them."

Randy followed him in. "It'd have to be the foaling barn. It's the only one with a toilet."

"Shit, yeah," Tom said. "You gotta have a toilet of your own."

They all laughed.

Wendy got up to get a little more salad and motioned to Ben's plate. He handed it to her. "A little more spaghetti, thank you." He nodded when it was enough, and she handed his plate back to him.

It was the simplest of actions, but didn't go unnoticed by either Dawn or Glenda. They looked at one another and smiled. "So," Dawn said, glancing first at Wendy and then Tom. "Have you given thought to staying on with Ben after you get married?"

Tom looked at her with the same deer in the headlights expression he had on his face the other night in Wendy's driveway. "No," he said. "We haven't talked about it, have we?"

Wendy shrugged casually. "Not really." She reached for another piece of bread, noticed them all looking at her, and added, "I'm so excited. I lost four pounds and I'm not even trying. Unbelievable. I think it's all the stairs."

Everyone smiled. Tom patted her on the head in passing, and they all went back to eating. "So," Ben said, with that still same "thinking" look on his face. Dawn had to keep herself from laughing. "If we form this alliance, would you like your house to be here?"

Wendy stared and then glanced over her shoulder at Tom. He too was awaiting her response. "Ben, I'm sorry." Silence descended upon the kitchen, the living room, the house, the farm. "I love it here, I really do. And I'm sorry I didn't get to know Meg. I see her everywhere here."

Ben lowered his eyes, swallowed hard.

"I know how Tom feels. I do," she said, looking in at him. "This is his home. My house has nothing to offer him; it has nothing to offer me, not anymore."

Big tears slid down Ben's face.

Wendy hesitated. "I don't want Tom to leave his home. I guess I was hoping there would be enough room there for me."

Tom looked away; he had to, and bit at his trembling bottom lip.

Ben looked at Dawn, he couldn't speak, he couldn't.... He motioned for her to speak for him, to say what he was thinking, what he was feeling. "He says there's room."

Ben nodded, and nodded again.

Dawn smiled and wiped her eyes. "He says welcome home."

Chapter Forty-Three

Wendy stared at her computer screen, hit Save, and downloaded the new racing program cover onto a compact disc. Ben entered Bo-T for Sunday. Tom ponied three horses aside from the ones in their barn. Dawn did up three horses, Tom, two. A load of hay was delivered, an order of grain. Randy stopped by. Dusty stopped by, Spears stopped by. The blacksmith stopped by to check on Bo-T's hind shoe. All was well.

Dawn left for home around noon. The farm blacksmith was due around one-thirty. Leaving now, she'd have time to eat lunch with the children. It was going to be a full day. Her Aunt Maeve was in town and all her family would be gathering at her cousin's this evening.

She was also hoping to take a nap sometime this afternoon. She and Randy had talked well into the night last night about the possibility of his parents building a home on the farm. They talked about where might be the best location, how close, how far, his parents needing their privacy, Randy and Dawn needing theirs. "I think privacy is largely overrated," Dawn had said softly just before falling asleep.

"That's easy for you to say; you grew up with servants and nannies."

"I miss my mom and dad."

"I know. Shhhh...."

Wendy and Tom had talked well into the night as well. "What attic?" Wendy had asked when Tom mentioned it. "Where?"

"Right behind this room?"

"Where's the door?"

"I'll show you in the morning."

Wendy lay next to him, staring up at the ceiling. "Are there lights in it?"

Tom chuckled. "Yes."

"I'll be right back." She tiptoed out of the bedroom, down the tiny hall and opened the door somewhat warily. She turned on the light switch. "Oh my...." The attic was practically empty, just some boxes, cobwebs, dust everywhere. The walls and ceiling had been insulated, but that was all, no drywall, no paneling.

When she crawled back into bed and under the covers, Tom tucked her in nice and close and kissed the back of her neck. She sighed contentedly.

Dusty had done night check with George and "Just for the hell of it" he decided to climb the ladder to the loft in the foaling barn. There were a couple of old bales of straw in the center. He sat down, looked around and listened. He could hear Dawn's ponies munching hay below. He could see the moon through the window. It looked almost close enough to touch. He could see the yearlings grazing in the pasture. He could see the dogs on Ben's porch; Rotty curled up on the welcome mat outside the door.

Surely Wendy was meant to be here. Surely he was meant to be here. He climbed down the ladder and as he walked to his truck, thought about solar heating. He glanced back. The south bank on the roof of the barn would be perfect for heat-conductor panels.

Tom and Wendy had their first real date Friday evening. They had dinner at a local steak house and band bar. They even danced. They talked about their day. They talked about the racetrack. They talked about Wendy's sons. They talked about the rest of their lives.

Dawn and Randy visited with Aunt Maeve at Linda and Harland's. As always, Aunt Maeve looked wonderful and had lots of stories to tell. She held little Alice Marie, cooed and sang songs, played with Maeve and D.R. She sat talking with her brother Matt. It was a catered affair: appetizers served on trays, drinks in long-stemmed glasses, a three-course meal, a choice of four different desserts.

Whenever Aunt Maeve visited, the visits were usually short. "She belongs to the world," her father always said. If there was a "cause" Aunt Maeve was "on it." If there was a "need," she was "right there."

"You okay?" Randy asked, as they rode home. Both children were sound asleep in their car seats. "You look sad."

Dawn sighed, staring out the window at the overhead street lights. "Just thinking."

"About what?"

"My mom and dad and how the kids will never know them."

Randy nodded. He figured as much.

The further they drove closer to home, the less street lights. Randy glanced at her. "Have I told you lately that I love you?"

She looked at him and smiled. "Yes."

"Good. I don't want you to forget."

"Never," she said.

The lights were all off at George and Glenda's except for the porch light. Ben's farmhouse was dark, both porch lights on. The night lights in the barns shone softly. The moon sat high above the trees. Randy parked the car, got out, and reached in for his sleepy son.

"Come on, honey," Dawn said, unbuckling little Maeve's car seat. "We're home." At the sound of her voice, Beau Born whinnied.

Sixty soft whips arrived Saturday morning by courier. Dawn and Dusty ran a video of Rupert opening the box, holding up one as a model and describing the dimensions and humane features. Dusty delivered them to the jockeys' room from there. With the Miller barn having horses running today in the third, sixth, and seventh races, training was light. The only horse to go to the racetrack was Wee Born. There was a race for her on Wednesday. Ben followed her back to the barn, pleased with how strong she galloped.

"With a little luck and a fast racetrack..." he said.

"She feels good. She feels real good," Johnny said, walking along with him.

It took longer than they would have liked for her to recover from that nick on her hock after her poor performance on the sloppy racetrack. She was almost a hundred percent. Ben wasn't one to rush a horse. "When they're ready, they'll let you know," he liked to say.

Johnny waved. "I'll see you later, Ben." He was riding Born All Together "Batgirl" in the seventh race today. Juan was riding Winning Beau "Whinny" in the third, and Native Beau Born "B-Bo" in the sixth. Back when Ben ran a public racing stable it wasn't all that uncommon to have this many horses running in a day, let alone back-to-back; one race right after another. They had the routine down pat.

Prior to the first race, Bud Gipson made the announcement to the fans in the grandstand that the jockeys would all be riding today with a soft whip. "The jockeys, the management, and the ownership of Nottingham Downs are dedicated to the safety of the horses and our jockeys. Ladies and gentlemen, today is a new day in Thoroughbred racing."

When the jockeys came out to the paddock, the crowd cheered, and they all waved their whips. The photographer flashed one photo after another. The race film photographer zoomed in on them.

Several of the owners and trainers could be seen smiling and shaking their heads in awe. Not only was there a crowd, the crowd seemed to care. Jeremy Blane, trainer of the three horse in the race; the favorite, wasn't smiling at all. He turned his back to the fans and leaned down close to his jockey. "This ain't a ride in the park," he said.

The jockey adjusted the Velcro on his sleeves.

"You hear me?"

The jockey looked up at him, he just looked at him, and there was something about the way the jockey just looked at him.

"I mean," Jeremy Blane said. "It's not fair. We trainers had no say."

"You trainers aren't riding. I don't tell you how to train."

"Riders up!"

The horse's fate, this race, this moment in time, never depended more on the rider. "Just hope I don't fucking fall off," the jockey said. "Carrying a big stick is not all I do."

It was a nine horse field.

The bugle sounded!

"Ladies and gentlemen, the horses for the first race here at Nottingham Downs are on the racetrack." He announced the name of each horse, each jockey, each trainer.

Wendy and Spears watched from their glass-front office. "What do you think's going to happen?" Wendy asked.

Spears shook his head and pointed to Ben, Tom, Dawn, Dusty, and Randy, all walking toward the Ginny stand. The bugler played "When the Saints go Marching in." Several people in the crowd started dancing.

"I think we'll all be happy when this day is over," Spears said.

Wendy had hoped to have the new program cover for today's racing, but when she made a last-minute change in the design it pushed the pilot time back until tomorrow. Ben said that was probably a good thing, commemorating a new day, a new week, a new beginning. She looked at the Forget Me Nots, thought of Renegade Man, thought of Karen and Veronica and Shifting Gears Thoroughbred Rescue Farm, the horses there, the Thoroughbreds at Ben's farm....

"I think tomorrow would be a good day to announce the free admission – free parking vouchers. Are they ready?" Spears asked.

Wendy nodded. "That was a brilliant idea, by the way, absolutely brilliant."

He laughed. "I think it was a stroke of genius, if I must say so myself." Fans leaving after the ninth race will receive a voucher for free admission and free parking any day of the racing season. And there was no limit. A fan staying until after the ninth race could essentially have free admission and parking each and every time they came, so long as they stayed until after the completion of the ninth race to get their voucher.

"How will they get them?" Ben asked, when Spears phoned him earlier.

"Easy," Spears said. "They'll get them from the pari-mutual tickets sellers, along with a 'Hope to see you again soon,' friendly greeting. It's a win-win! Even if we never see that fan again, at least they'll know we appreciate their business."

The horses were being loaded in the gate. Wendy glanced at the Ginny stand again, where for all practical purposes the powers-that-be sat amongst the other owners, trainers, and grooms, right where they wanted to be.

"And they're off!"

Wendy and Spears watched with trepidation. Wendy at one point actually feared a horse or two just might stop running, if not all of them. But that didn't happen.

Tom glanced up at the monitor in the Ginny stand. They'd run the half in 45.4, good fractions. The race for home had horses five wide down the stretch. They could hear the crowd. They could hear Bud calling the finish.

"And it is Tick Tack by a neck!"

Tom stepped down out of the Ginny stand to watch the horses pull up and turn around back toward the grandstand. The race was run in 111.4, a decent time. "Well?" Tom said, to Miguel, rider of the winner.

The jockey cocked his whip. He was looking forward to seeing the expression on Jeremy Blane's face. "No problem," he said. "Everything's good."

As Jeremy Blane led his horse into the Winner's Circle, Miguel saluted the Stewards with the new and improved whip. "Great ride," the trainer said. "I apologize."

The jockeys' room was abuzz after the race, the general consensus being "It didn't seem to make too much of a difference when considering the time of the race." One said his horse didn't flinch like always and actually ran better. "She no squirrely like usual."

Second race, same thing. The race was run in good time. There was no surprise horse behavior, no upset. By the time Tom, Red, and Dawn led Whinny over for the third race, the whip seemed already to be a non-issue. Juan came out of the jockeys' room all smiles.

"Only complaints, some jocks don't like the grip." He shrugged. "They'll fix them." When the call sounded, Dawn gave him a leg up and led Whinny out onto the racetrack and handed her over to Tom. Her race was 6 furlongs and she was coming off a win. This was her first wide-open race since winning all three of her lifetime conditions.

Ben and Dawn walked to the fence in front of the grandstand, their usual place to view a race and watched Whinny warm up. "Ladies and Gentlemen, I'd like to bring attention to the owner of Nottingham Downs. Ben Miller."

Ben stared at Dawn. "Are they playing a video?"

"No, I think this is live. I think you should turn around and wave," she said.

Ben turned and waved. The crowd cheered.

Dawn looked at him out of the corner of her eye. "Smile." He smiled.

"Thank you, Ben Miller," Bud Gipson said. "Thank you."

Ben smiled again, nodded, and turned back around. "Can we fire him?"

"What?" Dawn asked. "For doing his job? You told him to talk more."

Ben laughed.

"One minute to post," Bud said. "Do not get shut out."

Wendy stood at the window, debated going down to join them, and decided she'd better not. There were still those who might think having an owner of the racetrack allowed to race his or her own horses at that racetrack could be a conflict of interest, let alone the Assistant General Manager down there on the rail rooting along with them. "They're loading in the gate," she said.

Spears got up from his desk and stood at her side. Whinny's odds were 3-1.

When his cell phone rang, he glanced at the number and took the call. He could hear the track announcer - he could hear the crowd - he could hear Wendy.

"Come on, Whinny. Come on. I can't believe I haven't gotten binoculars yet. Come on, Whinny."

The filly laid third down the backside, took over second at the head of the stretch, and came up a nose short for the win at the wire. "She run big!" Ben said. Good fractions, a strong finish. The photo sign flashed, giving some bettors hope, but Ben could clearly see Whinny finished second. A horrible thought ran through is his mind, "What if they put her on top because of me?"

Dawn and he walked out onto the racetrack, waiting for Whinny's return. Tom and Red led her and Juan back. Juan dismounted. "Almost," he said. "She sure is game."

Ben heaved a huge sigh of relief when the winner's number was posted. "I'll see you back at the barn," he told Dawn and Tom, and walked along with Juan. "How was the soft whip?"

Juan twirled the whip and smiled. "It made no difference. She ran her race."

Ben nodded, agreeing, thanked him and walked back to the barn. It dawned on him that he could have gone up to his office and watched the next couple of races there. But old habits die hard. He laughed at himself and decided Meg would have laughed at him too.

"Ah, Mr. Miller," she'd say.

When he heard the crowd roar, he was still close enough to see the tote board and smiled. The trifecta paid $1225, the highest paying trifecta in months. He stopped by the spit barn, stood talking to Dawn and Tom for a moment while he looked Whinny over. Then he took Red to the barn, put him in his stall, slipped off his bridle and loosened the girth.

"You're a good boy," he said, patting him on the neck.

Spears hung up the phone and looked at Wendy. "We made the national news."

"You mean about the whips?"

He nodded. "And not just national sports news, the national news - news."

Wendy smiled. "Will it be positive?"

"Very."

Tom bed Whinny's stall when he returned to the barn and filled her water bucket and hay net. By the time Dawn returned, they were calling for horses for the fifth race. Race days, she wrote once, was like playing connect the dots. Go here, go there, do this, do that, come back over here again, go back over there. While she did up all four of Whinny's legs, Tom ran stalls, topped off water buckets, and quietly, very, very quietly, mixed the horses' dinner feed.

Done, he put running bandages on B-Bo and brushed him off. Dawn put Red's bridle on, tightened his girth, and led him down the shedrow and outside the barn, ground tied him, and walked back to get B-Bo. Tom had him all ready and bridled. He put on his helmet and mounted Red: Dawn met him at the end of the shedrow.

"Good luck," she said. "Bring him back safe."

Tom patted the colt on the neck and nodded. "There's three mares in the race. This should be exciting."

Dusty was set to meet them in the paddock. Ben could still saddle a horse, even with his weak arm from the stroke. But at times, he had trouble giving the jock a leg up. Tom dismounted Red outside the paddock, led B-Bo in, and gave wide berth to the stalls that held the mares. B-Bo kicked the wall. When the colt was saddled, Tom walked back out to the track and mounted Red. As Dawn would say, back and forth, back and forth, over here, over there….

"Riders up!"

"Good luck," Ben said to Juan.

"Thank you." He glanced back at Ben and smiled. He liked riding B-Bo. He was a big strong colt, took some handling, but always ran his heart out. He appreciated the mount.

The bugle sounded.

The crowd cheered as the horses walked onto the racetrack.

Dusty and Ben made their way down to the fence in front of the grandstand. Ben had forgotten about being announced from this vantage point, but fortunately Bud didn't announce him again. The race was a flat mile. "He looks like a million bucks," Mim said, walking up next to them with her cane. "I see you're starting Beau All Together tomorrow."

"I'm going to run him a couple of times and send him home. He's such a big colt."

"He's impressive."

Ben smiled. "He's headstrong."

"The good ones always are," Mim said.

The horses were loaded in the gate. The one horse started acting up.

"No, Boss! No, Boss!" the gate crew handler said. "No, Boss!"

Then silence.

"And they're off!"

B-Bo broke with the pack, laid fourth through the turn and down the backside. At the head of the stretch Juan clicked to him, asking for more run, and he dug in. When he passed the quarter pole, he was second. An eighth of a mile left to go he took the lead and win drawing away.

Tom helped pull him up and led him and Juan back to the Winner's Circle, dismounted, and they all got their picture taken. Dusty followed them to the gap and took B-Bo for a moment while Dawn handed "Batgirl" to Tom.

"Bring her back safe," Dawn said. She always said that for luck.

Tom nodded and winked, always - for luck. Connect the dots; connect the dots, superstitions run deep. Dusty handed B-Bo to Dawn. "You got him?"

She nodded. He was all pumped up, dancing and prancing. She finessed him to the spit barn by letting him dance and prance. There, he was more interested in having a drink of water than having his tattoo checked. He nipped at the attendant.

"Be careful," Dawn warned.

The man grabbed hold of B-Bo's lip again, confirmed the tattoo, and Dawn led him into the stall. His halter and shank were tied to her belt loop. It would have been bad luck to bring them down before the race, even if the odds were that he was going to win.

She allowed him a good long drink of water and took him outside for hosing off and a bath. By the time she got him back inside the spit barn, his breathing was practically normal. When he fast approached the filly that ran second, who was slowly walking around the shedrow in front of him, Dawn led him into the stall to give the filly time to get on the other side, and then brought him back out.

She couldn't hear the call of the race from inside the spit barn with everyone talking, but at every turn she thought she could make out the announcer calling Beau All Together's name. "You know, a monitor in your office would be nice," she told the state veterinarian.

"Ask the boss," he said, smiling.

Dawn led B-Bo into the stall to have his urine sample taken. When he "obliged" she put his lead shank back on him, led him outside, and here came Tom and Batgirl, all proud of herself and pushing against Red. "Did she win?" Dawn asked.

"Second," Tom said, doing that dismount of his, with Batgirl's reins over Red's head and leading her into the spit barn all in one fell swoop. Dusty walked Red down to the barn alongside Dawn and B-Bo.

"She run good."

"Did she have the lead?"

He nodded. "The horse just got to her. It was a photo."

Dawn smiled. It was a good day for the Miller barn. Randy stopped by a few minutes later. Yes, plans were to all go to the Rib for dinner to celebrate.

"I'll see you all there."

Spears was the last to arrive at the restaurant. He'd gone home to change clothes and was quite surprised when his wife said she'd like to join them. They sat by Ben at the end of the table across from Wendy and Tom. Dusty sat at the other end, Dawn on one side, Randy the other.

Horsemen passing the table, sitting nearby or way across the room, the waitresses and cooks, all congratulated Ben. He waved, thanking them, and then they all got down to the business of ordering. Spears' wife Heather studied Wendy and Tom while appearing to be looking at her menu. Finally, she had to ask. "Are you two a couple?"

"Yes," Tom said, winking at Wendy. "We're going to be married soon, someday, someway, somewhere...."

They all laughed. He'd sung that last part.

"Oh," Heather said. "That's so nice to hear. I used to worry all the time with Richard working so late and his saying how pretty you are, and you are."

Wendy blushed. "Me and Richard? I'm old enough to be his uh...older sister."

Everyone laughed again. Then here came the waitresses.

Heather looked at her husband when he ordered a tall glass of water. They were both heavy drinkers. "I'll have water too," she said. When it came time to make a toast, Ben stood and they all raised their glasses. "To the new Nottingham Downs!"

"Hear! Hear!"

Chapter Forty-Four

Sunday morning at the Miller barn was a breeze. With three horses running yesterday and Bo-T in the sixth race today, that left only Wee Born to go to the racetrack. By ten-thirty, all five horses were back in their stalls, done up, and the shedrow raked.

"I'll see you around two," Dawn said, as she left.

Ben sat down to read the racing form while Tom went up to Sunday Service at the racetrack chapel. The sermons were always short, in keeping with the horsemen's busy schedules. There were about twenty-two in attendance, a good turnout. Tom bowed his head and prayed. He had a lot to be thankful for. He took in every word. "Amen."

Pastor Mitchell shook everyone's hands as they filed out past him. "Next week we should be in our new chapel. Tell your friends."

Tom was last to go through the line. "It'll be nice. We'll try and get it all moved over by Tuesday."

"Thank you." Pastor Mitchell said. "Do you think we can use some of the Billy Martin Fund to purchase a real altar?"

Tom smiled. "I'm sure we can work something out."

Pastor Mitchell shook his hand. "You're a good man, Tom."

"Thank you. Funny thing is I don't talk about the Lord so much anymore."

"That's because your actions speak louder than words."

Tom just looked at him and then nodded. "Thank you."

Randy pulled up next to him as he walked back to the barn. "How is he?"

The *he*, he was referring to went without saying. Bo-T was the man of the hour, man of the day. "He's not happy with not having any hay, but aside from that he's as ready as he's ever going to be."

"How's Ben?"

333

Tom chuckled, chewing on a toothpick. "He says this is just another race, but we all know better. This is Bo-T were talking about."

"Yep," Randy said. "I'll see you later."

Wendy walked down to the receiving dock, had the shipping clerk open a box, and took out one of the programs. "Oh my!" She reached in for three more. "Thank you," she said, and headed for the Miller barn. She stopped mid-way in the parking lot, took a photo of the cover, front and back, and texted it to Dawn and Glenda. "What do you think?" she asked.

She phoned Dusty next. "Can you meet me at the Miller barn?"

"I'll be there in a few minutes." He arrived leading Renegade Man, the retired horse in his care. He liked grazing him and just walking him around every day. Renegade Man liked it too.

Wendy drew a breath, holding the programs next to her heart. "Okay, here it is," she said, passing them out.

"Nottingham Downs" it read across the top. "Where no Thoroughbred will ever be Forgotten." Below that statement, that creed - was a photo of a racehorse in the Winner's Circle with a blanket of Forget Me Nots draped over his neck.

Her phone rang. It was Dawn. "I love it!"

"Thank you!"

When she hung up, it rang again. It was Glenda. "We love it!" she said, meaning both her and George.

Dusty turned away with tears in his eyes. "Look at this," he said, to Renegade Man. "You're famous."

Tom shook his head. "How'd you do that?"

"Graphic arts, permission from the photographer; Rickety never paid him for it, so he was happy to give it up. Do you like it?"

"I love it."

"Ben?"

He'd turned the program over, something Dusty and Tom hadn't done yet. There were ads in the middle and on the bottom, but across the top was a collage depicting the stages of a Thoroughbred's life: a foal standing at its mother's side, a young horse in training, a horse race, a horse being shown over a jump, a cowboy, and finally, horses grazing in a pasture. He looked up. "I don't know what to say." His voice cracked. "This says it all."

"Awesome!" she said, and took off down the shedrow. She glanced back over her shoulder. "Oh, those are yours. They're on the house." The three of them laughed. She was already texting the photo to someone else. "What do you think?" she wrote to Linda Dillon.

A message came right back. "I love it!"

"How are you doing?"

"Good. Me and Maria miss you all, but we're hanging in there."

"Keep in touch."

By the time Wendy got back to her office, Linda had texted again. "Rec'd photo from Dawn and Glenda too. Love you all."

Wendy smiled, sat down at her desk, and looked up when Spears walked in. He had a copy of the program in his hand. "I didn't think you were coming in today," she said.

"Are you kidding me?" He smiled. "You're not the only one with things to do. Besides, Heather's meeting me for lunch in the clubhouse. We're going to make a day of it. She wants to see Bo-T win."

"You're both still coming to dinner tonight at Ben's, right? I'm making lasagna, remember. Meg's recipe. Ben's all excited."

By the time they led Bo-T over for his race, Dawn was a nervous wreck. Tom dismounted Red and led the colt into the paddock. Dawn walked alongside him as memories flashed in her mind. Beau Born, their tears the day Ben retired him. All Together, the day she broke her leg, the pain, the anguish, the

335

triumph. Beau Together was their son, their progeny. He was their legacy.

The big colt stood looking up at the fans as he was saddled. "I think he grew another inch overnight," Ben said, reaching for the overgirth. Johnny came out of the jockeys' room and, for a moment, just stood looking at the colt. Memories…. He had ridden Beau Born to a win in the last race of Beau's career. He was riding All Together the day she broke down.

"The most important thing," Ben said. "Bring him home."

Johnny nodded. "He's going to make you proud, Ben."

"Riders up!"

The bugle sounded.

Dawn gave Johnny a leg up and led Bo-T out onto the racetrack to Tom.

"Ladies and gentlemen," Bud announced. "Here come the babies! The future of Thoroughbred racing." Bo-T, the first-time starter was the odds on favorite. "I want to remind all you race fans, as you leave here today after the last race, don't forget to stop by a ticket window and get your free admission and parking voucher for your next visit."

As the crowd cheered, Ben and Dawn made their way to the fence. Dusty walked down next to them. Spears and his wife Heather sat looking out the clubhouse window. Wendy stood in her glass-front office, a new pair of binoculars in hand. Randy pulled up next to the Ginny stand, got out of his truck, climbed up the steps, and took a seat inside. When Frank Nixon, a trainer sitting next to him asked, "Do you think he'll win?" Randy shook his head at first. There was a whole lot of buzz going on about this colt. And as always he was protective of the family connection.

"I think he's going to run big."

The man nodded. "This is nice," he said, holding up the program. "I ran in the first, the fans are liking it too."

Randy smiled. "I agree." He heaved a breath and sighed. He also was thinking of Beau Born, thinking of All Together, the hard fight she fought to live, to go on. He thought about

336

the morning Bo-T was born, the softness of his skin and that steel look in his eyes.

"They're at the gate!"

A collective silence descended upon the racetrack, the starting gate far, far away.

"And they're off! …. Charging to the lead is Beau Together!"

"Is that good? Is that good?" Wendy asked out loud to herself. "Is he supposed to do that? I need to learn more about this!" She had her binoculars glued to him. "Go Bo-T, go," she said.

Dawn gripped the fence, straining to see the horses behind the tote board. Bo-T was still out in front.

"Coming into the clubhouse turn, it is Beau Together by six. Beau Together by seven, eight…."

"Oh no! Is he going to get tired?" Dawn asked.

Ben shook his head.

"Go Bo-T," Dawn yelled. "Go!"

"Come on, Bo-T," Dusty shouted, up on the fence and rooting him on with each stride. "Come on, Bo-T!"

Heather was on her feet up in the clubhouse, clenching her tickets and waving her arms. "Go, Bo-T, go!!"

"With a furlong left to go," Bud announced, "it is Beau Together by ten lengths! Bo-T! All alone! Bo-T!"

The crowd roared!

"Bo-T! pulling away. Bo-T by eleven lengths! It is Beau Together at the wire in complete command! Bo-Teeeeee!"

Dawn hugged Ben and Dusty, hugged them both hard, wiped her eyes, and looked up and waved at Wendy. She waved back, big tears running down her face. Heather waved to Dawn from the clubhouse. Dawn waved back, waved to Spears, and then turned and waved to Randy with both arms.

He waved back. Bo-T and Johnny galloped out in front of him. The big colt looked good. Tom and Red helped pull him up and turned them around.

"Ladies and gentlemen, Beau Together, better known as Bo-T is a homebred. He is out of Stakes winner All Together and the champion Beau Born." He cleared his throat,

337

attempting to regain his composure. He remembered both those horses, called their races, called the race the day All Together lay on the track injured. "Ladies and gentlemen, let's all hear it for your new 6½ furlong track-record holder, Bo-T!"

"What?" Ben looked at the tote board. Bo-T had bettered the track record by 2/5ths of a second. Dawn jumped up and down, waved to everyone again, and just about everyone in the crowd waved back.

Tom dismounted Red and led Bo-T and Johnny into the Winner's Circle. Johnny saluted the Stewards. The photo was snapped. Johnny jumped down and shook Ben's hand, shook Dusty's hand, shook Dawn's hand and gave her a hug.

"Ladies and gentlemen," Bud Gipson announced. "Remember this day. Remember Nottingham Downs' commitment to the safety and success of Thoroughbred racing. Remember our commitment to the life of a Thoroughbred. Hold on to that program you have in your hand. It's a promise. Nottingham Downs, where no Thoroughbred will ever be forgotten."

15811115R00180

Made in the USA
Lexington, KY
18 June 2012